IN PURSUIT
OF PROFIT

MARYLAND BICENTENNIAL STUDIES

Sponsored by the Maryland Bicentennial Commission
The Honorable Louise Gore, Chairman

EDITORIAL BOARD

Jack P. Greene, The Johns Hopkins University (Chairman)
Rhoda M. Dorsey, Goucher College
Benjamin Quarles, Morgan State College

MONOGRAPHS

A Spirit of Dissension:
Economics, Politics, and the Revolution in Maryland
by Ronald Hoffman

In Pursuit of Profit:
The Annapolis Merchants in the
Era of the American Revolution, 1763–1805
by Edward C. Papenfuse

DOCUMENTARY EDITIONS

Maryland and the Empire, 1773:
The Antilon-First Citizen Letters
by Peter S. Onuf

IN PURSUIT
OF PROFIT

THE ANNAPOLIS MERCHANTS
IN THE ERA OF THE
AMERICAN REVOLUTION,
1763–1805

EDWARD C. PAPENFUSE

THE JOHNS HOPKINS UNIVERSITY PRESS
BALTIMORE AND LONDON

Publication of this volume was assisted
by the Maryland Bicentennial Commission.

The Johns Hopkins University Press, Baltimore, Maryland 21218
The Johns Hopkins University Press Ltd., London

Library of Congress Catalog Card Number 74-6835
ISBN 0-8018-1573-8

Library of Congress Cataloging in Publication Data

Papenfuse, Edward C
    In pursuit of profit.

    (Maryland bicentennial studies)
    Bibliography: p.
    Includes index.
    1. Annapolis—Commerce—History. 2. Merchants—
Annapolis—History. 3. Annapolis—Economic conditions.
I. Title. II. Series.
HF3163.A4P36   330.9'752'5602   74-6835
ISBN 0-8018-1573-8

TO SALLIE

CONTENTS

ILLUSTRATIONS

TABLES

PREFACE

THIS book could not have been written without the cooperation of many people. Morris L. Radoff, recently-retired Archivist of Maryland, gave me free access to the stacks of the Hall of Records and lent me microfilms of materials I needed. His staff, especially Phebe Jacobsen, an authority on the early history of Annapolis, was extremely helpful. P. William Filby, director of the Maryland Historical Society, and Nancy Boles, former curator of manuscripts, also extended me every courtesy. Mrs. J. M. P. Wright and Historic Annapolis, Inc., materially supported research on chapter 4.

My advisor, Jack P. Greene, and Robert Forster read the manuscript carefully and offered many helpful suggestions. Gregory Stiverson has been a salutary critic and good friend. R. K. Webb, editor of the *American Historical Review*, has been a constant source of inspiration and encouragement. If there has been any improvement in my writing style over the past four years, he is responsible.

My family have come to my support in a variety of ways, although I owe special debts to Aunt Sara, who fostered my interest in history, and to my wife, Sallie, who contributed more than she will let me acknowledge.

PROLOGUE

THIS book has two objectives. The first is to present a case study of the structure of mercantile opportunity in Maryland during the latter half of the eighteenth century as reflected in the careers of Annapolis merchants; the second is to analyze the behavior of merchants as they coped with changes in the nature of opportunity. Between 1763 and 1805, fundamental alterations took place in the direction and control of the economy of Maryland. Prior to 1763, the major source of capital in the colony was tobacco, an export handled quite adequately and sufficiently without urban centers. The nature of the crop and the method of its marketing probably even militated against urbanization. After 1763, there began to be a concentration of capital in Annapolis, and the expanding market for tobacco created a sustained level of affluence for a great portion of the planter class served by Annapolis. As a result, a merchant community developed that began to accumulate capital from retail sales and had connections with a planter elite willing to place their crops and surplus funds in the merchants' hands. With capital of their own and some that was borrowed, the leaders of this numerically small but financially and entrepreneurially important business community successfully challenged the existing mercantile hegemony that controlled and financed the Maryland tobacco trade from London.

The leaders in this movement allied themselves with a new group of merchants in the Baltimore area who were, at the same time, venturing into the wheat trade. When war came, it was an Annapolis firm that served as one of the principal agents for the majority of Baltimore merchants in their quest for European goods and in their search for tobacco and grain markets. In effect, Annapolis capital and business leadership encouraged urbanization and crop diversification throughout the upper Chesapeake, extending their influence as far south as Richmond, but having their greatest impact on Baltimore, Alexandria, the Patuxent ports, and neighboring rural areas. Even during the war, however, the direction charted by the Annapolis merchant community was being followed by elements who wanted to be independent of Annapolis leadership. Tensions between the leading Annapolis merchants and their correspondents in Alexandria and Baltimore are clearly evident as early as 1782.

The Revolution offered opportunities to the Annapolis merchant community because of the town's position as an administrative center of the war effort. Government contracts, public service, and the use of public funds made it possible to acquire capital necessary for wartime speculation and postwar expansion. With peace, the Annapolis merchants, flush with wartime profits, had great expectations. They saw a market potential that had been beyond their wildest dreams less than a decade before. Their former British competitors had lost their property through confiscation and were in no position to return swiftly to the race for tobacco, a race in which speed was of great importance. But other Americans armed with capital derived from wartime speculations—for example, the Georgetown firm of Forrest and Stoddert—recognized the possibilities, too. The Annapolis merchants, in contrast to the prewar years, were no longer almost alone in being able to engage in the consignment trade or the outright purchase of tobacco, and they lost ground to their rivals.

Except for a brief period of unprecedented prosperity, Annapolis's position as an important center of native capital for commercial expansion was quickly eroded in the decade after peace was signed. Confronted with an influx of goods for which it could not pay, faced with competition for consignments of tobacco with which it could not effectively contend, the Annapolis merchant community was forced to adjust to constricting opportunity and to watch helplessly as its hopes for the future were dissipated by market forces and urbanization that its own capital and energies had helped to unleash. After 1793, the disastrous collapse of the tobacco market brought on by the European wars was but a *coup de grâce* at a time when Annapolis already had lost most of its transitory prominence in the Chesapeake.

Annapolis merchants, preoccupied by the trading world without, suddenly were forced to reexamine their prospects for survival at home. What they found was a much altered community. Once a city of rich planters and affluent government employees, Annapolis was quickly becoming little more than a market town for outlying farms and a residence for low-salaried government clerks. Merchants with limited assets shortened their sights and turned to the home market. They became what they had been in the colonial city: solely retailers, although now their source of supply was Baltimore instead of London, and their clientele had changed to the point where the prospects of great profits ceased. Those merchants who had been most successful in the halcyon days of international trade channeled their resources into domestic investments and rural development such as agricultural diversification. The planter's merchant now became the farmer's banker; and Annapolis became, in a quiet, visually imperceptible way,

a center of capital for agricultural improvement and rural development. It was a new role the town easily assumed. Sheltering the Farmers Bank of Maryland entailed no new growth and little opportunity
for any but the most affluent. The bank's impact was upon the countryside, and the townspeople were more than content that it be there.
Annapolitans had thus quietly adjusted to the new social and economic situation in which they found themselves. What is more, they
seemed to like the peace and quiet that came with the decline in commerce and gave the impression to all who visited that they would
wish it no other way.

In the following chapters the merchant community of approximately thirty individuals is viewed at three levels: in terms of its
composition and potential for capital accumulation in the late 1760s
and early 1770s, in terms of its most dynamic element represented
by the partnerships of Charles Wallace, Joshua Johnson, John Davidson, and John Muir, and in terms of the merchants' experience in
Annapolis in the context of the careers of other townspeople. Because
tax lists and other quantifiable data for the whole town exist only
for 1782-1783, it was not possible to compare the relative economic
standing of all people in town before and after the Revolution. But
by focusing upon the careers of those who were living in Annapolis
in 1783, at a peak in its growth, and by examining the pattern of
their successes and failures, an equally valid picture of the nature
and course of opportunity within the town emerges.

In order to move outside Annapolis and to demonstrate how the
community represents a case study of urban growth and mercantile
opportunity in the Chesapeake area, the activities of Wallace, Johnson, Davidson, and Muir are probed in detail. The initial partnership
of Wallace, Davidson, and Johnson was the first American firm to
break the British middleman's hold on the supply of goods to Maryland, and it was also the first to be active in the consignment tobacco
trade independent of British capital. The second partnership, of
Wallace, Johnson and Muir, formed during the war, found itself increasingly in competition with other American firms for the tobacco
trade. Although after the war they were perhaps the most important
tobacco firm operating in the upper Chesapeake, merchants in
Georgetown and smaller Tidewater towns challenged their leadership. The major threat to the consignment tobacco trade and to the
trade of urban centers like Annapolis and Georgetown came from
Baltimore where, after 1793, capital derived from the reexport trade
was channeled into the purchase of quality tobacco and other crops
from the Tidewater counties. As a result, the consignment trade
moved rapidly to extinction and what might have been flourishing

towns became decaying villages. Annapolis and Georgetown were saved from the status of ghost towns like Queen Anne's Town, Piscatta-way, and Port Tobacco because they still had government to sustain them.

How men cope with declining opportunity, especially in the context of eighteenth-century America, has rarely concerned previous historians. Usually the emphasis is on achievement within an expanding economy. Yet, with the earliest phase of urbanization in the Chesapeake, there was also urban decay and constricting opportunity of which Annapolis is only one case among many.

CHAPTER 1

THE STAGES of URBAN GROWTH AND THE EMERGENCE OF A MERCHANT CLASS, 1684-1774

S CHOLARS have long speculated about the reasons for the lack of urban centers in the Tidewater Chesapeake prior to the Revolution. The suitability of the soil, especially on the Western Shore, for tobacco and the existence of many streams navigable by the largest tobacco ships worked against the growth of central market places. Individual merchants, with perhaps one or two lesser competitors, dominated the trade of each of the several major landings, where little else than a few stores, half a dozen dwellings, and a warehouse or two stood by the water's edge. The relatively high price of tobacco, especially in the middle decades of the eighteenth century, inhibited agricultural diversification and restrained the development of marketing networks and urbanization of the type that developed only a relatively short distance away in southeastern Pennsylvania.[1] Urban centers were not likely to develop in the Tidewater so long as tobacco remained the principal cash crop.

But Annapolis proved an exception. Between 1684 and the Revolution, Annapolis grew from a landing hardly distinguishable from many others to a sizable community equivalent in terms of social life

---

[1]Lewis Cecil Gray, *History of Agriculture in the Southern United States to 1860* (Gloucester, Mass., 1958), I:443, discusses the lack of urban centers in the Chesapeake, as does Charles A. Barker, *The Background of the Revolution in Maryland* (New Haven, 1940), p. 52. For tobacco prices see Gray, *History of Agriculture*, 1:259-76. Central place theory and urbanization in nearby Pennsylvania are discussed in James T. Lemon, "Urbanization and Development of Eighteenth Century Southeastern Pennsylvania and Adjacent Delaware," *William and Mary Quarterly* 24 (October 1967), 501-42. See also James H. Soltow, *The Economic Role of Williamsburg* (Williamsburg, Va., 1965), pp. 2-5. In 1783, "A Merchant of Maryland" writing in the November 28th issue of the *Baltimore Maryland Gazette* argued that the Revolution made Baltimore into a central place of commerce in the Chesapeake, in sharp contrast to the past when merchants were separated and Maryland made no figure in the world of commerce. Cited by Mary Jane Dowd in "The Role of the State Government in the Economy of Maryland, 1777-1807" (master's thesis, Johns Hopkins University, 1959), p. 54.

and culture with most of the major colonial cities. It was a peculiar kind of urban growth, however: it derived from the town's political importance rather than its economic function. Throughout the colonial period, Annapolis never served as a major marketing center for a larger agricultural region. From the beginning, a number of its residents were employed as public officials or in supplying goods and services to those who were drawn to town by the business of government. For a time, some Annapolitans were also employed in essentially nonurban industries that happened to grow up about the town. But without government and the important role it came to play in both the political and social life of the colony, Annapolis probably would not have grown much beyond the hamlet that Londontown, Piscattaway, or Bladensburg was by 1774.[2]

From its founding until the Revolution, Annapolis passed through three distinct stages of growth. The first lasted from 1684 until 1715. During these years there was some doubt whether the town would be anything more than a small village which, after 1694, would swell each fall with the convening of the General Assembly and then shrink back to insignificant size some few weeks later when the assembly adjourned. The second lasted from 1715 to 1763 and can be characterized as an era of bureaucratic growth and small industrial expansion. In those years, the government grew to a year-round operation sustained by a permanent resident bureaucracy. Shipbuilding and, to a lesser extent, tanning employed a number of people in and about the town. The third stage, lasting from 1763 to 1774, was a period of affluence, and might appropriately be referred to as the townhouse era. During this brief period, shipbuilding and tanning declined sharply, but the population grew rapidly and conspicuous consumption, especially on the part of the rich who in increasing numbers resided in town, expanded dramatically.

Almost until the third stage of growth, merchants played a minimal role in the community. Annapolis had few exports, although tobacco may have been more significant in the first years of the eighteenth century than it was by the 1760s. As early as 1747, residents were complaining that most tobacco was being loaded up the

[2]By 1774, Londontown had no more than forty houses. Bladensburg and Piscattaway were mere landings, although the former boasted several stores because it was in the heart of the best tobacco-growing country. See Arthur Eli Karinen, "Numerical and Distributional Aspects of Maryland Population, 1631–1840" (Ph.D. dissertation, University of Maryland, 1958), appendix A; Edward C. Papenfuse, "Planter Behavior and Economic Opportunity in a Staple Economy," *Agricultural History* 46:2 (April 1972), 297–311, where one of the two stores at Piscattaway is discussed; and the Reverend John R. Biddle, "Historical Geography of Bladensburg, Maryland" (master's thesis, Catholic University, 1954).

Annapolis in the 1850s. Detail from a Sachse print, Maryland Hall of Records, Gift Collection. Photocopy by M. E. Warren, Annapolis.

bay.[3] In 1763, only seventy-five hogsheads of tobacco were inspected in Annapolis, while the four other inspection points in Anne Arundel County housed a total of 3,151 hogsheads.[4] By 1790, not even one hogshead was inspected in Annapolis and the inspection house had fallen down. Yet the other inspection points continued to handle as much, if not more, than they had twenty-seven years before.[5]

[3]*Maryland Gazette*, March 24, 1747.

[4]*Maryland Gazette*, November 17, 1763. There were five inspection points: Elk Ridge, 1,696 hogsheads; Land of Ease and Taylor's Landing, 426 hogsheads; Indian Landing, 309 hogsheads; Pigg Point and Spriggs, 720 hogsheads; Annapolis, 75 hogsheads. *Note:* This issue of the *Maryland Gazette* is not on the Yale University microfilm and must be consulted at the State Library in Annapolis.

[5]"1790 A list of the number of hhds of Tobacco inspected and shipped from the several Warehouses in the State of Maryland," Scharf Collection, Maryland Historical

The Annapolis market was largely for consumer goods bought on a cash basis, and until residents had sufficient amounts of cash to spend, few merchants were interested in establishing stores in town or in taking an active part in the town's development. Even of those who did, many were residents who had established themselves in industry or crafts and had relatively small amounts of capital that they invested in imports for sale to their neighbors. Only during the early 1750s and again after the French and Indian War did a significant number of merchants who actively traded elsewhere in the colony settle in the community, and they did so largely to maintain contacts with the affairs of government and with wealthy planters who were drawn to town for the social season.

THE UNCERTAIN YEARS, 1684–1715

During the first years of settlement, government played an insignificant part in the growth of the town. Richard Beard first surveyed Annapolis in 1684, as a result of an act of assembly creating "Anne Arundel Town," a port of entry.[6] The chances that it would grow much beyond the handful of houses and one tavern that were there in 1684 were slight. A town had been started across the Severn and had failed.[7] There was little reason to expect that the landing at Proctors, as Annapolis was then called, would do much better. Yet Beard laid out the lots as he was directed out of the 100 acres that had been given by Richard Hill, Robert Proctor, and the proprietor. Beginning at the end of what is now Duke of Gloucester Street, near Proctor's tavern, he drew straight lines for the principal streets and staked out lots along what were to become Market and Shipwright Streets.[8]

For the next ten years nothing happened. No houses were built and the stakes to the lots were lost, as was the transcript of the proceedings by which the land was originally given for the town. Then, in 1694, Governor Nicholson persuaded the legislature to move the capital away from the Catholics in St. Mary's County to a spot more central to the colony's population. He chose Anne Arundel Town,

---

Society, Baltimore, Md.: Elkridge Landing, 1,943; Taylor's Landing, 385; Tracy's Landing, 217; Indian Landing, 432. Annapolis is not mentioned. (Hereafter cited as Scharf Col.)

[6]Elihu S. Riley, *The Ancient City* (Annapolis, 1887), pp. 52–54.

[7]James E. Moss, "The Lost Towne at Severne in Mari-land" (paper on deposit at the Hall of Records, Annapolis, Md., 1938).

[8]See Richard Beard's original certificate of survey dated March 25, 1683/4 at "Anne Arundel Town," Annapolis Plats, Hall of Records, Annapolis, Md.

soon to be known as Annapolis. In haste, a committee was set up to determine title to the town lands, and Richard Beard was again commissioned to execute a survey and map, which he did after considerable prodding.[9]

Nicholson had a profound influence on the design of the town. He wanted to make his capital a model city, and he dramatically altered Beard's unimaginative plan by superimposing streets oriented to the points of the compass, and circles, features that were to govern the physical appearance of the town as it grew and were to provide it with a singular charm that has survived to the present.[10] When Nicholson left in 1698, Annapolis was beginning to resemble a town. The following year a correspondent of the Royal Society wrote:

There are indeed several places alotted for towns [in Maryland], but hitherto they are only titular ones except Annapolis, where the Governor resides. Col Nicholson has done his endeavour to make a town of that place. There are about 40 dwelling houses in it [c. 250 people], 7 or 8 of which can afford a good lodging and accommodations for strangers. There are also a state house and a free school, built with brick, which make a great shew among a parcel of wooden houses; and the foundation of a church is laid, the only brick church in Maryland. They have two market days a week, and had Governor Nicholson continued there a few months longer, he had brought it to perfection.[11]

The town had not reached "perfection" by 1707, and as far as the historian John Oldmixon was concerned, there was "no great probability" that it ever would.[12] Some of the uncertainty over the town's future was undoubtedly caused by the courthouse fire of 1704, which destroyed the land records; but it is significant that no action was taken to clear title to town lots until after 1715. In those eleven years,

[9]Riley, *Ancient City*, pp. 55-62. In March 1694/5, the "Speaker and Burgesses" demanded to see Beard's new map, but Beard answered "that for want of some Large Paper to Draw the same on, it is not yet done . . . ." In May, when Beard presented his bill, he still had not drawn the map and his account was "referred untill hee brings the Platt of the Towne to the Committee." Soon thereafter Beard complied in order to get his money. *Archives of Maryland* (Baltimore, 1883-), 19:96, 122, 195, 196. (Hereafter cited as *Archives*.)

[10]Nicholson's role in planning the town is discussed by John W. Reps, *Town Planning in Frontier America* (Princeton, 1969), pp. 129-43.

[11][John Oldmixon], *The British Empire in America Containing the History of the Discovery, Settlement, Progress and State of the British Colonies on the Continent and Islands of America* (New York, 1969 [reprint of 1741 edition]), 1:333, and Michael G. Kammen, ed., "Maryland in 1699: A Letter from the Reverend Hugh Jones," *Journal of Southern History*, 29 (1963): 371-72. The population figure inserted in the quote is based on the probable number of people per house. See table 1-1 and note 26 below.

[12]Oldmixon, *British Empire*, 1:338. Oldmixon's book was first published in 1708.

property acquired sufficient value to invite a challenge to ownership and two enterprising residents. Thomas Bordley and Thomas Larkin, decided to claim the whole town as their own.[13] Almost immediately the assembly responded by creating a commission to survey lots and ascertain titles. Although the claim was not rejected by the courts until 1733, landowners were quick to pay Bordley and Larkin what they demanded to secure their titles.[14]

INDUSTRIAL EXPANSION AND BUREAUCRATIC GROWTH, 1715–1763

Property had undoubtedly acquired value by 1715 because of the development of local industry and the prospect of increased governmental activity that came with the return of Maryland to proprietary control. Neither tanning nor shipbuilding was a necessary component of urban development. Both industries were to be found scattered about the bay, wherever natural resources were sufficient and people were so inclined. But they did offer employment for townspeople and supplied capital that eventually found its way into trade.[15]

The first tanyard, established as early as 1708, was followed by at least three others before 1763.[16] Shipbuilding and related trades, such as rope and block making, began to grow significantly after 1735 and attained their greatest influence on the economy in the 1760s. Ship-

[13]For the proceedings of the chancery case that arose over the Bordley and Larkin claim see Chancery Records, Hall of Records, Annapolis, Md. (hereafter cited as Chan. Rec.), 6 [IR#3]:293–414.

[14]Chan. Rec. 6:353. Stephen Bordley, Thomas Bordley's son, lists the amounts received by his father and Thomas Larkin from Annapolis residents.

[15]There has been no study of the tanning industry in Maryland, although the land and court records contain numerous references to tanyards in many parts of the colony far distant from any town. For example, see the subject indexes to Anne Arundel County Deeds and Judgments, Hall of Records, Annapolis, Md. Arthur P. Middleton, *Tobacco Coast* (Newport News, Va., 1953), deals with the shipbuilding industry throughout the Chesapeake. The illustration on page 252 of his book, showing the colonial shipyard at Spencer Hall, Maryland, is graphic evidence of the industry in its nonurban setting.

[16]Docura's tanyard on College Creek, Parcels 53 and 54, was the first in Annapolis, and on or near its site tanyards were in continuous operation under different owners and managers (e.g., Alexander Stewart, note 23 below), until the 1780s. About 1746, William Roberts opened his second tanyard, having previously purchased Stewart's; and, in 1775, leased it to Thomas Hyde (see Parcel 28, Section V). Hyde continued to operate this tanyard until the Revolution, when he leased it to the state. A third tanyard, although short-lived, was also erected on Parcel 24, Section II, some time before 1755 by Frederick Wolfe. The data about the location of tanyards and general land use in Annapolis between c. 1750 and 1800 are to be found in the three-volume study by Edward Papenfuse and Jane McWilliams, "Appendix F: Lot Histories and Maps, National Endowment for the Humanities Grant #H69–0–178," on deposit at the Hall

building lent a character to the life of the community that dominated it for at least a generation. While tanyards, for obvious reasons of smell, were built on the periphery of town, shipbuilding was carried on in the very heart of the community, and the dock area was filled with the hulls of ships in progress, a ropewalk, and blockmaker's shops. When the town was resurveyed in 1718, land was set aside specifically for shipbuilding, but it was not until 1735 that Patrick Creagh first entered his name for the area south of what is now Randall Street, then known as the "ship carpenters lot." Creagh was to become the best known of the Annapolis shipbuilders, although William Roberts was to erect a shipyard on the northern edge of town (near what is now St. John's campus), where he launched one of the largest ships ever built in the Chesapeake during the colonial period.[17] Creagh's operation was the hub of the Annapolis shipbuilding industry. As his business grew, any number of taverns were established nearby to cater to the needs of the craftsmen, and some, such as that owned by Samuel Horatio Middleton, proved so successful as to allow its owner to branch out into trade and other business enterprises.[18]

The extent to which tanning and shipbuilding could grow in and about the town was limited by natural resources and a relatively small demand for the products. No more than three tanyards were in operation at any one time throughout the eighteenth century. The two Annapolis shipyards faced stiff competition from Galloway and Steward at West River as well as diminishing supplies of local timber.[19] But tanners and saddlemakers, shipbuilders and ropemakers

---

of Records, Annapolis, Md. (Hereafter cited as Papenfuse and McWilliams, "Appendix F.") See the "Key to Summaries" in Papenfuse and McWilliams for an explanation of Parcels and Sections.

[17]For Creagh, see Papenfuse and McWilliams, "Appendix F," Parcel 39, introduction. For Roberts, see Middleton, *Tobacco Coast*, pp. 239, 262, 264.

[18]Papenfuse and McWilliams, "Appendix F," Parcels 15 and 16, Section XIV.

[19]For a much later period, some idea of the nature of the competition from other shipyards and the number of ships produced in Annapolis by the time of the Revolution can be derived from "Annapolis Registers, 1774–1798," Record Group 41, National Archives, Washington, D.C. The ships in the following table were all registered in 1774 and 1775, but some were built as early as 1771:

Shipyards

West River	Annapolis	Swan Creek	Severn	Herring Bay
1774 ship 180 t	1771 schnr 15 t	1771–1775	1771–1775	1775 ship 150 t
1774 schnr 20 t	1772 schnr 15 t	ship 220 t	schnr 23 t	
1775 brig 90 t	1773 sloop 22 t	schnr 35 t	schnr 34 t	
1775 ship 160 t	1775 ship 200 t		schnr 23 t	

Note: t=tons; schnr=schooner

recognized a growing market for goods in the town and began to invest their profits in imports to meet the demand.

The major reason for the increase in the market for imported goods after 1714 was the growth of the governmental bureaucracy, which brought customers to town and demanded goods and services for itself. Beginning in 1715, the proprietor in person and through his agents worked steadily to develop a bureaucracy centered in Annapolis to collect quitrents and hogshead duties, grant land patents, and handle a multitude of other business and administrative chores. The establishment of the proprietor's authority over the colony and the creation of an administrative structure for his affairs was a slow process. In the first years, the bureaucracy's economic impact on the town is difficult to measure with any degree of precision, but the major studies of the period agree that by the 1750s it was well developed and extracting a considerable annual income for the Calvert family.[20] In 1754, the first year for which there are comprehensive figures, at least £4,565 sterling was earned by public officeholders who lived part of the year in Annapolis and who had to support clerks and deputies to perform their functions when they were absent.[21] For the next twenty years, while the bureaucracy did not grow much larger, the volume of business handled and the value of the offices increased.[22] When it is considered that the cost of building a ship (Annapolis was, at the peak of production, launching three ships a year) was not more than £1,200 currency, that Annapolis's largest ropewalk probably had no more than £1,200 currency worth of business in a given year, and that a tannery probably did half as much, the

---

[20]Barker, *Background of the Revolution*, is the most complete account of the establishment of proprietary control. Donnell M. Owings, *His Lordship's Patronage* (Baltimore, 1953) is an exhaustive treatment of the proprietary, royal, and provincial bureaucracies, and includes information on who held the offices as well as what they were worth. Clarence P. Gould, *The Land System in Maryland* (Baltimore, 1913) and Newton D. Mereness, *Maryland as a Proprietary Province* (New York, 1901), should also be consulted. For an essay on other secondary sources relating to bureaucratic growth see Owings, *His Lordship's Patronage*, pp. 187–93.

[21]The figure is based on a civil list for 1754 and data found in Owings, *His Lordship's Patronage*. The civil list is in Executive Papers, Hall of Records, Annapolis, Md. (hereafter cited as Exec. Pap.), Portfolio #3, 30. The sums given in the civil list have been reduced to sterling at an exchange rate of £1.50 currency to £1 sterling. See Paul H. Giddens, "Trade and Industry in Colonial Maryland, 1753-1769," *Journal of Economic and Business History* 4 (May 1932), 537. The sum also includes a charge for a Rent Role Keeper, not noted on the civil list taken from Owings, p. 89.

[22]See Owings, *His Lordship's Patronage*, for the gradual rise in value of the offices as the volume of business increased. In 1784, the salaries alone of people on the civil list amounted to £3,795 sterling, a sum that did not include fees, which were a major source of income for some of the clerks. "List of Salarys for Civil List, . . . [1784]," Box 61, Exec. Pap.

government payroll looms large as an important component in the economy.[23]

Although the demand for imported goods began to grow after 1714, the market remained small for a number of years and was dominated by only a few merchants. From the first decade until his death in 1728, the most prominent and by far the most successful was Amos Garrett. In the words of a contemporary, "Amos Garrett was generally reputed to have greatly increased his fortune after 1714 . . . [and] did greatly advance in trade, but he never [had] more than one ship or sea vessell, except small craft."[24] Instead, Garrett built his fortune on lending money at interest and dealt in imported goods as a modest sideline. When he died he had no tobacco in his tobacco house (indicating that even then little tobacco was being brought to town) and only a small inventory of goods on hand for sale, but he left over £1,600 cash in his house and a large number of debts owed to him for bills of exchange drawn on his account.

Even after Garrett's death, it was a number of years before the prospects for the Annapolis import trade improved significantly

[23]Reverend Andrew Burnaby, *Travels Through the Middle Settlements in North America in the Years 1759-60* (London, 1775), p. 67: "They build two or three ships annually, but seldom more . . . ."

In 1771, Samuel Galloway hoped to get £1,200 for his ship *Caroline*. Middleton, *Tobacco Coast*, p. 240. The *Caroline* was 200 tons, 115 tons larger than the average size vessel built in Maryland between 1756 and 1775. Undoubtedly, the average price for a ship built in Annapolis was thus considerably lower than £1,200. Vaughan W. Brown, *Shipping in the Port of Annapolis, 1748-1775* (Annapolis, 1965), appended list of vessels that cleared Annapolis customs, 1748-1775, and Middleton, *Tobacco Coast*, p. 241.

The figure for the volume of business handled by an Annapolis ropewalk is derived from the Thomas Williamson Account Book, MS 913, Maryland Historical Society, Baltimore, Md., and pertains to the years 1748-1749. For similar accounts for the same ropewalk between 1759 and 1763, see Chan. Rec., 14:167ff.

When Alexander Stewart, the tanner, died in 1731 he had £276.10.0 worth of hides in his Annapolis tanyard. If it is assumed that the bulk of his business would be conducted in the spring and fall, the months when tanners were usually advertising in the *Maryland Gazette*, and that the volume of business handled in one year probably did not exceed twice what he had on hand in April, then Stewart probably did no more than £600 worth each year. Testamentary Papers, Hall of Records, Annapolis, Md. (hereafter cited as Test. Pap.), Box 37, Folder 14.

Here and throughout the chapter, unless otherwise noted, all sums are given as Maryland currency. Although the exchange rate between sterling and currency fluctuated throughout the colonial period, after the French and Indian War, one pound sterling was generally worth £1.67 Maryland currency.

[24]Test. Pap., Box 34, Folder 2. When Garrett died in 1728 he had developed part of the harbor area, had a "prizing" warehouse about 60 feet long and 40 feet wide, and owned approximately one sixth of the lots in town. The list of his lots as of 1726 is in the Carroll-Maccubbin Papers, MS 219, Box 13, Maryland Historical Society, Baltimore, Md. Garrett seems to have had a hard time adjusting to life in the new world and·became a chronic alcoholic, a disease that finally killed him. See his nephew's letter in Test. Pap., Box 34, Folder 2.

enough to attract more than a handful of merchants to the town. Surviving issues of the *Maryland Gazette* between 1728 and 1734 record but one merchant advertising drygoods for sale in Annapolis, and he faced competition from nearby Londontown.[25] But by the 1740s a change was apparent. The permanent population doubled between 1715 and 1740 (see table 1-1), and, as government became more important, people came in growing numbers from all over the colony to conduct their affairs and to stay for a brief time.[26]

Table 1-1 Population Growth in Annapolis, 1699–1783

Year	St. Anne's Taxables (#)	Regression (#)	Rate of Regression (%)	Total Population of Annapolis (#)	White (%)	White (#)	Black (%)	Black (#)
1783	1,400	-50	+3.6	1,280	64.9	831	35.1	449
1775	1,450	233	83.9	1,326				
1768	1,217	82	93.3	1,113				
1764	1,135	32	97.2	1,038				
1760	[1,103]	75	93.2	1,008				
1755	[1,028]	117	88.6	939	67.4	633	32.6	336
1740	[911]	61	93.3	832				
1730	850	106	87.5	776	68.0	528	32.0	248
1725	744	230	69.1	679				
1720	514	71	86.2	469				
1715	443	13	97.1	405				
1710	430	67	84.4	393	75.8	298	24.2	95
1705	363			332	88.4	293	11.6	39
1699				252				

Source: See chapter 1, note 26.
Note: 1740-1755 number of increase: 107; percentage increase 12.8
    1764-1775 number of increase: 288; percentage increase 27.7
    1764-1768 number of increase: 75; percentage increase, annual average: 1.8
    1768-1775 number of increase: 213; percentage increase, annual average: 2.7

[25]See appendix A, "Merchants Advertising in the *Maryland Gazette*, 1728-1774," in Edward C. Papenfuse, "Mercantile Opportunity and Urban Development in a Planting Society: A Case Study of Annapolis, Maryland 1763-1805" (Ph.D. dissertation, Johns Hopkins University, 1973).

[26]Except for the census returns for 1782 and 1783 in the Scharf Col., there are no separate population figures for Annapolis before 1800. The figures given in table 1-1 are based on the rate of regression from 1783 to 1705 in the number of taxables in St. Anne's Parish, of which Annapolis was a part. Taxable data were taken from Appendix A of Karinen, "Maryland Population," except for 1740, 1755, and 1760, when the known ratio of St. Anne's taxable population to that of neighboring St. James Parish (a constant throughout the colonial period) was used to ascertain the probable number of taxables for St. Anne's. The rate of regression was then multiplied by the known 1783 population to determine the population for the previous year for which there was taxable data, and so forth backwards until the year 1705 was reached. Expressed as formulae: the rate of regression (R) equals $\frac{T'-T''}{T'}$ when T'=taxables for one year, and T''=taxables for any previous year. The regressed population (RP) equals

Minor craftsmen and servants were quick to recognize the opportunities presented by the growing market. Letters captured during the French and Indian War written by Annapolis residents to their relatives in Britain all sound the same note of optimism about the prospect of selling drygoods and luxury items. Richard Tuggett had prospered as footman to Benjamin Tasker, prominent planter and government official, and was writing to encourage his relatives to send him "some knives, some buckles and butens and anything you think proper for I can make you money here . . . ."[27] Edward Watts, who from the tone of his letter had never succeeded at anything, nevertheless pleaded with his brothers to send such goods as "shirts stocking breeches hats and all things that is fitting thereto," for, he argued, "I could, if it whas posable you could believe me after my manyfould transgressons to you all, sell your goods to great advantage."[28] But those with capital fared best in meeting the increasing demand for goods and, of those who had it, shipbuilders and tanners were prominent. Between 1745 and 1753, the number of people advertising drygoods in the *Maryland Gazette* grew from three to twelve. Of these, Robert Swan, Robert Couden, and Thomas Hyde had been tanners. William Roberts was first a saddler-tanner and then a shipbuilder before becoming a merchant. As Patrick Creagh prospered, he combined shipbuilding and housebuilding with mercantile interests, and dealt in slaves and servants as well as goods.[29]

$100-R'\times P'$, $R''\times P''$, . . . when P'=a known population, P''=$100-R'\times P'$, . . . R'=the first rate of regression, R''=the second rate of regression, and so forth.

The percentage of the total population that was black was calculated by using the census data for 1704, 1710, and 1730, cited in Karinen; the census for 1755 published in *The Gentleman's Magazine* 34 (1764), 261; and the census of 1783, adjusting for the slightly lower concentration of blacks in the town than was the case in the county. The calculation for 1699 is based upon the number of people per family, assuming single family dwellings, times the number of houses. (Expressed as a formula: $\frac{P'}{H}\times D=P''$ when P'=the total population of the county (4,512), H=the number of heads of households (716), D=the number of dwellings (40), and P''=the projected population of Annapolis.) The result is close to the population regression estimate for 1705 and suggests that the regression method works with some degree of accuracy. The county data come from the census of 1704 cited in Karinen and the number of houses is taken from·Oldmixon, *British Empire*, 1:333.

[27]Great Britain, Public Record Office, High Court of Admiralty Papers (hereafter cited as PRO, HCA), 30/258. The letter is dated November 2, 1756, and is written to Tuggett's mother and father.

[28]PRO, HCA 30/258. The letter is dated Annapolis, December 24, 1756, and is written to his brother.

[29]Not all tanners went into trade. Allen Quynn, one of the town's leading citizens, began his career as a shoemaker in the 1760s, bought Robert Swan's tanyard, and died a wealthy man, without investing any capital in mercantile activities. For Quynn's career see Papenfuse and McWilliams, "Appendix F," Parcels 5 and 6; *Maryland*

After 1754, as the French and Indian War grew in intensity, the import trade slowed dramatically. When the Reverend Andrew Burnaby visited Annapolis in June 1759, he wrote "there is very little trade carried on from this place and the chief of the inhabitants are storekeepers or public officers."[30] By August 1762, there had been little change. Another traveller, Benjamin Mifflin, noted that there was "very little trade stirring. No sea vessel in port, three building by a Bermudian [Patrick Creagh] . . . there are no wharfs about the town except in a little bason where the vessels are building. . . ."[31]

THE AGE OF AFFLUENCE, 1763–1774

The end of hostilities in 1763 brought unprecedented prosperity to Annapolis, despite the fact that tanning, shipbuilding, and related trades suffered a marked decline. By 1771, the once prosperous blockmaking establishment of Nathaniel Adams, near what had been Creagh's shipyard, was in a sad state of decay.[32] Thomas Hyde had difficulty in renting his tanyard until the Revolution brought a renewed demand for leather products. But even the Revolution failed to help the town's shipbuilding industry.[33] During the war, when contracts were granted for the construction of galleys and barges, they went to Stephen Steward at West River and not to the yards in Annapolis, where only one ship was launched during the eight years of conflict.[34]

Prosperity was based not on industry but on the concentration of political power in Annapolis, as growing numbers of socially or polit-

Gazette, July 26, 1764, and November 10, 1803; Anne Arundel County Deeds, Hall of Records, Annapolis, Md., BB#3:622; and Chancery Papers, Hall of Records, Annapolis, Md. (hereafter cited as Chan. Pap.), 3002. For Patrick Creagh, see Joy Gary, "Patrick Creagh of Annapolis," *Maryland Historical Magazine* 48 (1953), 310–26.

[30]Burnaby, *Travels*, p. 67.

[31]Benjamin Mifflin, "A Journal of Benjamin Mifflin on a Tour from Philadelphia to Delaware and Maryland, July 26–August 14, 1762," edited by Victor H. Palsits, *Bulletin of the New York Public Library* 39 (June 1935), 431–34.

[32]Papenfuse and McWilliams, "Appendix F," Parcels 15 and 16, Section I.

[33]*Ibid.*, Parcel 28, Section V.

[34]Exec. Pap., November 18, 1776, Box 5, #15; 1778, Box 12; May 14, 1781, Box 37; October 13, 1781, Box 33. Auditor General's Journal B, Hall of Records, Annapolis, Md. (hereafter cited as AGJB), January 27, 1781, p. 248; March 23, 1781, p. 263; September 14, 1782, p. 347.

The only ship known to have been built in Annapolis during the war was the *Willing Tom*, built by Thomas Rutland and registered in July 1783. See the papers of the *Willing Tom* in the Vertical File, Maryland Historical Society, Baltimore, Md. (hereafter cited as Vert. File).

ically oriented wealthy planters were drawn to town. The market for imported goods that had begun to grow before 1763 mushroomed in the following decade because of increased spending by the rich and the ensuing impact of such expenditures on the incomes of the resident population. The affluent purchased large quantities of luxury goods and the wages they gave also enabled their employees to patronize local merchants.

The enormous importance of the spending habits of the affluent to the prosperity of the town can be demonstrated and measured in at least two ways: by the amount of private construction and the size of individual store accounts. After 1763, the rich began to build in the town as they had never done before, and they bought great amounts of goods to make life in what they built as comfortable as possible. Between 1764 and 1774, at least fourteen major townhouses and four combination residence/businesses were erected, releasing an estimated £57,374 currency into circulation, an average of £5,737 per year (see table 1-2).[35] How much one townhouse cost and the means used to finance it are detailed in an account book kept by Colonel James Brice.[36]

---

[35]The construction estimates in table 1-2 are based on the ratio of the known cost of building the James Brice townhouse (see note 36 below) to its 1798 valuation times the 1798 valuation for the other Annapolis townhouses. Expressed as a formula: $C=R\times V$ when C=construction cost, $R=\dfrac{\text{cost of Brice House}}{\text{1798 valuation of Brice House}}$ and V=1798 valuation. The dates for the building of the townhouses and the names of their owners are taken from data compiled by Historic Annapolis, Incorporated (in most cases the work of Phebe Jacobsen, Hall of Records), which is on file at Historic Annapolis and the Hall of Records.

There were few townhouses built before 1763. Perhaps the most prominent architect prior to that time was Simon Duff. Duff was brought to Annapolis in 1744 for the express purpose of erecting a suitable dwelling for the governor, Thomas Bladen. After £4,000 and considerable squabbling between the governor and the assembly, the project, known by then as "Bladen's Folly" was abandoned. Duff remained in town, however, and built a number of private dwellings, although only one, a townhouse erected for the merchant Daniel Wolstenholme, even approached the scale and magnificence of the mansions of the 1760s and 1770s. By 1751, Duff found the prospects for business were not very good. On May 15, he advertised in the *Maryland Gazette* that "Having been many years an inhabitant of this town, and having built a number of houses in it, which he hopes were always done to the satisfaction of his employers, finding now the business much slackens," he was determined to break up housekeeping and sell all that he owned. For Duff's career see Riley, *Ancient City*, p. 302; Aubrey C. Land, *The Dulanys of Maryland* (Baltimore, 1968), pp. 161ff.; and Papenfuse and McWilliams, notes to "Appendix F" on the Naval Academy grounds. To determine the 1972 dollar value of 1774 Maryland pounds multiply by 22.17. For conversion from sterling to 1972 dollars multiply by 37.34.

[36]James Brice Account Book, microfilm copy at the Hall of Records, Annapolis, Md.; original in the possession of Jerusalem Royal Arch Chapter No. 9, Masonic Temple, Baltimore, Md., to whom grateful acknowledgment is made for permission to cite this document. (hereafter cited as Brice Account Book), M 1207.

Table 1-2 Annapolis Townhouses and Their Original Owners, 1764-1774

Owner	Occupation	Built	Location, "Appendix F"	1798 Valuation	Estimated Construction Costs (Md./ currency)
Charles Carroll of Carrollton	Lawyer	c.1764–	Parcel 34, Section II	$2,900	£6,467
Samuel Chase	Lawyer	1769–	Parcel 19, Section I	$2,500	£5,750
Mathias Hammond	Lawyer	1774	Parcel 24, Section I	$1,800	£4,014
James Brice	Planter	1776–	Parcel 23, Section I	$1,800	£4,014[1]
William Paca	Lawyer	1764–	Parcel 24, Section II	$1,800	£4,014
Charles Carroll, Barrister	Lawyer	c.1764–	Parcel 35, Section III	$1,650	£3,679
Upton Scott	Doctor	1765–	Parcel 34, Section III	$1,600	£3,568
John Brice III	Lawyer	c.1766–	Parcel 17, Section IV	$1,200	£2,676
John Ridout	Government official	1764–	Parcel 35, Section VI	$1,400 $3,000	£3,122 £6,690
Wallace, Davidson and Johnson	Merchants	1771–	Parcel 13, Sections V–VIII	$4,000	£8,920
Lloyd Dulany Thomas Rutland	Planter	1771–	Parcel 12, Section VI	$1,000	£2,230[2]
	Planter	c.1772	Parcel 25, Section III	$1,000	£2,230
Total					£57,374

Source: See chapter 1, note 35.
[1]Actual cost
[2]In 1783 Lloyd Dulany's house sold for £2,745, Sale Book of Confiscated Property, Hall of Records, Annapolis, Md., p. 59.

James Brice was born in Annapolis in 1746, the second son of John Brice, planter-merchant and judge of the Provincial Court. During the 1750s, the father kept a store in Annapolis next to his house on Prince George Street, but James, although admitted to the bar, chose the life of the country gentleman, relying on inherited estates and, after 1780, income from government to supply him with funds to support his lifestyle.[37] When his father died in 1766, James was left plantations in Cecil and Kent counties and two lots in Annapolis with "bricks, lime, stones, plank and timber . . . for the purpose of building a dwelling house and out houses."[38] For the next eight years much of James's time was spent overseeing the construction of the house. It cost £4,014.8.0 currency to build; £2,825 represented cash outlays

[37]St. Anne's Parish Register, 1, 147; Will of John Brice, June 17, 1766, Wills Box B, Folder 84; Annapolis Records 5, 247–48, 253, 255; Register of Civil Officers, 1777–1794; all at Hall of Records, Annapolis, Md.
[38]Will of John Brice, June 17, 1766, Wills Box B, Folder 84, Hall of Records, Annapolis, Md.

Top: John Brice II House, built ca. 1730. Late nineteenth-century view, Maryland Hall of Records, Gift Collection. Photocopy by M. E. Warren, Annapolis. *Bottom:* James Brice House. Recent view, M. E. Warren Collection, Annapolis.

Top: Charles Carroll of Carrollton House. Early twentieth-century view, Maryland Hall of Records, Gift Collection. Photocopy by M. E. Warren, Annapolis.
Bottom: Samuel Chase–Edward Lloyd House. Early twentieth-century view, Maryland Hall of Records, Gift Collection. Photocopy by M. E. Warren.

Top: Matthias Hammond House. Late nineteenth-century view, Maryland Hall of Records, Gift Collection. Photocopy by M. E. Warren, Annapolis. *Bottom*: William Paca House and Gardens. Recent view, M. E. Warren Collection, Annapolis.

Top: Upton Scott House. Recent view, M. E. Warren Collection, Annapolis. *Bottom*: John Brice III House. Late nineteenth-century view, Maryland Hall of Records, Gift Collection. Photocopy by M. E. Warren, Annapolis.

Top: John Ridout House and Row Houses. *Ca*. 1930 view, Maryland Hall of Records, Gift Collection. Photocopy by M. E. Warren, Annapolis.
Bottom: Thomas Rutland House. Late nineteenth-century view, Maryland Hall of Records, Gift Collection. Photocopy by M. E. Warren, Annapolis.

Lloyd Dulany House. Photo taken in 1970 by the author.

of Brice alone, the remainder being the value of supplies left by his father and money from his mother. (See table 1-3.)

Brice's chief source of income during the time he was building his townhouse was an estate of 1,042 acres in Cecil and Kent counties, from which he received no more than £360 per annum.[39] In 1771, Brice took on an additional financial burden when he bought a second plantation on the north side of the Severn River for £1,000. He probably hoped it would be self-sustaining and would supply his table in nearby Annapolis, but over the next four years he proceeded to expend £1,068 on capital improvements and expenses, receiving only £200 in return, a net loss of £868 over and above his initial investment.[40] No wonder that Brice borrowed money from the loan office and failed to pay the Visitors of King William's School the £1,155 he owed them as treasurer.[41] Even by borrowing he probably had diffi-

[39]Brice Account Book, p. 10.
[40]IB#3, p. 159, Anne Arundel County Deeds, Hall of Records, Annapolis, Md.; and Brice Account Book, p. 29.
[41]Brice Account Book, and Anne Arundel County Testamentary Papers, Box 96, Folder 2, Hall of Records, Annapolis, Md.

Table 1-3 James Brice's Account of the Cost of Building His Townhouse

Category A:	"Sundries for buildings for which no *cash* was paid and which were furnished by Sarah and James Brice and left by Jno Brice dec'd"

	£. s. d.	
190,000 bricks made on Severn at 30/- (deducting therefrom 48.10.2 for flatting from Turners Neck, paid for)	237.07.10	
23,800 bricks brought by flatt at 30/-	35.14.00	
Carting the above bricks at 4/- per thousand	42.17.08	
Carting 3M bricks bought of Hammond 12/-; 35,400 of Rutland, 7.01.07	7.13.07	
Carting 18,500 bricks bought of Christian Librant at 4/-	3.14.00	
4M bu of lime at 6d; carting it at 50 bushels to a load at 2/-	108.00.00	
Carting 80 loads of sand £8, carting 240 1/2 tonns stone at 1/- =£12.00.00	20.00.00	
60 tons brown stone £9; carting it £3	12.00.00	
		467.07.01
Digging foundation of the house 49'by 44', 6' deep	20.00.00	
4 labourers 8 weeks about Stone Work	28.16.00	
5 labourers 5 months 9 May to 9 October, when about brick work at £3 a month each	75.00.00	
1 hand three years attending Thomas Harvey, Plaisterer at £30	90.00.00	
1 hand 2 years attending bricklayer when about kitchen stable, outhouses, garden wall	60.00.00	
2 hands 6 months attending Masons about Stonework, garden wall, at £3 a month each	36.00.00	
Negro carpenter 5 years at £36 a year	180.00.00	
		489.10.00
4M feet of plained and jointed flooring plank free from knots at 20/-, 1 1/2" thick	40.00.00	
Boarding:		
John Matthews, Carpenter 9/1766-6/1770 at £16	60.00.00	
Daniel McCritch, Carpenter 8/1766-10/1769 at £16	18.13.04	
Thomas Harvey Plaisterer	49.06.08	
Henry Jackson, 4 years	64.00.00	
		232.00.00
Grand Total		£1,189.03.01

Category B: "Cash Outlays"

	£. s. d.
Labor	
Bricklayers	227.12.07
Masons	66.18.00
Carpenters and Joiners	597.12.00
Servants [purchased labor]	81.10.00
Carver	17.16.00
Painters and Glaziers	40.12.11
Materials	
Shingles	102.05.01
Plank	200.03.00
Rum	17.00.00
Rope	7.07.09

Table 1-3 (continued)

Category B: "Cash Outlays"

Laths	11.00.00
Hair	9.13.00
Stone	154.12.60
Bricks	243.07.09
Nails	110.08.06
Screws	3.16.01
Locks	24.07.07
Hinges	14.14.05
Bolts	2.03.10
Lead	9.08.02
Bell	3.13.06
Jack for kitchen	13.01.02
Scotch oven	8.16.03
Iron stoves	3.13.00
Copper	5.10.00
Cranes	4.06.07
Plaister of Paris	57.14.01
Stucco tools	19.13.08
Sweet oil	1.08.06
Ironware	32.05.10
Lightning conductors	7.10.00
Window glass	52.01.03
Paints, oil	46.07.07
Glue	2.01.00
Shell lime	222.10.00
Stone lime	23.07.06
Spades	3.04.00
Marble	67.19.04
Scantling	5.00.00
Wells	21.08.11
Stable	12.12.10
Garden	47.07.00
Sundries	220.02.05
Grand Total	£2,825.00.04

Summary of Expenditures, 1766–1770

	Cost	Percentage of Whole
Labor	£1,715.11.06	42.8
Materials	£2,298.15.11	57.2
Total	£4,014.07.05	

Source: James Brice Account Book, microfilm M 1207, Hall of Records, Annapolis, Md., loose sheet.

Note: All sums are in Maryland currency.

culty making ends meet, for the account book reveals only capital investment and tells nothing of the cost of maintaining his lifestyle.

There is no question that the rich spent a great deal on themselves. Walter Dulany purchased £1,731 worth of goods at Nathan Hammond's store between 1764 and 1767, an average of £433 per year

(7.2 times the yearly income of the typical Annapolis craftsman).[42] When Governor Eden fled town in 1775, he owed one firm £360 for debts incurred between 1771 and 1773, not to mention accounts outstanding at other stores.[43] Lloyd Dulany, another prominent loyalist who was said to have put £10,000 into his Annapolis townhouse before the war, left £636 (an average annual debt of £127) unpaid to local merchants.[44] If what Walter Dulany, Governor Eden, and Lloyd Dulany spent each year represents the range of what the affluent might spend, the occupants of Annapolis's townhouses alone were lavishing £2,000 to £8,000 annually on the consumption of imported goods.[45] Coupled with what their employees bought, the resulting demand for luxury goods in Annapolis was truly impressive.

Government employees continued to be a source of income for local merchants, as did those who came to town for court days and the meeting of the General Assembly; by 1771, workmen employed in the construction of townhouses and others who catered to the needs of the affluent also proved to be an important clientele. Almost half the customers of William Coffing were Annapolis residents, most of whom derived their living from supplying the rich (see table 1-4). Of those who lived out of town, over half had occupations similar to the townspeople and probably worked in the community from time to time. Nearly all of Coffing's customers paid in cash, as did those who patronized other merchants for whom account books have survived. Such cash sales are in sharp contrast to the normal pattern at stores elsewhere in the Chesapeake, where planters usually exchanged their crops for credit. In Annapolis, where no commodities were exchanged for goods, Coffing's business depended upon the buying habits of the rich or upon customers who worked for cash and who in turn looked to the affluent for employment.[46]

---

[42]Hammond Account Book, MS 429 (hereafter cited as Hammond Account Book), pp. 88, 209, 255, 286, 304, Maryland Historical Society, Baltimore, Md. The average annual wage of the Annapolis craftsmen employed on the Brice house was about £60 currency (assuming a daily wage of 5/6 and a maximum work year of 214 days) in 1766. See Brice Account Book for details.

[43]"Confiscated Property, Accounts against the Property of Lloyd Dulany, Sir Robert Eden . . . . ," Scharf Col.

[44]*Ibid.*, and Land, *Dulanys of Maryland*, p. 296.

[45]£120 and £433 times the eighteen townhouses. There were four older townhouses owned by the Ogle, Dulany, Bordley, and Tasker families and they were included in this calculation in the place of the four business/residences. For the location of the older townhouses, see Papenfuse and McWilliams, "Appendix F" and project notes.

[46]The account book of Nathan Hammond, MS 429, Maryland Historical Society, Baltimore, Md., covering the period 1764-1768, contains mostly cash entries. The vast majority of Hammond's customers were probably Annapolis residents. He gives the residence of only ten percent of his customers, and most of these lived only a few miles

Table 1-4 Occupations of Customers at
William Coffing's Store in Annapolis, 1770-1771

Occupation	Resident	?	Nonresident
Architect	1		
Artist-planter	1		
Baker	1		
Barber	3		
Blacksmith	3		1
Bricklayer	1		
Brickmaker			1
Britches maker	1		
Builder	1		
Butcher	2		
Cabinetmaker	1		
Carpenter	4		
Carter	1		
Clerk	2		2
Cobbler	2		
Cooper	1		
Court Cryer	1		
Doctor	1		1
Ferrykeeper			1
Gentleman-planter	4		
Goldsmith			1
Harnessmaker	1		
Hatter	2		
Innkeeper	6		2
Lawyer	2		
Laborer	5		
Merchant	4		7
Minister	1		
Musician	1		
Painter			1
Planter			27
Sailmaker			1
Sawyer	1		
Schoolmaster	1		
Servant	1		
Shoemaker	1		
Shoesupplier			1
Shipsmaster, mariner	2		5
Slave trader			1
Staymaker			1
Tailor	2		
Tanner	1		
Turner			1
Other:			
Widow or wife	3		3
Unknown		10	
Total	64	10	57
Percent of total*	48.9	7.6	43.5

Source: Coffing Account Book, MS 249, Maryland Historical Society, Baltimore, Md.
*Percent of total nonresident planters: 20.6; percent of total in nonagricultural occupations: 71.8.

The attraction of good wages and the demand for services had a noticeable effect on population growth. Between 1740 and 1755, population rose by only 12.8 percent; but between 1765 and 1775, it grew by 27.7 percent, with the greatest concentration of growth occurring after 1768 (see table 1-1). In the seven years between 1768 and 1775, population increased at an average annual rate of 2.7 percent, as compared to the 1765–1768 average of 1.8 percent a year. As Joshua Johnson observed in 1771, when writing to a friend who had departed town about three years before, "Annapolis cuts quite a different figure to what it did when you left it, it increases fast, both in inhabitants and society."[47]

Craftsmen and others who worked for the rich supplanted shipbuilders and tanners. The newcomers were more numerous, earned more, and together with their rich patrons, spent what they had with increasing fervor.[48] To meet the demand, Thomas Hyde, tanner turned merchant, bought £511 worth of goods in 1766, £675 worth in 1767, and £903 worth in 1768 from the London firm of Perkins, Buchanan and Brown.[49] Another merchant, Lancelot Jacques, purchased £1,032 of goods from the same firm in 1766 and, by 1771, when Perkins, Buchanan and Brown sought greater profits by opening their own store in Annapolis, commissioned almost £3,000 of goods from one of

---

away "over Severn." The others probably were neighbors for whom he felt no need to note where they lived. Another account book having mostly cash entries is that of John Wilmot and James West, who were in business together on West Street (D553, Gift Collection, Hall of Records, Annapolis, Md.; it covers the period 1774–c. 1781).

The normal Tidewater pattern of exchanging crops for credit can be seen in any number of store accounts, but a good sample are the journals and ledgers in the Glassford Papers, Library of Congress, Washington, D.C. They cover a number of stores in Maryland and Virginia during the years 1755 to the early 1800s. At each store credit was advanced for the promise of the principal cash crop, usually tobacco, and the number of cash transactions on the books was few. For a discussion of the Piscattaway store in Prince George's County, Maryland, and its customers, see Papenfuse, "Planter Behavior." Also see Soltow, *Economic Role*, p. 125.

[47]Joshua Johnson to James Gibbs, London, November 12, 1771, Private Account Books, Wallace, Davidson and Johnson Letter Books, 1:34, Private Account Records, Hall of Records, Annapolis, Md. (hereafter cited as WDJ 1). Gibbs was in Annapolis between 1765 and 1767, when he had an account with Nathan Hammond (see Hammond Account Book, p. 190). It is likely that he left town shortly thereafter.

[48]See table 1-4. Not a single customer of William Coffing called himself a shipcarpenter, blockmaker, or ropemaker. These trades seem to have disappeared almost completely from Annapolis by 1771.

Wages increased faster than inflation. For example, the index of wholesale prices for Philadelphia [1850-59=100] rose only three points between 1768 and 1771, when wages in the housebuilding trades rose twenty percent. In other words, a bricklayer who could earn 5/6 a day in 1768 was earning 6/6 in 1771. For the wholesale index see the evidence of George Rogers Taylor and Ethel D. Hoover in U.S. Congress, Joint Economic Committee, *Study of Employment, Growth, and Price Levels, Part Two: Historical and Comparative Rates of Production, Productivity, and Prices* 86th Cong., 2nd sess., 1959, p. 394. For data on the increase in wages, see Brice Account Book.

[49]Hyde Papers, MS 1324, Maryland Historical Society, Baltimore, Md.

their London competitors.[50] Business was so good that some found it hard to believe it would last. In 1771, as Joshua Johnson dispatched almost £4,000 sterling of merchandise from London to his Annapolis partners, he wrote, "I hope the run may not be over so that we may come in for part."[51]

Johnson's fears were not without justification. In 1772–1773, merchants found that they had overstocked themselves and could not make remittances fast enough to suit their London and Glasgow suppliers.[52] But while the supply outran the demand temporarily between late 1772 and the summer of 1773, stocks were depleted enough by the fall of 1773 so that some merchants once again were importing large quantities of goods, although not quite so much as in the peak year of 1772. For example, Wallace, Davidson and Johnson imported nearly £8,000 sterling worth of goods into Annapolis in the fall of 1772, but only about £5,000 worth in the fall of 1773. Yet the latter was still worth over £1,000 more than the fall cargo for 1771, the first year of business for the firm.[53]

By 1774, Wallace, Davidson and Johnson was probably the largest of the sixteen importing firms then in Annapolis. In 1728, when Amos Garrett died, he was undoubtedly the most important merchant in town. Yet he had an inventory of goods on hand worth no more than £1,300 sterling, a sum that is roughly equivalent to one quarter of the value of the goods Wallace, Davidson and Johnson offered as their fall selection in 1773.[54] Business prospects for Annapolis merchants had improved enormously in the forty-five years since Garrett's death, with the years of greatest demand concentrated in the period after 1763.

There are a number of reasons why the age of affluence occurred when it did in Annapolis. People were able to build townhouses and purchase luxury goods because Maryland was prospering. Noninvolvement in the French and Indian War contributed to the economic growth of the colony. Unsaddled with major war debts such as those confronting Virginia, and with good markets for its principal exports (grain, tobacco, and iron), per capita income grew.[55] For instance, be-

---

[50]"Shipping Invoices of Lancelot Jacques, 1766–1774," D 387, Folder 283, Gift Collection, Hall of Records, Annapolis, Md.

[51]WDJ 1, p. 18.

[52]James Dick and Anthony Stewart to William Lee, June 30, 1773, James Dick and Stewart Company Letter Book, Duke University Library, Durham, N.C., p. 64.

[53]"Statement of Goods Shipped by Joshua Johnson to Wallace, Davidson and Johnson," 1771–1779, Chan. Pap. 2893.

[54]*Ibid.*

[55]For the relative unimportance of Maryland's war debts, see Lawrence Henry Gipson, *The British Empire Before the American Revolution* (New York, 1961), 10:91–100.

tween 1768 and 1771, the sterling value of exports increased by 39 percent at a time when the population of the colony increased by only 8.9 percent.[56]

But the affluent who chose to build townhouses in Annapolis after 1763 did so for more specific reasons than the generally prosperous state of the economy. An important side effect of the establishment of proprietary authority in the colony's affairs was the growing ability of the proprietor to grant lucrative posts to his supporters. As a result, a "court party" grew up in the colony with Annapolis as its focus and principal watering place.[57] Much of the credit for the establishment of a powerful court party belongs to Horatio Sharpe, governor from 1753 until 1769. Sharpe was an able administrator who zealously supported the proprietor's prerogative and made effective use of the bureaucracy that had been developing in the colony since 1715. The best example of his success was the well-organized and well-run administration he set up to supervise collection of the quitrents, manor rents, and alienation fines, the chief source of the proprietor's income. Although it took him almost fifteen years to do it, Sharpe wrested control from Edward Lloyd, who had inefficiently supervised the land revenue since 1753. After a series of extensive investigations, Horatio Sharpe and Secretary Cecilius Calvert (uncle of the proprietor) formulated and implemented a system that by 1769 was centered in a new "Revenue Office" in Annapolis and was extracting 20.1 percent more income for the proprietor than in 1753.[58]

[56]Calculated from data given in James F. Shepherd, "Commodity Exports from the British North American Colonies to Overseas Areas, 1768-1772: Magnitudes and Patterns of Trade," *Explorations in Economic History* (Fall 1970), p. 18; and population figures for the colony found in Evarts B. Greene and Virginia Harrington, *American Population before the Federal Census of 1790* (Gloucester, Mass., 1966), pp. 126-27. The total value of Maryland exports between 1768 and 1771 rose from £214,004 to £297,524 or £83,520 sterling, an increase of 39 percent. Population between 1761 and 1775 grew by 86,003 or 6,143 a year on the average. The projected population for 1768 using this average annual growth would have been 207,008 (seven times 6,143 plus 164,007), and the growth over the following three years using the same average annual growth would have been 18,429, or 8.9 percent.

[57]See note 20 above for a general discussion of secondary sources relating to the rise of the bureaucracy, and Barker, *Background of Revolution*, pp. 174-77.

[58]Sharpe's struggle with Lloyd is discussed in Barker, *Background of Revolution*, pp. 258-59, 262-64, 266-67. There are a few sources not used by Barker that are relevant to Sharpe's administration of the land revenue, including a recently discovered letterbook of the investigating body he and Calvert set up (see Warrants I.C.#1, Liber 45, 1781-1782, rear of volume, upside down, Hall of Records, Annapolis, Md.) Letters describing Sharpe's efforts in establishing control over the land system and suggestions he made for improvements are to be found in his published correspondence, *Archives*, 6:522; 9:116-17, 403.

The percentage increase in income between 1753 and 1769 is based on income from land only as given in Barker, *Background of Revolution*, p. 380, adjusted for inflation

Rigorous enforcement of proprietary rights such as quitrents, alienation fines, escheat, and title to vacant lands, coupled with increased prosperity throughout the colony, also proved a boon for lawyers who were drawn to Annapolis to handle cases involving land and debts.[59] Of the eleven people who built townhouses between 1764 and 1774, six were lawyers and three more were closely connected with the proprietary or court party (see table 1-2). Undoubtedly, there were people who could have afforded to build townhouses before 1763 (such as Richard Bennett or Edward Lloyd) who never did; it was not until the French and Indian War that political and social power were so centralized that sons of wealthy planters who had taken up the law found Annapolis an ideal place to display their wealth while they pursued their work.

William Paca is a case in point. Born into a prominent Western Shore planter family, he, like so many of Maryland's noted lawyers before the Revolution, attended the Inns of Court. While in London he was undoubtedly influenced by the townhouse and garden architecture then in vogue. When he returned to practice law in Annapolis, he not only undertook to build the first of the splendid townhouses, but also designed a garden to go with it that was a technical masterpiece of which even "Capability" Brown would have been proud.[60] Paca set the standard. Over the next few years others competed to build even more imposing structures, although no one ever attempted to improve upon his garden.

The Age of Affluence had a profound influence on the character and composition of the Annapolis merchant community. Prior to the French and Indian War, mercantile activity was more of a sideline than a career, and it was often of short duration. Between 1750 and 1754, twenty-six people advertised drygoods for sale in the *Maryland Gazette*. Of these, six were selling goods on a one-time-only basis to establish themselves in an occupation other than merchant, one was a ship captain who occasionally stopped at Annapolis, another was a goldsmith dealing in goods periodically, three were tanners,

---

using the English wholesale price index in John J. McCusker, "The Current Value of English Exports, 1697–1800," *William and Mary Quarterly* 28 (October 1971), 619. The British wholesale index was used because sums cited in Barker are in sterling and were destined for the proprietor in England.

[59]Evidence for this statement is to be found in a forthcoming dissertation being written by Alan F. Day, under the supervision of Jack P. Greene, Johns Hopkins University.

[60]Papenfuse and McWilliams, "Appendix F," Parcel 24, Section II, summarizes the available evidence about Paca's property, and notes the major study of the Paca house and garden by Stanley South. The garden was built over the remains of a tanyard, symbolic of the dramatic changes that had taken place in the town's development since the beginning of the eighteenth century.

and one was a shipbuilder. Only two were tobacco export merchants who had their main business elsewhere, but maintained stores in the town in order to take advantage of the growing retail market. Nineteen of the twenty-six had short mercantile careers; only seven, or just over one-fourth, remained in business ten years later.[61]

By contrast, the merchant community of 1774 was remarkably enduring. Most were newly-established; three quarters entered business after 1763. Of the twenty-two merchants who advertised in 1774, fourteen, or over three-fifths, remained in business in Annapolis for a decade or more (see table 1-5).

Endurance was not their only characteristic. Some proved to be highly successful entrepreneurs. The concentration of wealth and

Table 1-5 The Annapolis Merchant Community, 1774

Name	Year of First Ad in *Md. Gaz.*	Year of Ad Closest to 1774	Residence in 1783
Robert Buchanan	1771	1774	?, loyalist
Colin Campbell	1763	1773	?, loyalist
Robert Couden (tanner)	1752	1771	Annapolis
James Dick	1728–34	1773	Deceased
Thomas Gassaway, storekeeper for Perkins, Buchanan, & Brown	1771	1773	Annapolis
Nathan Hammond	1759	1772	Frederick Co.
Thomas Harwood	1768	1773	Annapolis
Thomas B. Hodgkin	1765	1774	Annapolis
Samuel Harvey Howard	1771	1773	Annapolis
Thomas Hyde (tanner)	1760	1774	Annapolis
Lancelot Jacques	1749	1772	Frederick Co.
Nicholas and John Henry Maccubbin	1749, 1774	1774	Annapolis
William Potts	1774	1774	West Indies
Anthony Stewart	1764	1773	?, loyalist
Charles Wallace, John Davidson, and Joshua Johnson	1771	1774	Annapolis & London (1)
William Wilkins	1763	1774	Annapolis
Thomas Charles, James, and Joseph Williams	1766	1774	T.C., a deceased loyalist; other two, Annapolis

Source: Maryland Gazette ads and "Merchants of Annapolis to Governor Robert Eden . . . April 19, 1774," Black Books, 9:154, Hall of Records, Annapolis, Md. Residence information is based on the tax list of 1783 and other biographical data.

Note: Total: 22 merchants; loyalists: 23 percent.

[61]Based on an analysis of advertisements in the *Maryland Gazette*.

the desire of the wealthy to consume conspicuously created unparalleled opportunities for the retail sale of goods in Annapolis, and it also provided capital for basic changes in the organization and funding of trade. In 1771, two prominent members of the Annapolis merchant community, Charles Wallace and Joshua Johnson, in partnership with John Davidson, a clerk in the Naval Office, launched an attack on what had been the traditional preserve of the British middleman. In three years, the new partnership established itself in firm opposition to past methods of conducting business and as a result contributed to the growing tension between Great Britain and her colonies.

CHAPTER 2

TOWARD INDEPENDENCE: CAPITAL ACCUMULATION AND THE CHALLENGE TO THE BRITISH MIDDLEMAN, 1763–1776

THE decade after the French and Indian War saw a dramatic increase in the consumption of goods in Maryland, which greatly affected the structure of opportunity for merchants throughout the colony. It had an especially pronounced impact in Annapolis, where the concentration of wealth allowed significant alterations in the traditional means of organizing and capitalizing trade. Change centered on the role of the London tobacco merchant in handling the bulk of Maryland's import and export trade, and led to a form of economic independence for a few Annapolis merchants that would have been impossible less than a generation before.

In contrast to developments in Virginia, Maryland's economy continued to be dominated by London throughout the colonial period. In Virginia, Scottish factors supplied with goods from Glasgow invaded the market and, by 1771, controlled approximately half the tobacco trade; but in Maryland, they managed to corner no more than 30 percent.[1] As a result, most of Maryland's goods

---

[1]Jacob M. Price, *France and the Chesapeake* (Ann Arbor, Mich., 1973), I:668, provides data on Maryland and Virginia tobacco imports into Scotland, which were used in conjunction with tobacco export data for Virginia and Maryland given in U.S. Bureau of the Census, *Historical Statistics of the United States, Colonial Times to 1957* (Washington, D.C., 1960), pp. 766-67 to arrive at this percentage. The Scottish merchants catered to the poorer class of planters and, after the Revolution, had more difficulty collecting their prewar debts than did the London merchants. Even so, only 42 percent of the total prewar debt still owed by Marylanders in 1790 was held by Scottish firms. See Great Britain, Public Record Office (hereafter cited as PRO) 30/80/343.

The thesis based on the Price data about the relative unimportance of the Scottish tobacco trade from Maryland is confirmed by other sources. In 1772, 7,070 hogsheads of tobacco, 21 percent of the crop for that year, were exported from the Annapolis trading district, an area that was bounded by the Patapsco on the north and the Patuxent on the south. Of these 7,070 hogsheads, 1,107, or 16 percent, were cleared for Glasgow. See Port of Entry Records, Annapolis, Microfilm M 1002, Hall

Table 2-1 The Pound Sterling Value of
Maryland Tobacco and Grain Exports, 1768-1772

(in £1,000 units)

Exports	1768	1769	1770	1771	1772
Wheat					
to Great Britain	2,153	3,285	1,728	2,732	1,560
to Ireland	1,641	12,441	20,372	9,990	4,786
to Southern Europe	28,237	47,400	39,783	12,492	18,785
Bread and Flour					
to Ireland	1,765	9,304	19,772	12,665	1,507
to Southern Europe	8,383	18,222	25,292	11,744	25,558
Corn					
to Great Britain	1,130				
to Southern Europe	7,961	4,395	2,990	3,399	6,266
Grain total	51,270	95,047	109,937	53,022	58,462
Tobacco	182,867	219,145	231,768	266,096	231,720
Grand total	234,137	314,292	341,705	391,118	290,182
The value of grain exports as a percentage of the value of tobacco exports	28	43	47	20	25

Source: Data in James F. Shepherd, "Commodity Exports from the British North American Colonies to Overseas Areas, 1768-1772, Magnitudes and Patterns of Trade," *Explorations in Economic History* (Fall 1970), pp. 5-76.

came from London and were paid for in proceeds from tobacco sold on the London market. Grain exports, principally from Baltimore, increased dramatically (if somewhat erratically) after the French and Indian War, but their value never equaled half, and averaged close to a third, of the value of tobacco between 1768 and 1772 (see table 2-1).[2] The concentration of Maryland imports and exports

---

of Records, Annapolis, Md. In 1761, Governor Sharpe wrote that of an annual production of 28,000 hogsheads of tobacco, Maryland exported "near two-thirds . . . to the London market and the rest to Glasgow except about 200 hhds. to Bristol, Liverpool, Beddeford and Whitehaven." Executive Papers, Hall of Records, Annapolis, Md. (hereafter cited as Exec. Pap.), Portfolio 3, Folder 12 (i). The literature on the Scottish merchants in Virginia is extensive. See Jacob M. Price, "The Economic Growth of the Chesapeake and the European Market, 1697-1775," *Journal of Economic History* 24 (1964), 496-511; and James H. Soltow, *The Economic Role of Williamsburg* (Williamsburg, Va., 1965), which contains an extensive bibliography on the subject.

[2]For a discussion of the grain trade as the growth factor in the Chesapeake during the same period see David Klingaman, "The Significance of Grain in the Development of the Tobacco Colonies," *Journal of Economic History* 29 (1969), 268-78. From

in the hands of London merchants placed these merchants in an important position within the structure of the Maryland economy. Those who sold tobacco in London became the principal middlemen in the handling of goods imported into the colony, and bills of exchange drawn on London merchants were eagerly sought after as a medium of exchange.

Maryland merchants generally paid their London suppliers in bills of exchange, which were drafts drawn on merchants in London to be paid at a certain time, usually in thirty, sixty, or ninety days, if the drawer had sufficient funds or credit with the merchant. If he did not, the bill was protested and returned to the person to whom the money was supposed to be paid. He, in turn, sent the bill back to the Maryland merchant for prosecution of the drawer, adding the charges of the protest. It was a process not unlike a modern checking account, except that the account was with a merchant rather than a bank and payment could be demanded only on the expiration of the period of time stated on the bill.

Bills of exchange were obtained by Maryland merchants in a variety of ways. For example, people who had accounts at Thomas Hyde's store in Annapolis paid in bills of exchange or cash. If they paid in cash in the form of currency—that is, Maryland pounds, shillings and pence as distinct from their counterparts in sterling—Hyde could redeem it at the colony's loan office where the currency had originally been issued on the strength of mortgaged land and investments the colony had made in the stock of the Bank of England. Bills purchased from the loan office in this manner would be drawn on the trustees of the stock and would be paid in sterling out of dividends from the stock or its sale. If Hyde received coin, he purchased bills of exchange from planters or merchants who had credit balances with London firms. The bills used in paying for goods are an indication of the degree to which the London merchants were involved in

---

1749 until 1763, the most grain exported from the Annapolis trading district (which included Baltimore) was 91,527 bushels of wheat in 1753. In 1765, 194,477 bushels of wheat were exported and in 1769, 288,529 bushels were exported. Vaughan W. Brown, *Shipping in the Port of Annapolis, 1748-1775* (Annapolis, 1965), p. 29. These figures undoubtedly reflect the reorientation of the Eastern Shore grain trade to Baltimore, and thus are not a perfect measure of the expansion in Maryland grain exports, but there is no question that most of the increase in grain exports was from newly developing areas in the province. See Edward C. Papenfuse, "Economic Analysis and Loyalist Strategy during the American Revolution: Robert Alexander's Remarks on the Economy of the Peninsula or Eastern Shore of Maryland," *Maryland Historical Magazine* 68 (1973), 173-95; and Clarence Gould, "The Economic Causes of the Rise of Baltimore," in *Essays in Colonial History Presented to Charles McLean Andrews by his Students* (Freeport, N.Y., 1966), pp. 225-51.

the tobacco trade, and to some extent measure their success. In any given year the bills purchased by an importer of goods, such as Thomas Hyde, would be a cross section of bills available from people having credit balances with London tobacco merchants. The greater the amount drawn on a firm, the more extensive its tobacco business probably was that year. Assuming that bills remitted by Thomas Hyde between 1765 and 1771 represent a random sample, they provide a profile of the British merchant community active in the Maryland tobacco trade (see table 2-2).[3]

Another measure of the extent to which British firms were engaged in the Maryland tobacco trade is the distribution of the debt owed by Marylanders to British merchants as of 1776 (table 2-3).[4] Although amounts due include interest to 1790, the percentage of the total debt held by each firm indicates its relative position in the Maryland trade. From both Hyde's bills of exchange and the account of the prewar British-held debt, it is clear that only a small number of London and Glasgow merchants played major roles in the import-export trade of the colony in the years immediately preceding the Revolution, and that London firms predominated. Even accounting for six percent interest over the fourteen years between 1776 and 1790, the principal owed to both London and Glasgow merchants in 1776 was equivalent to approximately 1.8 times the sterling value of goods imported into Maryland in 1774. To what extent the debt held in 1776 was incurred as a result of imports before 1774 is difficult to determine, but without question the bulk of Maryland's import and export trade was handled by London tobacco merchants such as the Buchanans, the Mollesons, Mildred and Roberts, and James Russell. In fact the Glasgow trade with Maryland was almost exclusively confined to the Potomac River and the Eastern Shore. In 1774, for example, out of the five naval districts in Maryland, all but a small fraction of the tobacco exported to Glasgow came from North Potomac and the two Eastern Shore districts of Pocomoke and Oxford. Only one ship carrying 507 hogsheads of

[3]For a good discussion of how bills of exchange operated as the "principal instrument in large commercial transactions," see T. S. Ashton, "The Bill of Exchange and Private Banks in Lancashire, 1790–1830, in T. S. Ashton and R. S. Sayers, *Papers in English Monetary History* (Oxford, 1953), pp. 37–49. For a profile of most of the London merchants see Katherine Kellock, "London Merchants and the Pre-1776 American Debts," forthcoming in *The Guildhall Miscellany*. I am greatly indebted to Mrs. Kellock for the loan of materials relating to London merchants active in the Maryland tobacco trade. Hyde purchased bills of exchange to pay for the goods he sold retail because he was not an export merchant sending tobacco to a London merchant in return for goods.

[4]Table 2-3 is taken from PRO 30/80/343, a copy of which was loaned to me by Katherine Kellock.

Table 2-2 Bills of Exchange Purchased by Thomas Hyde and Remitted to London, August 1765 to October 1771

(in pounds sterling)

On Whom Drawn	1765		1766		1767		1768		1769		1770		1771	
	#	Amt.	#	Amt.	#	Amt.	#	Amt.	#	Amt.	#	Amt.	#	Amt.
London merchants														
Anderson, James and/or William	2	139			1	20			1	8	1	75		
Buchanan, John	3	36	5	61	7	144	8	179	4	268	1	38	3	45
Buchanan, Thomas									1	16	1	42		
Day, Richard and John	1	2					1	27						
Ewer, William and John									1	125				
Grove, Silvanus	3	212	6	47	6	43	2	2	2	191	2	68	2	27
Hanbury, Capel and Osgood or Osgood Hanbury and Co.	2	90	4	158	2	75	4	351	2	271	2	350		
Jordan and Maxwell					1	8			1	7				
Ketty, John													1	54
MacLane, Thomas A.	1	25												
Mildred & Roberts			1	5			1	20	2	28	3	90		
Molleson, William							1	20	3	41			1	30
Perkins & Company			1	68	1	333			2	52				
Philpot, Thomas			1	23					1	32				
Russell, James			6	77	5	83	3	110	1	15	2	207	2	171
Russell & Molleson	3	31												
Thomas, Thomas & Son											1	80		
Glasgow merchants														
Buchanan, George & Andrew											1	100		
Glassford, John			1	30							1	37		
Gordon, John					1	17								
Jameson, John and James					1	40								
Liverpool merchants														
Gildart, James							1	50						
Whitehaven merchants														
Hartley, John and Thomas			1	60	1	50								
Skyrin, William			1	25										
Total	15	535	27	554	26	813	21	759	21	1054	15	1087	9	327

Source: Hyde Papers, MS. 1824, Maryland Historical Society, Baltimore, Md.

British Firms	Amount £ Sterling	Percentage of Total Debt
London		
John & Gilbert Buchanan	73,384	12.84
William & Robert Molleson	66,878	11.70
Mildred & Roberts	52,897	9.25
James Russell	33,580	5.88
Christopher Court	24,719	4.33
Thomas Philpot (estate)	14,349	2.51
Duncan Campbell	12,500	2.19
Perkins, Buchanan & Brown	11,711	2.05
Anthony Bacon	6,088	1.07
Nash, Eddowes & Co.	4,000	.70
Thomas Eden & Co.	2,469	.43
Eddowes, Petrie & Co.	2,083	.36
Davis Strachan	1,687	.30
Robert Smith	1,380	.24
William Clarke	925	.16
Dyson & Rogers	699	.12
Champion & Dickson	514	.08
Richard & John Samuel	304	.05
Harrison & Ansley	242	.04
Total	310,407	54.31
Glasgow		
Speirs, French & Co.	71,944	12.59
John Glassford & Co.	70,370	12.31
Cunningham, Finley & Co.	27,724	4.85
Colin Dunlop & Son & Co.	13,948	2.44
James & Robert Buchanan	13,437	2.35
Oswald Dennistown & Co.	9,520	1.67
James Brown & Co.	9,657	1.69
James Jamieson	8,330	1.46
Henry Glassford	4,152	.73
George & Andrew Buchanan	4,250	.74
Brown, Scott & Co.	4,085	.71
Cunningham, Brown & Co.	2,471	.43
Colin Dunlop & Co.	2,174	.38
Patrick Telfair	21	.01
Total	242,084	42.35
Bristol		
Stephenson, Randolph, Cheston	14,000	2.45
William Dighton	2,227	.39
Total	16,227	2.84
Leeds		
Samuel Elam (executors)	1,556	.27
Emanuel Elam	282	.05
John Elam & Son	18	.01
Total	1,856	.33

Table 2-3 (continued)

British Firms	Amount £ Sterling,	Percentage of Total Debt
Liverpool		
Clay & Midgley	197	.03
Whitehaven		
John Hicks	715	.13
Grand total	571,485	100.00

Source: Great Britain, Public Record Office 30/80/343.

tobacco to Speirs, French & Co. cleared the port of Annapolis and none sailed from the Patuxent.[5]

While he supplied Maryland with goods, the London tobacco merchant also served the colony as investment banker and shepherd of its credit. Maryland called on tobacco merchants Osgood Hanbury, Sylvanus Grove, and James Russell to invest its surplus funds in order to support its currency, which they did with remarkable success by purchasing stock in the Bank of England and other securities.[6] James Russell, John Buchanan and Son, and other London merchants helped to develop Maryland industry by putting capital into such successful ventures as the Nottingham Ironworks.[7] In addition to the gratitude of those Marylanders who profited from such capital outlays, London merchants expected not only the normal commission of two and one half percent for goods they sent, but they also expected to dominate the Maryland tobacco trade, resenting and resisting the intrusion of any Maryland entrepreneur who dared venture into the market. Until the burgeoning prosperity of the early 1770s, the efforts of the London tobacco merchants to maintain a strong hold on the tobacco trade and to remain the prin-

[5]The sterling value of goods imported into Maryland in 1774, the last year before effective implementation of nonimportation by the colony, was approximately £171,502, assuming that the ratio of Maryland tobacco exports to that of Virginia can be applied as well to the importation of goods. U.S. Bureau of Census, *Historical Statistics*, pp. 757, 767. The accounts of the naval officers are scattered among collections in the Hall of Records and the Maryland Historical Society. The data for 1774 were collated from materials in the Calvert Papers #1030, p. 14, MS 1668, MS 638 and MS 21, all in the Maryland Historical Society. Assuming 6 percent interest over 14 years, the principal of the British-held debt in Maryland in 1776 was £310,590 sterling.

[6]For an excellent study of the successful effort to retrieve the bank stock after the Revolution see Morris L. Radoff, *Calendar of Maryland State Papers, No. 2: The Bank Stock Papers* (Annapolis, 1947).

[7]Great Britain, Public Record Office, Audit Office (hereafter cited as PRO, AO) 13/39, p. 152.

cipal source of imported goods were successful, although they did this within the context of a change in the nature of opportunity that permitted Americans to establish themselves as preeminent in the retail trade.

During the early years of the colony and on into the eighteenth century, London merchants dominated both the retail sale of imported goods and the tobacco export trade. In the 1720s, Samuel Hyde, Robert Cruickshanks, Joseph Adams, John Hanbury, William Hunt, Gilbert Higginson, and John Falconer purchased tobacco "in the country" or solicited consignments from the planters at the same time they were supplying their own factors in the colony with goods to sell.[8] During the 1740s, however, significant numbers of independent resident merchants began to appear who had sufficient resources to establish stores and order goods on commission from London. In the beginning, most were successful planters who ventured into trade, such as the Brices, Galloways, Ringgolds, and Worthingtons; or immigrants, such as James Dick, who came to Maryland from Edinburgh with sufficient capital to establish a store and engage in the export trade.[9] Later, especially after 1763, when a wealthy clientele created a lucrative market for goods in Annapolis, tradesmen, such as the tanner Thomas Hyde and the staymaker, Charles Wallace, accumulated sufficient capital to commission goods and open stores, confining themselves almost exclusively to the retail trade, that is, the sale of goods for cash or its equivalent.[10]

[8]Charles A. Barker, *The Background of the Revolution in Maryland* (New Haven, 1940), p. 74.

[9]Aubrey C. Land, "Economic Behavior in a Planting Society: The Eighteenth-Century Chesapeake," *Journal of Southern History* 33 (1967), 469-85; and *ibid.*, "Economic Base and Social Structure: The Northern Chesapeake in the Eighteenth Century," *Journal of Economic History* 25 (1965), 639-54. Land points to the general trend of wealthy planters becoming merchants. Information about the Brices, Galloways, and Worthingtons can be found in J. D. Warfield, *The Founders of Anne Arundel and Howard Counties, Maryland* (Baltimore, 1905), although Warfield is often wrong and must be used with care. Much better is H. W. Newman, *Anne Arundel County Gentry: Twenty-two Pioneers and Their Descendants* (Baltimore, 1933). For William Worthington, see his inventory in Inventories, 81:25, Hall of Records, Annapolis, Md., taken in July 1772; and a list of debts received by his estate in Accounts, WD #14, Hall of Records, Annapolis, Md. For James Dick's origins and the fact that he had capital enough to open a store soon after his arrival, see All Hallows Parish Register (1722-1857), p. 56, Hall of Records, Annapolis, Md., and *Maryland Gazette*, July 12, 1734. For the Ringgold family, see Barker, *Background of the Revolution*, pp. 24, 76, 98, 114n, 295, 341.

[10]Except for selling freight on ships in which he had an interest, Wallace did not become involved in the tobacco trade to any great extent until just a year prior to the commencement of the Revolution. An Annapolis retailer is identified as a "merchant" here and elsewhere in the text if this is how he was referred to by himself and contemporaries.

The change from dependent factor, salaried by a London merchant, to independent retail merchant free to seek connections with any number of suppliers is contrasted in the careers of Isaac Hyde and his son Thomas. Isaac came to Maryland in 1716 as a factor for the London merchant Gilbert Higginson. Higginson's business took Isaac on trips to New England and Barbados, but by 1721 he had settled as a storekeeper in All Hallows Parish near Annapolis. Isaac was paid travel expenses and £60 a year, half of which Higginson sent in goods. But Isaac preferred to be his own employer. Lacking the capital or the credit for independent storekeeping, Isaac moved to Queen Anne's Town, Prince George's County, where he rented a tavern and kept a ferry. When Isaac died in 1734, he left a small estate.[11] His children were still minors and his son Thomas, age fifteen, was apprenticed to learn to read, write, and make shoes. For the next eleven years, Thomas all but disappeared from the records, emerging again in 1745, at the age of twenty-six, as a shoemaker and tanner in Annapolis. By 1764, the shoemaking business had prospered to such an extent that Thomas was able to build a store on Church Street, secure £300 in bills of exchange drawn on the London tobacco merchants and bankers, Capel and Osgood Hanbury, and order a stock of goods from the London firm of Perkins, Buchanan, and Brown.[12]

Thomas Hyde was a relative latecomer to the ranks of the independent retail merchant class in Maryland and, as a merchant, was a product of an age of affluence which made it profitable to concentrate on retail sales to the exclusion of engaging in the export trade. The older generation of independent merchants, like Samuel Galloway or James Dick, did not derive their independent status from exclusively retail sales, but from an import-export trade that existed in a symbiotic relationship to the work they did as agents for London tobacco merchants. This older type of independent merchant sought out consignments from the wealthier planters, purchased tobacco outright, and handled such matters as arranging for charters of ships to carry the tobacco, or fitting out and load-

---

[11]Anne Arundel County Judgments, 1720–1721, pp. 271–74; Prince George's County Judgments, 4:83; 10:120; Prince George's County Inventories, Box 9, Folder 35; Hall of Records, Annapolis, Md.

[12]Prince George's County Judgments, 10:102, Hall of Records, Annapolis, Md. By 1739, Hyde was in Annapolis, as he is listed in the inventory of Humphrey Meredith, Annapolis Cordwainer, with one year and nine months to serve. Inventories (1739), 24:249, Hall of Records, Annapolis, Md. In 1745, he was established in business as a tanner and brought suit against someone by the name of Stansbury. See Anne Arundel Court Records for 1745, Hall of Records, Annapolis, Md. For Hyde's accounts see Hyde Papers, MS. 1324, Maryland Historical Society, Baltimore, Md.

ing ships owned by the London merchant. In turn, the London merchant would supply the Maryland merchant with credit and secure whatever goods he cared to import. The relationship of independent merchant to his London supplier was mutually beneficial, and neither had reason to consider any other method of doing business. A good example of such interdependency is the connection of the Annapolis firm of Dick and Stewart with the London supplier and banker, John Buchanan and Son.

James Dick, who had been an active export merchant in the Annapolis area since 1734, was, by 1772, the Maryland agent for John Buchanan and Son, with his son-in-law Anthony Stewart. In this capacity, Dick and Stewart handled a considerable volume of tobacco, managed John Buchanan and Son's one third interest in the Nottingham Ironworks, and pursued John Buchanan and Son's debtors through the courts. Dick and Stewart solicited consignments of tobacco and purchased tobacco when it seemed advantageous. In 1772 and 1773, they purchased and shipped tobacco worth £1,583.11.11 and obtained pledges of "upwards of 3,000 hhds" more (approximately one tenth of the annual Maryland tobacco crop) to be shipped on consignment.[13] During the same time period, Dick and Stewart provided £1,478 sterling worth of pork, corn, and other commodities used by the ironworks. In addition, they bought freight for John Buchanan and Son's £375 sterling share of the iron produced in 1772–1773.[14] In all, Dick and Stewart estimated that in the course of one year they would clear almost £1,000 sterling in commissions from transacting John Buchanan and Son's affairs in Maryland.[15] Until the depression of 1773 this arrangement worked well, and Dick and Stewart were able to pursue a number of other business ventures that relied heavily on their ability to draw on London capital.

As agents for John Buchanan and Son, Dick and Stewart were entitled to draw large amounts in bills of exchange on the London firm, depending on the amount of tobacco secured and their London balance. Between the fall of 1772 and the summer of 1773, for example, they could have drawn almost £4,400 worth, although in fact they drew only £2,959.[16] The ability to draw such large amounts in bills on their London correspondents provided Dick and Stewart access to short-term credit (30 to 90 days), which they employed in three ways:

[13]James Dick and Stewart Company, Letter Book, 1773–1781, Duke University Library, Durham, N.C. (hereafter cited as JDS), pp. 58–62.
[14]*Ibid.*
[15]*Ibid.*, p. 126.
[16]*Ibid.*, pp. 63–65.

a ropewalk; retail stores in Annapolis, Londontown, and Frederick Town; and an import-export trade to the West Indies, Europe, and Madeira.

Hemp for the ropewalk came clandestinely from Virginia where it was purchased with bills of exchange drawn on Buchanan and Son, or from Frederick Town, Maryland, where it was received as barter for goods Dick and Stewart had bought from the same firm.[17] Buchanan and Son were also the principal source of goods for two other retail stores Dick and Stewart kept in Londontown and Annapolis, but on the whole, neither the retail trade nor the ropewalk figured as prominently in their business affairs as did their commerce with southern Europe, Madeira, and the West Indies.[18] For example, in 1772 they considered enlarging their store in Annapolis with the idea of dislodging their largest competitor, but even the competitor doubted that they would pursue the scheme very far. When told of Dick and Stewart's announced plans he wrote to assure his partners: "You mention J. Dick and Stewart's Importation with intent to rival us dont be afraid of them Anthony [Stewart] will soon be gone [from London] when matters will get in the old Channell again . . . ."[19]

Significantly, the retailing of goods from London was secondary to many Maryland export merchants, and some were reluctant to engage in it at all. Samuel Galloway, acting as agent for Silvanus Grove and James Russell in the tobacco trade, exported corn, wheat, and ships, and imported wine, rum, and servants. Only when his son John was idle and in need of work did Galloway think of opening a store in the capital. In August 1771, he wrote his London correspondent that he was sending an invoice for £1,500 sterling worth of goods, explaining: "I am not fond of the retail business of goods but as he [John] is Idle and has a great inclination to be employed in that way I have agreed to it."[20]

The most time-consuming and seemingly most important aspect of Dick and Stewart's business, aside from the management of John Buchanan and Son's Maryland affairs, was their trade to the West Indies, southern Europe and Madeira. Although 1773 was a difficult year for the firm, the ventures they undertook during that

---

[17]*Ibid.*, pp. 5, 73–74, 148, 159–60, for the Virginia trade, and *ibid.*, pp. 135, 241, for the Frederick Town, Maryland store.

The Frederick Town store was an abysmal failure. *Ibid.*

Wallace, Davidson, and Johnson Letter Books, 1:56, Private Account Records, Hall of Records, Annapolis, Md. (There are two letter books covering the period 1771–1777, each with separate pagination. Hereafter they will be cited as WDJ 1 and WDJ 2.)

[20]Samuel Galloway to James Russell, July 21, 1770. Galloway, Maxcy, Markoe Papers, Box 75C, Library of Congress, Washington, D.C.

year give some indication of the nature of this side of their business and the extent to which it was an integral part of their relationship with John Buchanan and Son.

Dick and Stewart insured every vessel they sent to sea, whether their own or on charter. As Dick put it in a letter to a friend: "You may have heard me say that I never venture above £10 sterling at sea without Insuring, which is the reason for our Insuring our property in this venture tho such small sums [a total of £410 currency] are generally riskd by many people in trade."[21] As a result the records of how much they shipped and its minimum value were carefully noted in letters to the insurers. In 1773, Dick and Stewart chartered a schooner to Barbados and a brig to Spain and purchased a brig which they sent to Madeira.

The Barbados venture was the least successful of the three voyages, and may have proved a loss. In August, Dick and Stewart wrote:

Our vessel from Barbados is arrived but unfortunately the cargo sent in her was near totally damaged so that for £300 we had only a return of 3 hhd rum, 1 hhd spirit, 6 bbls sugar this misfortune was occasioned by the Captain going out of his senses & jumping over board at sea, the passage being protracted to upwards of 70 days thro the mates ignorance. . . .[22]

The charter to southern Europe was undertaken at the suggestion of a London merchant, Mr. Quarles Harris, who wanted Dick and Stewart to ship Indian corn to his firm, Harris and Archdeacon, in Oporto. In May 1773, they dispatched 4,743 bushels of Indian corn and 160 barrels of flour on the brig *William and Hopewell.* The total invoice value of the cargo was £728.18.2 sterling, half of which Dick and Stewart immediately drew in bills of exchange on Harris payable to John Buchanan and Son as partial remittance for their debts with the London firm. The cargo reached its destination safely and apparently netted a good profit to all concerned.[23]

Dick and Stewart also gained from a third voyage undertaken in 1773. Together with William McGachen, a merchant in Baltimore, they purchased the brig *Peggy Stewart,* a three-year-old vessel that had hitherto been employed in the bay trade and had never been to sea. They loaded the brig with 3,000 bushels of Indian corn, 300 bushels of wheat, 138 barrels of flour, and 30 bushels of beans. The brig was insured for £900 and dispatched to Madeira, consigned to Lamar, Hill, Bisset and Company.[24] The Philadelphia partner of the firm, Henry

[21] JDS, p. 209.
[22] *Ibid.,* pp. 12, 13, 22, 27, 75.
[23] *Ibid.,* pp. 10, 38, 39, 46, 50.
[24] *Ibid.,* pp. 14, 17, 19, 20, 29, 34, 68, 82.

Hill, had hoped to be able to share in the voyage, but Dick and Stewart felt they could afford to assume all risks, and agreed instead to seek orders for wine from people in the Annapolis area, taking a five percent commission as compensation.[25]

Lamar, Hill, Bisset and Company were to sell the cargo and, after deducting their commission and other charges, remit the proceeds to Annapolis in wine. Richard Jackson, captain of the *Peggy Stewart*, was given explicit instructions on how to handle the return cargo, for it appears that Dick and Stewart intended to make the most of the voyage by avoiding payment of import duties and smuggling in part, if not all, of the wine. They cautioned Jackson that secrecy was of the utmost importance:

From Madeira you are to return directly to this port and when you come on shore bring all your letters and papers of every kind to us and before you see us do not mention what quantity of wine you have on board or to whom any of it belongs.[26]

The *Peggy Stewart* made the journey to and from Madeira safely, although on the passage back to Annapolis she was severely battered by a storm. Dick and Stewart were enthusiastic about the prospects of profit. They wrote Henry Hill that "our cargo arrvd in tolerable order and we have reason to expect the sales will turn out to our entire satisfaction. . . ."[27] Undoubtedly, if the times had been better, Dick and Stewart would have ventured even more in other cargoes in 1773 but when John Buchanan and Son failed in June of that year, they found themselves in a most difficult position.

When John Buchanan and Son stopped payment and went into the hands of trustees on April 27, 1773, they were owed over £30,000 sterling in debts on open accounts and over £51,832 sterling on bond by people in Maryland.[28] Among the largest single debtors were Dick and Stewart, who still owed £6,350 as late as 1775.[29] The failure of John Buchanan and Son came as a complete surprise, and Dick and Stewart were both pained and annoyed when they wrote to the firm on June 30, 1773:

We are truely sorry and feel very sensibly for your misfortunes the first intelligence of which was conveyed us by our friend Mr. Edward Anderson as contained in a letter from his brother under Date the 6th May and on

[25]*Ibid.*, p. 14.
[26]*Ibid.*, p. 34.
[27]*Ibid.*, p. 82.
[28]PRO, AO 13/39, pp. 190–91.
[29]*Ibid.*

Friday last confirmed to us in your letter by the Pacquet. . . . We think from our long correspondence we had a right to expect more explicit information from you on the state of your affairs.[30]

Dick and Stewart explained the debt represented goods ordered through John Buchanan and Son for their retail stores, and argued that, "The longest date of any part . . . does not exceed twelve months at this time," which meant that it was not past due. They acknowledged that their remittances had been slow but, because the times were difficult, they were forced to give large and long credits as other merchants had done.[31] To counter accusations that the cause of the large debt was an excessive number of bills of exchange drawn during the previous summer, Dick and Stewart reviewed their dealings with John Buchanan and Son between 1772 and the summer of 1773. They pointed out that they had assumed payment of a £1,000 debt owed by John Buchanan and Son, purchased and shipped tobacco worth £1,583,11.11, and sent iron valued at £375. These transactions entitled them to draw £2,958.11.11 sterling, but they had actually drawn only £2,411. In addition, as agents for John Buchanan and Son in the Nottingham Ironworks, they could legally have drawn another £1,478.3.2, for the pork, corn, and other commodities they had supplied the manager of the ironworks.[32]

The most disturbing aspect of the failure to Dick and Stewart was the opportunity that had been lost by the firm's declining to continue in business. They had been hard at work securing "upwards of 3,000 hhds" of tobacco which would have been consigned to John Buchanan and Son, and which now, they wrote, "your friends are at a loss to whom they will consign," as they had received no word of encouragement from the trustees. As a result, John Buchanan and Son's ships that were already in Maryland were chartered out to William Molleson and James Russell, two of their competitors. Dick and Stewart wrote to John Buchanan and Son:

Had it been signified to us that there was the least probability of your being able to manage the Sales of tobacco we could have with the greatest ease procured a loading for both. . . . Had your house been suffered to go on we are well convinced from our knowledge of your business in this province you would have been able by the ensuing Spring to have discharged one half if not two thirds of the claims against you.[33]

[30]JDS, p. 59.
[31]*Ibid.*, p. 64.
[32]*Ibid.*
[33]*Ibid.*, p. 105.

The failure of John Buchanan and Son was a tremendous blow to Dick and Stewart. For the first time in forty years of business, James Dick was dunned by creditors, including John Glassell, to whom Dick wrote:

Our friend & correspondent Messrs John Buchanan & Son having failed & and general stagnation of credit in Britain will make it very difficult to procure bills of Exchange but this you may depend on we shall make the payment of the Hemp as soon as convenient to you as we can allowing for the distress'd Situation of the times.[34]

But neither Dick nor Stewart felt compelled to alter a mode of business that relied heavily upon the London tobacco merchant. When John Buchanan and Son went into the hands of trustees, Dick and Stewart entrusted their London affairs to one of the most prominent of the London tobacco merchants, James Russell, a former partner of John Buchanan and Son in the Nottingham Ironworks.[35]

Because of the difficulties caused by the bankruptcy of John Buchanan and Son, in 1774 Dick and Stewart considerably reduced their usual order of goods for the Londontown and Annapolis stores, and curtailed their ventures to the West Indies and Europe. Instead, they chartered their brig *Peggy Stewart* to an Annapolis firm and addressed her to Russell's care. If the brig could not be sold, Russell was to charter its return to Annapolis. Unfortunately for Dick and Stewart, the vessel was not sold for the £550 sterling they thought her worth. Russell, by assuring the captain that he had hidden it well, stowed a considerable amount of tea on board, consigned to one of Dick and Stewart's Annapolis competitors.[36] The events surrounding the burning of the ship and its cargo when it arrived in Annapolis in the fall of 1774 are well known.[37] Significantly, Dick and Stewart did not blame

[34]*Ibid.*, p. 74.

[35]*Ibid.*, pp. 133–34.

[36]WDJ 1:447. In this letter Johnson did what he could to rouse people against Russell and one of Wallace, Davidson and Johnson's Annapolis competitors: "I should not be surprized to hear that you have made a Bon Fire of the Peggy Stewart as I have a hint that a certain J[ames] W[illiams] has ship'd Tea on Board of her & that Capt. Jackson applied to old Russell & told him that he was suspicious of it but Russell told him it was not his business so that he got the 2 1/2% Freight, on Jacksons persisting to be uneasy Russell satisfied him by telling him it was Linens. I am suspicious that it is done up in that way to deceive, if he has been hardy enough to do so daring a thing I hope that you will adopt a proper punishment for him and old Russell who has been assistant in the affair." Johnson wrote the letter on August 4, in plenty of time for his partners to have received it before the *Peggy Stewart* arrived, and possibly they were the cause of the ship being burned.

[37]For example, see Arthur Meier Schlesinger, *The Colonial Merchants and the American Revolution* (New York, 1957 [1918]), pp. 389–92.

Russell; their hearts were with the old order. As they wrote Henry Hill in Philadelphia:

The loss we sustained by the destruction of the Peggy Stewart falls heavy and the tide of popular clamour has run much against us on account of the part our A.S. was innocently led to act in that transaction but when calm reason resumes her empire we trust our conduct will appear in a different light not only to our friends but even to the conviction of our enemies.[38]

To Russell they offered only a mild rebuke:

We wish you had acted more cautious & not have suffered Captain Jackson to take the tea on board but we suppose you was not aware of the consequences. The loss falls heavy but its what we must put up with.[39]

The burning of the *Peggy Stewart* brought the business of Dick and Stewart to an abrupt close and, in 1775, they advertised the dissolution of their partnership. Dick, who was "determined never to join in any thing which I think an act of Injustice," retired to Londontown and was known familiarly as "the old Tory," until his death in 1782.[40] "The ravages of Civil war" frightened Stewart, who thought that "countries which have been visited by that dreadful Hydra would, I fancy, be at more pains to avoid it."[41] Stewart fled to London in the fall of 1774, abandoning his family and his partner.[42] In a letter to James Russell, dated September 1775, Dick wistfully looked ahead to a return to normalcy and the reestablishment of the firm in the familiar pattern of trade.

Our A.S. who will deliver you this is under the necessity of leaving us for a time there being no business at present and as he will be ready to come out when things are better and will be at hand to enter into any new plan of business to help make up for loss of time.[43]

Dick and Stewart's business world depended upon the cooperation and support of the London tobacco merchants. When that world was threatened, they longed for the restoration of trade into its old channels and resisted both economic and political change. Their attitude appears to have been typical of most Maryland export mer-

[38] JDS, p. 166.
[39] *Ibid.*, p. 165.
[40] *Ibid.*, p. 135.
[41] *Ibid.*, p. 183.
[42] *Ibid.*, p. 199.
[43] *Ibid.*

Table 2-4 *Known Suppliers of Annapolis Retail Merchants in 1770*

Merchant	Supplier	Supplier's Location
Robert Couden	William Molleson	London
James Dick and Anthony Stewart	John Buchanan & Son	London
Nathan Hammond	John Buchanan & Son	London
Thomas Harwood	James Russell	London
Thomas Hyde	Perkins, Buchanan & Brown	London
Lancelot Jacques	Perkins, Buchanan & Brown	London
Joshua Johnson	James Russell	London
Charles Wallace	Osgood & Capel Hanbury	London
Thomas Charles Williams	William Molleson	London

Source: Wallace, Davidson and Johnson Letter Books, Private Account Records, Hall of Records, Annapolis, Md., vols. 1 and 2; *Maryland Gazette*, May 27, 1766 and April 13, 1775; Hyde Papers, MS. 1324, Maryland Historical Society, Baltimore, Md.; Katherine Kellock, "London Merchants and the Pre-1776 American Debts," forthcoming in *The Guildhall Miscellany*.

chants dealing in tobacco. To maintain a successful business in the Chesapeake, such merchants found it necessary to depend heavily on their London correspondents. For Dick and Stewart and others, like Samuel Galloway, the London middleman was a crucial component of their manifold business interests and a challenge to his role was not seriously considered.

When the demand for imported goods increased dramatically after 1763, it was largely met by the new type of independent merchant, exemplified by Thomas Hyde, who confined himself primarily to the retail import trade and did not maintain such a complex or beneficial relationship with his London supplier as did export merchants like Dick and Stewart. Dick and Stewart were more concerned with profits in exports than the sale of imports; but retail merchants, such as Thomas Hyde, Athanasius Ford, and Charles Wallace, concentrated on selling goods at their stores. As the table of known suppliers of Annapolis merchants active in 1770 points out (see table 2-4), the retail merchant's source of goods was London, as was the export merchant's.

Initially, London merchants insisted that retail merchants have sufficient capital before they would agree to commence shipping goods. During 1764, Perkins, Buchanan, and Brown shipped only slightly more in goods than Thomas Hyde advanced in bills of exchange.[44] But because the demand for goods was so great and the price

---

[44]Hyde Papers, Maryland Historical Society, Baltimore, Md. (cited hereafter as Hyde Papers), MS. 1324; see also Kellock, "London Merchants."

of tobacco high, by 1771 some firms, including John Buchanan and Son, Perkins, Buchanan and Brown, and Christopher Court and Company, were shipping cargoes of goods on easy terms and for little or no down payment, making it relatively simple for aspiring merchants to establish themselves.[45] For instance, in 1771, Athanasius Ford, planter in Charles County, sent Christopher Court a shipment of tobacco worth only £210 sterling. In turn, Court shipped Ford goods worth nine times the value of the cargo received.[46]

In the decade prior to the Revolution, tradesmen who could afford to become independent retail merchants because they had accumulated capital or had sufficient property to borrow from the colony's loan office, were joined by a great number of small operators, both tradesmen and planters, who were able to establish business with only a small down payment of commodities or cash. By 1773, there was a profusion of such small retail merchants throughout the colony, but one of the best and most concentrated markets was in Annapolis. Striking, almost singular, new opportunities in trade were developing there for a few people.

The margin of profit that a retail merchant could expect was greater than the six percent his capital would earn if loaned out. On a typical cargo Thomas Hyde paid a two-and-one-half percent commission to his London supplier, paid ten percent of the wholesale value in freight, and cleared a maximum profit of twenty-one percent over cost, once all the goods were sold and all the accounts were paid.[47] From 1766 to 1771, Hyde ordered six shipments of goods worth a total of £5,225 sterling from the London firm of Perkins, Buchanan and Brown; and, at best, would have realized a return of £235 sterling per annum.[48] Such an income was not great enough to fund any effort to challenge the London tobacco merchants in their role of middlemen procuring goods for the Maryland retail market. Capitalizing such a venture would require about £3,000 sterling, and even in the halcyon days of conspicuous consumption, three Annapolis merchants were able to venture forth independently only by joining together.[49] Attracted by the two-and-one-half percent commission, the five percent discount for cash purchases, and the opportunity to select only

[45]Jacob Price, "Capital and Credit in the British Chesapeake Trade, 1750-1775," in Virginia Bever Platt and David Curtis Skaggs, eds., *Of Mother Country and Plantations: Proceedings of the Twenty-Seventh Conference in Early American History* (Bowling Green, Ohio, 1971), pp. 34-35, notes the cargo shipments of Perkins, Buchanan, and Brown.

[46]PRO, Treasury 79/36, "Memorial of Christopher Court, London."

[47]Hyde Papers, MS. 1324; Kellock, "London Merchants."

[48]Hyde Papers, MS. 1324.

[49]WDJ 1:223-24; and Price, "Capital and Credit," pp. 13-14.

goods of quality (often a serious handicap when dealing with a London merchant who rarely saw what he supplied), Charles Wallace, John Davidson, and Joshua Johnson pooled their resources and decided to seek goods from London on their own.

Charles Wallace, the chief promoter and engineer of the new firm of Wallace, Davidson and Johnson, began his career in Annapolis in the late 1740s as a staymaker.[50] By the 1760s, he had given up stay-making and had opened a store, securing goods from Osgood Hanbury and Company.[51] Wallace had great plans for the town of Annapolis. In 1769, he purchased a large tract of undeveloped land that ran from the marshy basin at the foot of Church Street and up the hill to State House Circle. Almost immediately he laid out the property into lots along two new streets, which he named Fleet and Cornhill, that ran from the circle to the water. Undoubtedly he chose the names of the streets carefully, hoping that the area would soon resemble (at least in miniature) its London counterpart. At the foot of Fleet and Cornhill Streets Wallace envisioned an impressive row of four stores situated on the new wharf that would house goods transferred by open shallow draught craft from ships anchored out in the Severn.[52] His plans were too big for successful completion by one man alone, and he convinced Joshua Johnson, a fellow retail merchant who had been commissioning goods from James Russell in London, and John Davidson, deputy naval officer of the port of Annapolis and registrar of the Annapolis Free School, to join him.[53]

On March 22, 1771, the three signed a partnership agreement covering the period from April 1771 to January 1776. Each contributed £1,000 sterling and held equal shares. Johnson was to go to London to purchase goods and was to remain there for the duration of the agreement, except for one short visit home.[54] Johnson left Annapolis on the 25th of April and arrived in Bristol on the 29th of May. From Bristol he journeyed to London, armed with a number of introductions, to begin the process of sending goods back for sale in the new stores on the dock.[55]

---

[50]*Maryland Gazette*, August 30, 1749.

[51]WDJ 1:7.

[52]See Edward Papenfuse and Jane McWilliams, "Appendix F: Lot Histories and Maps National Endowment for the Humanities Grant #H69-0-178," (hereafter cited as Papenfuse and McWilliams, "Appendix F"), on deposit at the Hall of Records, Annapolis, Md. For the Wallace property see Parcels 13, 14, and 15.

[53]WDJ 1:6; *Maryland Gazette*, May 22, 1766, and April 13, 1775.

[54]Chancery Papers 2893, Hall of Records Annapolis, Md. (hereafter cited as Chan. Pap.).

[55]WDJ 1:4, 6-7. For Johnson's career in London see also Jacob M. Price, "Joshua Johnson in London, 1771-1775; Credit and Commercial Organization in the British-

Annapolis in the 1850s, showing the Wallace, Davidson, and Johnson Build-
ing facing the dock and the area behind it to State Circle developed by
Charles Wallace. Detail from a Sachse print, Maryland Hall of Records, Gift
Collection. Photocopy by M. E. Warren, Annapolis.

In London Johnson was eager to begin, but also somewhat apprehensive and even a little homesick. In a letter to Charles Wallace he remembered fondly the evenings when the venture was only in the planning stage and he was safe by the fire enjoying good company.

When you are in a writing mood be pleased to bestow a few lines on me & tell me in them how the House Building &ca goes on and & what progress you have made on the Wharf it will be exceedingly welcome to me . . . it will enliven the thoughts & Freshen the memory of those Jocoas evenings that you used to sett at your House with your feet up against the Jam & plan for the Publick oh Charles all those days are gone at least from me I fear I live much retired here not a friend nor even a Person that I dare open my mouth too.[56]

Johnson's first task was to convince Osgood Hanbury that he had no intention of entering into the tobacco trade, and that Hanbury should help him become acquainted with the London tradesmen. Hanbury was very candid and told Johnson that if he had any intention of meddling with the tobacco trade, he "could not consistently recommend" him, "as the gentlemen of the trade would say he acted ungenerous in taking a stranger by the hand to rival them in the business." Johnson told Hanbury that he had no thought of competing with the tobacco merchants; Hanbury was convinced and sent his cousin to the tradesmen to introduce and recommend Johnson. The rest of the tobacco merchants were not as kind and began to view Johnson with "a jealous eye."[57] James Russell, who had supplied Johnson with goods up to the time he came to London, was especially chagrined. Johnson described the encounter, "I dined with Russell who took every occasion of diverting me until he found that he was to have know more 2 1/2% of me, then there was an end of that over fondness."[58] Thanks to strong recommendations to Hanbury written by Daniel Wolstenholme, naval officer for the North Potomac District, and Thomas Sprigg, a prominent Anne Arundel County planter, and the fact that Hanbury's fortune "put him above doing those mean things that some do," Johnson began work under

---

Chesapeake Trade," in Anne Whiteman, J. S. Bromley, and P. G. M. Dickson, eds., *Statesmen, Scholars and Merchants: Essays in Eighteenth-Century History presented to Dame Lucy Sutherland* (Oxford, 1973), pp. 153–80. Although Price covers some of the same ground as this chapter, his emphasis is quite different and his conclusions need to be revised or amplified, especially with respect to the volume of trade the firm handled, both in goods and commodities, and the nefarious way in which Johnson conducted his later tobacco sales.

[56]*Ibid.*, pp. 12–13.
[57]*Ibid.*, pp. 1–2.
[58]*Ibid.*, pp. 1, 6.

(in pounds sterling)

To Whom Goods Were Sent	Value £.s.d.
1771	
George Cook	33/10/11
Thomas Johnson, Jr.	26/19/08
William Lux	31/12/06
Charles Wallace	15/05/05
Charles Wallace for the State House	15/18/08
Wallace, Davidson, and Johnson	6,436/16/01
Total	£6,559/17/03
1772	
John Davidson	45/07/01
James Edison	14/19/05
Thomas Harwood	15/02/00
James Johnson	7/10/00
Roger Johnson	16/01/02
Thomas Johnson	5/05/00
Lloyd Tilghman	12/10/00
Charles Wallace	25/06/08
Wallace, Davidson, and Johnson	13,385/17/05
Total	£13,527/18/09
1773	
Charles Carroll, Barrister	10/10/00
John Davidson	7/17/00
Richard Tilghman Earle	1,516/13/01
Thomas Johnson	2/00
James Johnson	5/05
William Lux	8/12/01
Matthew Ridley	12/14/00
Charles Wallace	3/16/06
Wallace, Davidson, and Johnson	7,483/05/00
Total	£9,043/15/01
1774*	
Sarah Bateman	9/01/00
William Bond, son of Joshua	684/08/02
William Bowie	6/16/04
Clement Brooke	431/13/06
Henry Brooke	9/17/10
Buchanan and Cowan	1,686/19/01
Archibald Buchanan	2,112/14/01
Nelly Buchanan	41/02/11
John Burgess	12/05/05
Charles Carroll, Barrister	49/18/00
Charles Carroll of Carrollton	904/05/11
Mary Carroll	38/02/07
James Chalmers	14/06/00
Greenbury Chiney	13/07/11
Joshua Clark	14/05/08

Table 2-5 (continued)

To Whom Goods Were Sent	Value £.s.d.
Jacob Claude	62/14/01
George Cook	5/14/06
John Cowan	12/14/06
Ann Dorsett	6/00/00
Daniel Dulany	5/00/00
Hall Gilbert and Hall	768/12/03
Aquilla Hall	258/17/07
Benjamin Hall	14/10/01
Francis Hall	3/10/01
Gerrard Hopkins	8/08/09
Johns Hopkins	12/05/06
Joseph Hopkins	1/08/00
James Johnson	463/07/06
Thomas Johnson	12/10/00
Lux and Bowley	1137/16/06
Reuben Merriwether	19/10/11
John Muir	7/13/06
Ship Nancy, owners of	402/10/09
Alice Nicholson	90/12/03
John Paca	31/01/09
Thomas Ringgold	189/10/02
Lucy Smith	3/09/04
Charles Soaper	5/16/09
Vachel Stevens	8/17/00
Lloyd Tilghman	7/09/00
Robert Tyler	73/17/11
Samuel Tyler	32/15/03
Charles Wallace	7/10/00
Charles Wallace for the State House	1,233/12/01
Wallace, Davidson, and Johnson	6,707/00/06
Wallace, Davidson, and Johnson Nottingham Store	804/07/07
William Whetcroft	64/05/06
Thomas White	13/13/08
Total	£18,506/05/11
Grand total, 1771–1774	£47,637/17/00

Source: Chancery Papers 2893, Hall of Records, Annapolis, Md. Wallace, Davidson and Johnson Account Books, Ledger A, Account #1516, "merchandize exported," pp. 11, 114 and Wallace, Davidson and Johnson Invoice Book, 1771–1774, Account #4555, both in Private Account Records, Hall of Records, Annapolis, Md.

*Does not include goods shipped on the *Hope* which was wrecked in July 1774.

the best possible circumstances. Hanbury's credit with his tradesmen enabled Johnson to command what he thought were the best goods in London, and although the rest of the tobacco merchants "hung alough," Johnson found he was able to "defy them" and proceed with the loading of his first cargo.[59]

A month and a half after his arrival, Johnson dispatched £3,877 worth of goods to Annapolis on board the *Brothers* (see table 2-5).

[59]*Ibid.*, pp. 1–3.

He was anxious that his ship get off promptly, because he had heard rumors of one Annapolitan who recently sold £5,000 or £6,000 worth of goods, and Johnson was afraid that the market would be glutted before his cargo arrived.[60]

Once the first cargo was gone, Johnson took time to seek out better quarters than the two small rooms he had used since his arrival, and by November he had settled into a comfortable counting house between the Customs House and the Exchange. He felt the move was necessary to keep the "character of a Gentleman & a Partner to a house that will export 10 or 12 thousand p Annum."[61]

Johnson came with only £3,000 capital and with the first shipment of goods was obviously in need for further funds. In order to find the capital necessary to keep the firm going at the pace he desired, Charles Wallace hit upon a source unique to Annapolis and indicative of the special role that the colony's capital could play in funding a native enterprise. During the summer of 1771, he agreed to build the State House for the £7,500 sterling the legislature had appropriated for that purpose. It was a shrewd move on Wallace's part. He could lend the cash to the firm (at three percent interest) and pay the workmen in goods and credit at the store, reaping the profits from a retail sale as well. Johnson was a little annoyed that Wallace would charge the interest, arguing that his service to Wallace in supplying materials from London should be adequate compensation, but nevertheless he was delighted that the firm had an influx of cash with which they could buy bills of exchange to send to him.[62] In time he would be even more appreciative, when a severe economic depression occurred and money became difficult to find.

The competition to send goods to Annapolis was fierce. In December 1771, as he dispatched another large cargo of goods, Johnson described the scene:

There is a struggle amongst the merchts who shall get their ships out first Buchanan sends Christie out Russell sends Person Molleson has chartered a ship & West & Hobson is on the lookout for one they will Sail about the first of January I believe & everyone of them carry goods for Annapolis so that in all probability your town will be earlier supplied this year then usual and perhaps with larger quantities.[63]

[60]WDJ 1:18.
[61]*Ibid.*, p. 33.
[62]*Ibid.*, p. 24.
[63]*Ibid.*, p. 44.

Nevertheless Johnson was optimistic about the likelihood of a good sale if his cargo arrived before the others. He felt he had a distinct advantage over his competitors; he was able to secure the best tradesmen because he could pay in cash, while others were forced to deal with only those tradesmen who would give fifteen to eighteen months credit. He also saw the goods before they were shipped, unlike most of his competitors, and was able to insure that they were better "in quality, more fashionable and better chose" than most.[64]

Letters from Annapolis buoyed his spirits further with news of the great progress in the construction of the stores. He was told they rivaled the newest and most grand of the townhouses then being built, and he was eager to hear which of Annapolis's two architects, Joseph Horatio Anderson or William Noke, had executed the design. So confident was he that all was well, he even took time to tease Charles Wallace about the new "Merchiones" in Annapolis, Wallace's sister, who had chosen to order her goods from their competitors, West and Hobson.[65]

Unfortunately, this optimism was not altogether justified. The first cargo of goods did not reach Annapolis in time for the meeting of the Provincial Court that fall, when demand would have been at a peak, nor did the quality of the goods meet the expectations of the partners. Johnson was dismayed and blamed Hanbury for poor advice in the selection of tradesmen, and pledged his best efforts in the future.[66] He sent his next cargo in February 1772 (see table 2-5), at which time he expressed a concern that the partnership was shipping too much. The goods were invoiced at over £5,000 sterling, and Johnson was "of an opinion that the quantity will over do your place." He suggested that to insure the sale of goods on hand and those now being sent, it might be "requisite to send some to Baltimore or Frederic Town."[67] Subsequent reports from Annapolis, however, quieted his fears. A letter from a rival but friendly merchant dated January 5, 1772, told of good sales in spite of big inventories. Johnson was delighted and wrote his friend: "I congratulate you on the largness of your Sails & doubt not the truth of what you say about the quantity of goods in Town or the profits they are sold for."[68]

In order to improve the quality of some of the goods he sent to his partners, Johnson considered ordering directly from the manufacturers, and in April 1772 set out on a tour of the manufacturing towns.

[64]*Ibid.*
[65]*Ibid.*
[66]*Ibid.*, pp. 54–56.
[67]*Ibid.*, p. 58.
[68]*Ibid.*, pp. 64–65.

He visited Gloucester, Tewkesbury, Bromesgrove, Birmingham, Coventry, and Woodstock, but the trip was disappointing: "I never met with anything that fell so short of my expectations instead of finding large warehouses well stocked it was quite the reverse." He found that the London tradesmen had bought up all the best goods. Johnson concluded that a fellow merchant, Thomas Ridgate, had been right when he warned that one could always do better in London, and decided to limit his out-of-town orders to shoes from Bristol.[69]

Upon his return from the tour of the manufacturing towns, Johnson found no letters from his partners. The failure of a number of houses prominent in the continental corn trade compounded his uneasiness about hearing nothing from Annapolis. When at last a letter arrived from a friend in Baltimore, it told of a severe winter that made it likely corn prices would rise, and complained that Baltimore merchants were saddled with large inventories of goods they could not sell except at a loss. Johnson sent his condolences to the "young adventurers" who were working so hard to promote Baltimore in the grain trade and expressed his concern: "The account you give me of the dreadful situation of the drygoods merchants are truly alarming & I am very fearful of the consequences."[70] On May 25, 1772, Johnson heard from his partners for the first time in four months, and they too had discouraging news. The goods were not selling at all well, and Johnson panicked.

You say that the Quantity of goods per Page exceeded your expectations what will you say on the arrival of Nicholson & Richardson besides the Quantity now coming I assure you it makes me tremble for fear of the remittances & for the future I must decline taking Discounts & apply the money as I receive it to the discharge of the old ballances.[71]

Johnson was loath to give up the five percent profit he had made for the firm by paying for goods in cash, but he had no alternative.[72] He might even be forced to discount his bills as the "Scotch" did, taking a percentage loss on each for selling them before they came due.[73] He pleaded with his partners to use every means possible to sell the goods and collect payment, reviving the suggestion that they open a Frederick Town store.

[69]*Ibid.*, pp. 70, 73.
[70]*Ibid.*, p. 78.
[71]*Ibid.*, pp. 79, 82.
[72]*Ibid.*, p. 54.
[73]*Ibid.*, p. 79.

We never used to talk of trying Frederic Town I have often thought of it since here & am of opinion that it would be well worth our trying It appears to me that it would serve us in extending our acquaintance in the Inland Villages by which means the Shopkeepers would know where to apply for supplies from the recommendation of our Assistant in F Town and would not go to Philadelphia & Baltimore for their Goods & indeed it would not be amiss to have Patent Cards & that the one presiding in F Town shew it to the shopkeepers there & go from Town to Town occasionally with his Patents It is my opinion if he was cleaver it would answer our purpose . . . .[74]

By the end of June, Johnson had even greater reason to be concerned. In the same ship in which he sent the fall goods worth almost £8,000 sterling (see table 2-5), he sent a letter announcing the failure of a number of banks and merchants connected with the tobacco trade.

I am just returnd from Change, where it is current that the Glasgow Bank is stopd, the Banks & Merchts continue to stop here daily, what will be the Consequence God knows, but such a conflagration there never has been in the Memory of Man its suspected all you Scotch Factors Bills will go back therefore you cant use two much caution who you by off.[75]

A number of factors combined to produce a depression in 1772 and 1773. In 1771 and early 1772, Glasgow and London merchants competed for tobacco, pushing the price paid in Maryland to 30/- per cwt.[76] To pay for the tobacco they drew bills of exchange on themselves or bankers such as Thomas Philpot and Fordyce & Company, who advanced credit on the assumption that the sale of tobacco in Glasgow or London would cover the amount drawn with interest. The price of tobacco in the European market did not hold, however, and the London merchants were not able to pay the bills their agents in Maryland had given for tobacco.[77] Compounding the situation was the generous credit advanced by London merchants in 1771 and previous years to merchants in Maryland. Because the demand for imported goods was so strong, by 1771 London merchants such as Perkins, Buchanan and Brown and Christopher Court and Company supplied Maryland buyers with enormous quantities of goods with little regard to their ability to pay, trusting to a good market and rapid turnover in inventory to speed remittances. It was usual for goods to be sent on twelve months credit, but those British merchants who

[74]*Ibid.*, p. 81.
[75]*Ibid.*, p. 85.
[76]*Ibid.*, p. 95.
[77]*Ibid.*, pp. 112, 122–23, 165.

agreed to ship cargoes for little or no prepayment counted on their customers to pay sooner. As tobacco prices fell and the supply of money available to the colonists constricted, Maryland merchants found they were forced to give longer credit terms and ask lower prices if they were to sell their goods at all. As a consequence, remittances to British merchants slowed considerably and, in turn, the British merchants were unable to pay their suppliers. Although the colonists found it increasingly difficult to pay their debts to store-keepers, the depression had its greatest and most devastating effect on the British middleman, who supplied the Maryland merchants with goods and who sold the colony's tobacco. As Dick and Stewart, when pressed for payment, explained to the trustees of John Buchanan and Son, although they owed almost £7,000 sterling, none of their account was twelve months past due, a grace period they were legally entitled to, even if they had been able to remit sooner in the past.[78]

By "dabbling" in a "vile circulation of Paper"—bills of exchange drawn on sales expectations rather than cash or commodities already in London—and by speculating in cargoes of goods shipped to Maryland customers with dubious resources, the London tobacco merchant found himself in a desperate situation. During the fall of 1772, almost all the major London tobacco firms fell into financial straits. In January 1773 even Amsterdam, the major continental market for Maryland tobacco, was affected, and several prominent firms there failed. By February 1773, all the major London firms, including Perkins, Buchanan and Brown, James Russell, John Buchanan and Son, Christopher Court and Company, West & Hobson, and Barnes and Ridgate, were protesting every bill of exchange offered them.[79]

The Scottish merchants were able to save themselves, as Johnson had predicted in November 1772:

From the strictest observation & Inquiries, I am of opinion that the many failures in England & Scotland will not affect the [tobacco] trade in the manner you apprehend, insted of throughing the Business intirely in the London Channel I think it will increase to Scotland, especially if they can make their Purchaises with you for Goods & part Bills. I am the more Justifiable in my opinion from the Declerations of the Merchts here, that they will curtail their Exports & not Purchase any more Tobacco for the futer, many other reasons Prompt me to believe it will be so, the very considerable loss on this Purchase & and badness of Remittances will disable them in futer

---

[78]In addition to the examples of failures cited elsewhere in this chapter, also see WDJ 1:158, and JDS, p. 64.
[79]WDJ 1:112.

in pushing the Trade to such extreams, on the other hand, the Scotch Bankers (from Scotland) have acted with the usual craft (peculiar to that Country) in procureing Money on Annuities etc to Answer the purpose of supporting their Merchts.[80]

At the depths of the depression, in June 1773, a number of the London houses did, in fact, fail. A London merchant, James Anderson, described the magnitude of three of the failures to his friends in Maryland.

I have nothing new that is good to communicate; the late stoppages in our trade of Mr. Russell, Mr. Court and Mr. John Buchanan will, it is apprehended, cause confusion in Maryland, as such large sums of money will be immediately demanded—I hear Mr. Russell's debts amount to upwards of £50,000 and that he has near £100,000 owing to him by his books—Mr. Court's are about £52,000 and shows about £58,000 to pay them with—Mr. Buchanan's are about £70,000 and has about £120,000 in his books.[81]

As the depression worsened, Joshua Johnson's situation became more and more difficult. When London tobacco firms stopped payment, Johnson found himself faced with an increasing number of bills noted for nonacceptance, and he urged his partners to purchase as many drawn on Scottish factors as they could.[82] At times in 1773 remittances became so slow that Johnson began to have a morbid fear of incarceration, that was only heightened by a visit to his friend, John Barnes, in jail. In a letter written privately to John Davidson, Johnson related:

The times are beyond any description, all Punctuality is at an end, all Credit is stopt no Money amongst the People & an appearance of almost General Bankruptcy, good God, Joney . . . be very cautious about ordering Goods unless you can Remit a part at the time. . . . You must know doubt hear the fate of poor J[ohn] B[arnes] [of the bankrupt firm of Barnes and Ridgate] he poor fellow was three or four days a Constant Inhabitant of a polite place cal'd the Kings Bench & I am told and believe a nightly visitant still & God knows only when it will be otherways O Davidson think but one Moment what a difference it must & has made a fine Young fellow rob'd of every thing that is'dear think of him pity him & take care of poor me, I beg of you . . . .[83]

---

[80]*Ibid.*, pp. 113–14.

[81]Quoted by Ronald Hoffman, "Economics, Politics and Revolution in Maryland" (Ph.D. dissertation, University of Wisconsin, 1969), chapter 5, note 59.

[82]WDJ 1:121.

[83]*Ibid.*, p. 131. Over £1,400 sent Johnson was noted and of no use.

June and July of 1773 were especially bleak months for Wallace, Davidson and Johnson. At the end of April Johnson had written:

What I shall do or how to satisfy the Tradesmen much longer I can not tell for I am now in the power of them & they must do with me as they please, exert yourselves Buy or Borrow ten thousand pounds & remit me three immediately & the other Seven in all June & July or expect to hear I am fast in some Damd Dungeon living on Musty Mutton Chops . . . .[84]

From April to June Johnson received no bills of exchange. When at last on June 2 a little over £1,100 arrived, £833 was noted for nonacceptance.[85] In despair Johnson turned to Osgood Hanbury and Company who refused to help with a loan (even on the recommendations of Benedict Calvert, William Paca, and Thomas Johnson, three prominent Maryland planters), and went so far as to expose Johnson's plight to his creditors.[86] At the end of June, Johnson conferred with his largest creditors to no avail, and wrote plaintively to his partners:

I assure you there is nothing left to save us but your exertions in remitting me for Heavens sake ride or do any thing to save us my Sprits are exceedingly Broak & I can scarce hold up my head therefore again I beg you will depend on no one, but use your indeavours to save me . . . .[87]

No further bills arrived until the middle of July, and even then they were insufficient to meet the outstanding debts. As of July 17, the firm still owed £9,500 sterling, £1,800 of which was due the previous February, and £6,500 due the end of June.[88]

Wallace and Davidson struggled to meet Johnson's needs. At last in August and September 1773, good bills, largely borrowed from Annapolis sources and sufficient to save the firm, arrived in London. Johnson's position was improved so much in August that he could ship over £5,000 sterling worth of goods, and on September 4 he could write that the distribution of the last remittances "revived our credit somewhat" and a "continuance" would result in "top credit" for the firm.[89]

Even when times were at their worst, Johnson did not give up the hope of success in the London venture. If his situation was at times desperate, he took some comfort in the state of the London to-

[84]*Ibid.*, p. 162.
[85]*Ibid.*, p. 169.
[86]*Ibid.*, pp. 172–74.
[87]*Ibid.*, p. 175.
[88]*Ibid.*, p. 180.
[89]*Ibid.*, pp. 197–98.

bacco merchants, noting that they became increasingly "sowered," because they too were unable to pay their bills, and were swearing that they would not ship such immoderate amounts of goods in the future. Johnson saw the net effect as beneficial to his firm's sales: "You may be assured you'll not have such large importation in Annapolis for the futer & I think much fewer sellers to oppose us soon." He predicted that if Wallace and Davidson could remit fast enough, "a little time will leave us victorious in the Market & I hope crown us with the Laurel we so earnestly struggle for."[90]

So impressed was Johnson with the failures of so many London tobacco firms that he was bold enough to suggest again that his partners consider the consignment trade, a plan they had previously rejected when he first broached it seriously in July 1772.[91] In March 1773, Johnson wrote his partners that for 1,000 hogsheads of tobacco they could net a profit equivalent to that on £8,000 of goods. Only £3,000 additional capital was necessary, no more than the original investment made in accord with the current partnership agreement.[92] Johnson made it clear that he was only interested in consignment. The purchase of tobacco in the country had been one of the chief causes of the failure of the London tobacco merchants. They had so overcommitted themselves to buying tobacco in 1772, at prices too high for the London market to bear, that they were forced to renege on their own bills of exchange with which their Maryland agents had paid for the tobacco. With evident relish Johnson observed that:

The Situation of the Tobacco Gent is truly deplorable. There is few who can find money to pay their acceptances and for fear of meeting their immediate fate they protest everything, tho I incline to think that will

---

[90] *Ibid.*, p. 106.

[91] *Ibid.*, p. 87. Johnson favored the consignment business almost from the beginning of his stay in London. In November 1771, he wrote his partners that he saw "tho now two late, that there was a field opened for our making £1,500 or £2,000 on Tobacco this year had we accepted of the consignment Business & pushed it, a number was surprized we did not & a number was afraid we should. It is expensive here but the business just as easy managed as shiping of goods." *Ibid.*, p. 33. When Johnson seriously proposed the firm take on consignments in the letter he wrote the following July, Wallace and Davidson urged speculation in grain instead. Johnson, in turn, objected to this plan because of the risk, noting that one wheat importer had already "been thrown out of the Bank." Johnson advised his partners that it was "prudent to adopt the old Proverb that Drowning men would catch at Straws," and avoid such connections as they were proposing in the grain trade "for fear that we might sink sooner than we would chuse." *Ibid.*, p. 100. On this score, Johnson was shown to be perceptive and, in January of 1773, was found writing his grain merchant friends in Baltimore that "Was I in your Situation I would Raise Indian Corn, Eat Homina & curse the corn business."

[92] *Ibid.*, pp 118, 151.

operate like slow poison & must bring them to their end one day or other, for it must undoubtedly ruin their interest [with the planters].[93]

But if Wallace, Davidson and Johnson were to benefit from the failure of the tobacco merchants, they had to avoid the purchase of tobacco at all costs and devote themselves exclusively to consignments and to a more modest retail trade.[94]

Coming when it did, Johnson's advocacy of the tobacco trade was poorly received. In a letter dated June 30, 1773, Wallace and Davidson fell on him "without mercy" for even suggesting consignments when they were pressed to use every bit of credit they could find to pay the London tradesmen.[95] Only when business improved and loans from local sources proved bountiful did Wallace and Davidson weaken. In August, they began to see that the failure of so many firms engaged in both the retail and consignment trade (most recently Perkins, Buchanan and Brown) presented the unparalleled opportunity Johnson had claimed. By September, they were actively soliciting financial support from wealthy Marylanders and, in November 1773, Johnson received word that they no longer objected, having acquired sufficient funds to make expansion into the tobacco trade feasible.[96]

If Wallace, Davidson and Johnson were to compete effectively for the planters' favor and succeed in the consignment business it was necessary for them to borrow enough money to pay their London creditors and supply themselves with adequate capital to underwrite the costs of the consignment trade. For example, a consignment merchant, in addition to the cost of having shipping available when and where he needed it to load tobacco, also had to be prepared to advance as much as £5 sterling per hogshead in good bills of exchange on London before planters would even contemplate consigning.[97] This meant that if his business amounted to the 1,000 hogsheads

---

[93]*Ibid.*, p. 112.
[94]*Ibid.*
[95]*Ibid.*, p. 192.
[96]*Ibid.*, pp. 188–90, 212–13.
[97]*Ibid.* In December 1773, Johnson wrote "that some merchants were out to crush . . . us . . . therefore it is the more necessary to forward me a Sum sufficient to pay up our debts to answer the droughts of our friends with you. Can you effect which, we need not in a very little time care what they [the unfriendly merchants and tradesmen] can do, I do therefore recommend to you to lessen your imports, to add £3,000 to our stock [capital] & to keep two ships for our own in the trade of about 400 hhds each. They would be loaded early & You might always build or charter a ship to bring home the later tobacco. That would always be clevor business & which I could manage very well, tho after all that I have said, a great deal depends on the dispatch to Captn for if he is idle & not saving the ships will soon eat us out." *Ibid.*, pp. 223–24. Johnson agreed to advances of £5 sterling per hogshead (*ibid.*, p. 200).

a year that Johnson wanted, a merchant had to have as much as £5,000 sterling on hand in London to pay bills that fell due before the tobacco was sold. London merchants without adequate resources of their own usually funded such capital demands by resorting to loans from British sources. But Wallace, Davidson and Johnson's intrusion into the tobacco trade marked a radical departure from the norm. They found they could rely exclusively on Maryland money and, by 1775, owed £19,000 currency to a total of fifty-nine people in the colony (see table 2–6).[98] In that year, thirteen Maryland creditors held ninety-five percent of Wallace, Davidson and Johnson's total debt, claiming sums ranging from £538 to £6,346. The greatest single amount, one third of the total, was owed to Anne Tasker, a prominent Annapolis resident who loaned from a family fortune built on planting, office-holding, and the iron industry. The state held another 25 percent, consisting of advances for the building of the state house, loans from funds appropriated for the erection of a church, and bills of exchange borrowed from the provincial loan office. The remainder of the money was derived from a variety of sources, including Charles Wallace's sister, a retired Annapolis merchant, and a number of prominent planters such as Gerrard Hopkins (see table 2–7).[99]

With such backing and with careful management of affairs on both sides of the Atlantic, Wallace, Davidson and Johnson made

[98]At least two other Maryland firms, West & Hobson of Prince George's County and Barnes and Ridgate of Charles County, sent partners to London about the same time as Wallace, Davidson, and Johnson in order to buy their own goods. Barnes and Ridgate were insufficiently capitalized to weather the depression of 1773 and, although West & Hobson sold tobacco on consignment, they never equaled Wallace, Davidson, and Johnson's success, if Johnson's letters are any indication. Johnson's rivals were Molleson, Russell and Thomas Eden; other competitors were considered relatively unimportant. *Ibid.*, pp. 318–19, 322, 327, 411, 447. Neither Barnes & Ridgate nor West & Hobson relied exclusively on American capital to fund their business, although it is quite likely that West & Hobson were considered American interlopers in the tobacco trade as were Wallace, Davidson, and Johnson. For an indication of the diversity and extent of West and Hobson's business see Hannah West, executrix of Stephen West vs Clement Hill, General Court Judgments (Loose Papers) October, 1793, Hall of Records, Annapolis, Md. It is significant that in order to compete with Wallace, Davidson and Johnson and others, West & Hobson opened a store in Annapolis. *Maryland Gazette*, June 25, 1772. Joshua Johnson urgently pleaded with Wallace and Davidson to borrow. See WDJ I, p. 162. When the sums were borrowed is not known for certain, although the bulk was probably borrowed during the depression. For instance, in November and October 1772, Wallace and Davidson borrowed £1,000 currency from the commissioners appointed to erect a church in Annapolis. No money was paid on the loan until October 1775. See "Mr. Hydes State of Mr. Wallace's bond for £1,000 Church Money," 5/18/82, Box 35, Exec. Pap.

[99]It is important to stress that Wallace, Davidson, and Johnson, formed with American capital, was saved by American capital, the bulk of which was loaned to them by residents of Annapolis or from public funds.

Table 2-6 The Distribution of Wallace,
Davidson and Johnson's Debt among Creditors in Maryland, 1775

Range (£)	Creditors (#)	Amount of Debt (£)	Percent of Total Debt
0–49	40	412.04	2.17
50–99	5	323.85	1.70
100–199	1	168.15	.89
200–299			
300–399			
400–499	1	458.50	2.41
500–599	4	2,253.96	11.86
600–699	1	600.00	3.16
700–799	1	785.05	4.13
800–899	1	829.50	4.37
900–999			
1000–1999	3	3,637.22	19.14
2000–2999			
3000–3999	1	3,223.35	16.97
4000 +	1	6,308.00	33.20
Total	59	18,999.58	100.00

Source: "Balances due by Wallace & Co. taken Novem^r 10, 1775," exhibited as evidence in Chancery Papers 2893, Hall of Records, Annapolis, Md.

Table 2-7 Major Creditors of Wallace, Davidson and Johnson, 1775

Name or Agency	Occupation	Residence	Amount of Debt Held (£ currency)
John Ball	Shipcarpenter	Annapolis	558.90
John Clapham	Government clerk	Annapolis	458.50
John Davis	Planter	Anne Arundel County	1,469.51
Daniel Dulany	Lawyer	Annapolis	829.50
Gerrard Hopkins	Planter	Baltimore County	571.04
Mary Howard	Innkeeper	Annapolis	785.05
John Muir	Deputy naval officer	Annapolis	1,167.71
Margaret Murdock	Widow of Annapolis doctor	Prince George's County	543.98
Ann Tasker	Widow of planter-public servant	Annapolis	6,308.00
Thomas Wilson	Merchant	Annapolis	600.00
Church Commissioners			1,000.00
Loan Office			580.00
State House Account			3,223.07
Total outstanding loans from private sources			13,292.19
Percentage of total debt due from private sources			69.96
Total outstanding loans from public sources			4,802.07
Percentage of total debt due from public sources			25.28

Source: See table 2-6. Residence and source of capital derived from information in Wallace, Davidson and Johnson Letter Books, vols. 1 and 2, Private Account Records, Hall of Records, Annapolis, Md.

Table 2-8a Tobacco Consignments to Joshua Johnson, 1773-1775

Ship	Number of Hogsheads	Price Range (pence sterling)	Date
Sally	104	1 3/4-2	May 1773
Kitty and Nelly	275	2-3 1/4	January 3, 1774
Elizabeth	20	1 5/8-3 1/4	January 29, 1774
Sally	122	1 7/8-2 7/8	February 2, 1774
Morning Star	58		
Molly and Betsy	52	2-3	April 8, 1774
Snow Farmer	173		
Peggy Stewart	156	1 1/2-3 5/8	c. July 1774
Kitty and Nelly	545	2 3/4-6	October 29, 1774
Brothers	378	2 1/5-5 1/4	December 8, 1774
Nancy	423	3-4 7/8	January 9, 1775
Aston Hall	188	3 1/4-4	January 11, 1775
Richmond	95	3-4	January 1775
Generous Friends	120	3 3/8-4	January 1775
Patty	12	3 1/2-4	?
Annapolis	4		February 15, 1775
Nancy	431	3 1/4-6	July 31, 1775
Kitty and Nelly	531	6-9	October 1775
Eleanor	506	3 1/2-6	October 1775
Vanderstegen	363	3 1/2-5	November 1775
Brothers	23	4-4 1/4	November 1775
Total	4,475		

Source: See table 2-8*b*.

Table 2-8*b* Consignments to Joshua Johnson Other Than Tobacco, 1774-1776

Cargo	Amount	Consignee	Residence	Date
Pig iron	30 tons	William Buchanan	Elk Ridge	12/74
Pig iron	7 tons	Gerrard Hopkins	Baltimore	12/74
Pig iron	25 tons	William Buchanan	Elk Ridge	2/75
Pig iron	20 tons	Charles Carroll of C.	Annapolis	2/75
Pig iron	20.5 tons	Lux and Bowley	Baltimore	2/75
Bar iron	3 tons	Nelly Buchanan	Baltimore	
Pig iron	8 tons	Wallace, Davidson, & Johnson	Annapolis	
Pig iron	17 tons	Samuel Dorsey	Elk Ridge	
Pig iron	15 tons	Archibald Buchanan	Baltimore	
Pig iron	28 tons	Samuel Dorsey	Elk Ridge	
Wheat	617 quarters	Lux and Bowley	Baltimore	6/75
Wheat, corn, flour	4,065 bushels	Archibald Buchanan	Baltimore	4/76
Pitch	252 barrels	Lux and Bowley	Baltimore	
Indian corn	109 quarters	Lux, Bowley, & Ridley	Baltimore	12/75
Boards	6,590 feet	Archibald Buchanan	Baltimore	4/76

Source: Wallace, Davidson and Johnson, Ship Entry Book, 1774-1776 (Acc. #4544); and Account Sales for Non-Tobacco Cargoes (Acc. #1531), Private Account Records, Hall of Records, Annapolis, Md.

great progress in the consignment trade between the fall of 1773 and the adoption of Nonexportation in the fall of 1775. In two years, they handled 4,475 hhds. of tobacco (approximately 7 percent of Maryland's export) and managed several cargoes of wheat, corn, iron, and other commodities (see tables 2-8*a* and 2-8*b*). To promote their business they opened stores in Nottingham and Queen Anne's Town on the Patuxent River.[100] Johnson was particularly anxious that he receive consignments from Calvert County planters because they usually took their profits in goods and rarely drew on their London balances in bills of exchange. It was to Wallace, Davidson and Johnson's advantage to have planters consign tobacco to London and draw the proceeds in goods from the firm's country stores. In this way they gained a commission from the sale of the tobacco and a profit from store goods priced considerably above cost, without having to pay the consigner in bills of exchange or to ship him goods on special order. Most planters were not like those in Calvert County, however, and in order to obtain consignments, Wallace, Davidson, and Johnson were forced to allow their customers to draw bills of exchange in advance of the sale of the tobacco and to accept numerous small orders for goods from planters shipping only one or two hogsheads. Johnson's only caution was that Wallace and Davidson not pay out bills of exchange for a cargo until the ship had set sail, in order to minimize the amount of time he would be drawing on partnership funds before the tobacco was sold in London.[101]

The growth of Wallace, Davidson and Johnson's tobacco trade coincided with a general business revival. During 1774, a number of the London firms that had failed or reached the verge of bankruptcy in 1772 and 1773 returned to the competition with new capital and great zeal. Johnson soon found his greatest rivals in William Molleson, James Russell, and Thomas Eden. They used every opportunity to lure Johnson's customers away, arguing that Johnson was inexperienced and that the tobacco business could only be managed to advantage by merchants long familiar with the trade. Johnson constantly found it necessary to assure old and prospective customers alike that "Buckskins," or Americans, could handle tobacco as

---

[100]"A list of Balances due to Wallace, Davidson, and Johnson taken 10th November 1775," Chan. Pap. 2893.

[101]See Johnson's comments on the people who live near Pig Point in Calvert County, WDJ 1:226; also his letter to Charles Wallace in April 1773: "I must take the liberty of recommending your two, three, & four hhd Correspondents, in preference to any others. Their moneys are generally sunk in Goods on which we have 12 mo credit & of course that or more time, the use of their Money . . . ." *Ibid.*, p. 158. Johnson cautions about bills (*ibid.*, p. 200).

well, if not better, than the London merchants.[102] Fortunately, he could prove it. His tobacco sales satisfied most of his customers, and the services he rendered met with acclaim.

A measure of Wallace, Davidson and Johnson's success was the decision of Charles Carroll of Carrollton, perhaps the wealthiest planter in Maryland, to send much of his tobacco to Johnson and to entrust Johnson with orders for almost all of his goods ordered on commission. From the fall of 1773 to 1775, Carroll sent tobacco, iron, and other commodities worth almost £9,000 sterling to Johnson, and drew the proceeds in goods and bills of exchange to £3,600, leaving £5,400 in Johnson's hands, which undoubtedly he used to best advantage.[103] Carroll was pleased with the management of his affairs and sent his compliments to Johnson: "The attention you discover to my business, your readiness to oblige and the punctuality of your correspondence deserve my thanks."[104]

Johnson was a fierce competitor and entered into his work with a vigor that was diminished only by bad health. At one point when he became ill, William Molleson tried to force trade back into the old channel, and wrote Wallace and Davidson that he would be happy to take over Johnson's work. Johnson reacted vehemently.

You tell me you were allarmed on the arrival of Carcaud who brought you a letter from Molleson informing you of my illness & his readiness to take charge of our affairs here for which you are thankfull to him, he is one of the last men in the world whom I would trust & depend on it shoud that happen & I retain any sence I shall not put em in his hands.[105]

While competition with Molleson and other London merchants heightened Johnson's consciousness of being an American interloper in the tobacco trade, the passage of the Intolerable Acts in 1774 wrought great changes in his attitude toward political involvement. In 1771, when John Davidson became embroiled in controversy with a neighbor, Johnson observed that he had "learnt two things since I came to London, that is not to meddle with religion or

[102]*Ibid.*, pp. 318–19. In a letter of February 20, 1774, Johnson wrote to a consigning planter, "we have not sold your tobacco hoping that the Spring will enable us to obtain a better price for it than is or has been going for some time & that you will be convinced Buckskins are equally capable of managing your business as others." WDJ 1:254.

[103]Ledger A, Wallace, Davidson, and Johnson Account Books, Account #1516, "merchandize exported," Private Account Records, Hall of Records, Annapolis, Md. (hereafter cited as WDJ Ledger A), p. 111.

[104]Charles Carroll to Messrs. Wallace & Co., March 16, 1774, Charles Carroll Letter Book, MS 8173, Arents Collection, New York Public Library, New York, N.Y.

[105]WDJ 1:82.

politicks."[106] At that time, he was content to concentrate on business and ignore political matters—at least when it was to his advantage. Although Johnson had been a leading member of the Annapolis associators, who had agreed in 1769 not to import tea, the prospect of profit could easily overcome virtue if there was a chance of not getting caught. As he put it in a letter to Wallace and Davidson in 1771:

The Capt. tells me that Ja Russell has shipped five chests of Tea on board of him these two days for West River It puzzles me. I wish you would not be sparing to me of those hints for provided it is a general thing we ought to profit by it, Other wise the traitor ought to be exposed, Tho I wrote you before that the Baltimoreans had imported Tea for some time from Philadelphia.[107]

After the passage of the Intolerable Acts, Johnson's political perspective underwent a marked change. In sharp contrast to Dick and Stewart, who represented an element in the Maryland mercantile community that was content with the old order, Johnson became a strong advocate of resistance to Parliament's intervention in American affairs. Even the prospects of losses in the tobacco trade could not diminish this sentiment although he was not unmindful that his London competitors might be hurt more than he. In July 1774, Johnson wrote Gerrard Hopkins:

It is with every apprehension of dread, sorrow & fear that we behold the steps taken here to crush our fellow subjects that almost every Man we meet will tell us that the punishment is just *our deserts* & that we are even worse than the Scotch Rebels were. It is hard to be put up with, yet more hard to see those Rascals who are sucking your Hearts blood out [i.e., Johnson's competitors in the tobacco trade] join in the same sentiments & not stir a foot to preserve you. We have used our Weak endevours in denying the right this Kingdom has of enslaving our fellow & native Subjects in America by signing Petitions . . . & we would do more had we it in our powers. It is in yours. Continue Virtuous be cool and determinate and you will in spite of this Drunken Country hand down Freedom and happiness to your posterity that the great Creator of all intended for you & them. We are content & ready to meet any rebuff in our Trade. We began with but little, we are conscious that we have prudently used that little, so that unless unforeseen accidents, no one will have cause to say that they suffer by us, we are not drunk with success & can & will most readily submit to our low state for the Good of the whole in which sentiments we remain unalterably.[108]

[106]*Ibid.*, p. 33.
[107]*Ibid.*, pp. 17–18.
[108]*Ibid.*, p. 418.

Almost a year later, in June 1775, Johnson explained his position further to his partner, Charles Wallace. Commenting on the news from Lexington and Concord, he argued that the time had come for everyone at home to declare his sentiments:

All who are in the Interest of the Country will immediately take part with the Bostonians, for a declaration of Defence is now made & the terms that will be granted you depends totally on your own strength to oppose the Torrent of Ministerial revenge against you. It is hard on us, it is true, to be cut off of our expectations but why repine, what we possess was not left us by Parents or Friends, we earn'd it by honest industry, & if we part with it, it ought to go with our lives, for Life without Liberty is nothing.[109]

When colonial resistance came in the form of Nonimportation, effective for the fall of 1774, and Nonexportation, effective one year later, Wallace, Davidson and Johnson began to wrap up their business. In Annapolis, Wallace and Davidson were in a strong credit position. A surviving account current for November 1775 indicates that, although they owed £7,585 currency and £6,876 sterling in Maryland, they had balances due on store accounts of £15,171 currency and £17,376 sterling (see tables 2-9*a* and 2-9*b* for the range and distribution of the store debts).[110] Over the next few years, the partners were able to settle their accounts and remit good bills to Johnson.

With adequate remittances from Maryland, Johnson was able to pay the London tradesmen and hold the last shipments of tobacco for a good, if not the best possible, market. When war pushed tobacco prices to an exceptionally high level, between four and five times what they had been in 1771, Johnson sold what he had on hand for a good return.[111]

As Johnson brought the firm's affairs to a close in London, he undoubtedly found that his own efforts had been profitable to the partnership. He had shipped £47,638 worth of goods (see table 2-5) and could claim a commission of about £1,200 sterling. He also had sold 4,475 hogsheads of tobacco on consignment and acted as agent for cargoes of wheat, flour, iron, and a few other commodities (see table 2-8), which brought Wallace, Davidson, and Johnson another 2 1/2 percent commission.[112]

---

[109]*Ibid.*, p. 248.

[110]For the Nonimportation and Nonexportation agreements, see Schlesinger, *The Colonial Merchants*, pp. 505-9.

[111]Prices for tobacco are given in the Wallace, Davidson, and Johnson Ship Entry Book, 1774-1776 (Acc. #4544), Private Account Records, Hall of Records, Annapolis, Md.

[112]Some of Johnson's profits were consumed by a lifestyle his partners thought extravagant. In 1773, for instance, he spent about £600 for "house rent" and "expenses." WDJ

Table 2-9a The Range and Distribution of
Debts Owed to Wallace, Davidson and Johnson, Excluding
Debts Owed by the Partners and by the Stores at Queen Anne and Nottingham, 1775
(in local currency)

Range	Number of People	Amount of Debt	Percentage of Total
0–49	691	7,159.42	21.3
50–99	90	5,537.62	16.5
100–199	37	5,072.14	15.1
200–299	19	4,417.02	13.2
300–399	9	3,085.82	9.2
400–499	3	1,327.42	3.9
500–599	2	1,169.28	3.5
600–699	1	623.00	1.9
700–799			
800–899	2	1,703.40	5.1
900–999			
1000–2000	3	3,463.74	10.3
Total	857	33,558.86	100.0

Table 2-9b Debts Owed to the Firm by the
Partners and the Stores at Nottingham and Queen Anne, 1775
(in local currency)

Debtor	Amount of Debt
John Davidson	1,123.82
Charles Wallace	2,391.12
Ship Nancy	1,454.16
Nottingham Store	1,497.50
Queen Anne Store	3,114.12
Total	9,580.72

Source for tables 2-9a and 2-9b: "Balances due by Wallace and Co. taken Novem^r 10, 1775," exhibited as evidence in Chancery Papers 2893, Hall of Records, Annapolis, Md.

Ledger A, p. 155. He was not reluctant to ask for more money to support himself, nor were his partners reticent about declining. Once, when Wallace and Davidson suggested another occupation might be more honorable, and incidentally less expensive, Johnson responded: "You tell me that the calling of a Millener or Taylor is more recommendable in one than the consequences of a Merchant. Either of the professions are to me not dispiseable, but my opinion is let a Man act in what character he will, that there is a certain dignity to be supported in [being a merchant] without which he is presently reduced to the scoff of the people & called a miserly pretender of a profession he is not intitled to & when I can no longer support the Character I now personate, perhaps I may commence either Millener or Taylor, [although a Tailor] I don't think I can . . . . for when I try to sew, the needle always pricks my fingers and makes them sore." WDJ 1:58.

Johnson was reluctant to leave London and for two more years attempted to continue there as a merchant, apparently speculating in the last cargoes tobacco planters had consigned to him, as well as investing in a trading venture to Russia.[113] He speculated by selling the consigned tobacco to a firm in which he was a silent partner. The firm, Williams and Letillier, held the tobacco in anticipation of a continued rise in price and Johnson closed his accounts with the planters. How much Johnson made is not known, but the intensification of hostilities and the severe curtailment of shipping from the Chesapeake to London did force the price of tobacco up at least five pence per pound over what the planters had been paid. Presumably, Williams and Letillier sold what they had for a good profit.[114]

The conditions that caused tobacco prices to rise also served to curtail the opportunities for trade open to an American merchant in London. The supply of tobacco dwindled. Surveillance of Johnson's activities increased.[115] On the other side of the channel, prospects were brighter. France seemed ready to enter the war on the American side and, if an alliance materialized, would become a main source of supply for the war effort as well as a good market for Maryland tobacco.

In the spring of 1778, Johnson departed for Nantes. His leaving London marked the close of a most sucessful foray into a business long dominated by London merchants and London capital. Between 1771 and 1776, a vanguard of Maryland merchants effectively challenged the British middleman and proved that American capital could hold its own in the tobacco trade. What opportunities and changes war would bring remained to be seen, but the nature and organization of the tobacco trade in the upper Chesapeake would never be the same.

---

[113]The venture to Saint Petersburg was undertaken in July 1777. See WDJ 2:542-43.

[114]In the Matthew Ridley Papers, Box 4, Massachusetts Historical Society, Boston, Mass., there is a journal covering the years 1776 to 1778 in which Johnson and Ridley are noted as speculating in tobacco purchased from Wallace, Davidson, and Johnson. See especially the accounts for September 1776, in which Johnson, Ridley, Theop. Williams, and Jacob Letillier buy 40 hogsheads from Wallace, Davidson, and Johnson. In his Ship Entry Book, Johnson merely notes the sale to Williams and Letillier and makes no mention of the interest he has in the purchase in any of his surviving letterbooks or accounts. As the price of tobacco rose to over 12d sterling per pound, Johnson also failed to be strictly honest with his Maryland correspondents who had sent him consignments. While in one breath he could write to Lux and Bowley in Baltimore that "we had sold our last cargo at 7d at which we feel no regrets," in another he could boast to an agent in Holland that he was getting as much as 12d and still had a full third of the total London tobacco reserves in his possession. WDJ 2:422, 416, 508.

[115]On the matter of surveillance, see WDJ 2:250.

CHAPTER 3

A WARTIME ECONOMY: NEW SOURCES OF CAPITAL, NEW MARKETS, AND NEW OPPORTUNITIES, 1776–1783

E ARLY in 1775, Joshua Johnson was convinced armed resistance was inevitable, but as late as the twentieth of October, Annapolis and the Maryland Council of Safety were ambivalent. When it seemed likely that the British navy would soon make its appearance off Annapolis harbor, the city passed a resolution that "any of the King's ships arriving off and behaving peaceably shall be permitted to purchase provisions," and urged the citizenry to avoid any possibility of conflict by not "associating with the officers of such ships in order to preserve peace and to avoid entering into any political disputes."[1]

After the Maryland Convention met in December and resolved that the province be put immediately into the best state of defense, the prospects of averting conflict lessened, although for six months more the Council of Safety functioned under an uneasy truce with the proprietary governor, Sir Robert Eden. In March 1776, the council, in contrast to the action of the previous October, refused to provision British warships, but found it necessary to convey their sentiments through Governor Eden.[2] It was an awkward arrangement; power lay with the council, but the appearance of legitimate authority was with Eden. By June 1776, the council found the relationship with Eden no longer viable. Under pressure from Congress and Virginia, who demanded Eden's arrest, and faced with the need for consolidating and

---

[1]Papers Relating to Maryland, 1:49, Chalmers Collection, Manuscript Division, New York Public Library, New York, N.Y. (hereafter cited as Chalmers Col.). In March 1775, Johnson wrote to John Dorsey that it appeared troops would be sent to Virginia and that "these matters forebode nothing less than a Civil War & which we fear is almost inevitable therefore. Where & when it will end we cannot undertake to say, but this we are clear in that every resistance is Justifiable & ought to be made....," Wallace, Davidson, and Johnson Letter Books 2:157, Hall of Records, Annapolis, Md. (hereafter cited as WDJ 2).

[2]*Archives of Maryland* (Baltimore, 1883–   ), 11:233 (hereafter cited as *Archives*).

legitimizing their position, the council allowed Eden to depart for London.[3]

Within a month mobilization began in earnest. In July, at a meeting of the townspeople who supported the war, plans were made for fortifying Annapolis. Just outside the city, troops from all over the province arrived to join the "Flying Camp."[4] The change in the physical appearance of Annapolis was dramatic. A year later, William Eddis, a loyal supporter of the Crown, described the scene to Governor Eden:

Annapolis has assumed a very different appearance since your Excellency left it. The rebels have formed a battery from Mr. Walter Dulany's lot, round the water's edge to the granary adjoining your garden. The cannon are mostly 18–pounders. The works appear strong, and, I am told are so. From your wharf to the hill where Callihan lived they have thrown up a covered way to communicate with that part of town adjacent to the docks. They have another fortification on Hill's point and a third on Mr. Kerr's landing on a high cliff called Beaumont's Point. Three companies of artillery [about 180 men] are stationed at the respective forts, and in spite of inexperience they talk confidently of making a vigorous resistance in case of any attacks.[5]

The Revolution transformed Annapolis from a town of wealthy consumers and their suppliers into an armed camp and distribution center for the war effort. At least a quarter of the most wealthy residents were loyalists or loyalist sympathizers, and were compelled to leave when the war broke out. Some, such as John Ridout, the former naval officer and secretary to Eden's predecessor, Governor Sharpe, retreated to plantations in the country. Others, such as most of the Dulany family, fled to England.[6] At the same time, preparations for war and British threats to the town dissuaded others of the affluent from coming to town and buying goods in the manner to which merchants had become accustomed.

[3]*Ibid.*, pp. 354–56.
[4]Executive Papers, Box 1, Folder 84, Hall of Records, Annapolis, Md. (hereafter cited as Exec. Pap.).
[5]Great Britain, Public Record Office, Audit Office 12, Volume 144, William Eddis to Sir Robert Eden, July 23, 1777.
[6]Of the twelve people noted in Chapter 1 who built townhouses before the war (see table 1–3), three (25 percent) remained loyal supporters of the crown. Two of these, John Ridout and Upton Scott, managed to hold on to their property even though they fled Annapolis, but Lloyd Dulany was not as fortunate, nor were his relatives Daniel of Daniel and Daniel of Walter. When loyalist property was confiscated and sold beginning in August of 1781, the Dulany family lost land in Annapolis worth £12,555 specie. To save her property, Mary Dulany was forced to buy it back from the state at the market price of £2,500. In 1783, two years before the state sale, the property was valued at

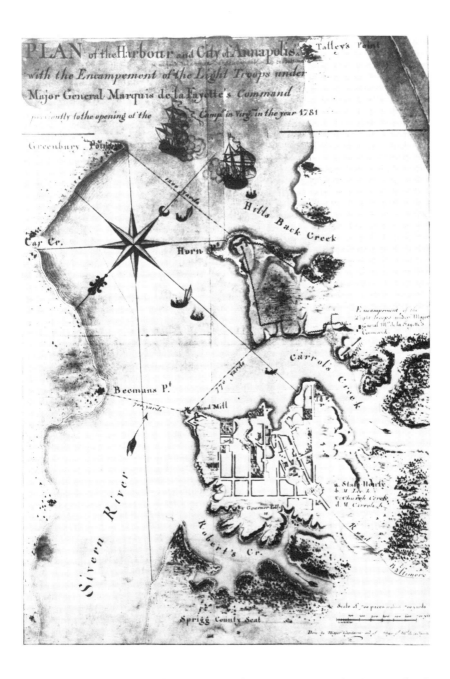

Plan of the Harbor and City of Annapolis, 1781. Photostat in the Maryland Room, Enoch Pratt Library. Original in the Archives des cartes, Dépôt de la Guerre, Paris. Photocopy by M. E. Warren, Annapolis.

The support the wealthy gave to the economy of Annapolis was supplanted by government spending on the war effort. Cabinetmakers such as Shaw and Chisholm, and blacksmiths such as Isaac Harris, turned their talents to war, assuming paid public posts and channeling their skills into the manufacture of war materiel.[7] Of the merchants who chose to remain in town (63 percent of those in business in 1774) and of those who entered trade between 1776 and 1782, over half took public employment (see table 3-1). Included among these were the most wealthy and influential, such as Charles Wallace, who became paymaster for the Maryland troops; Thomas Harwood, who was made treasurer of the Western Shore; and William Wilkens, who was chosen one of the commissioners for emitting currency. If merchants did not assume public posts, they lent their resources to the state. Nicholas Maccubbin, who had retired from trade before fighting broke out, contracted to mill flour for the army and loaned the treasury large sums of money.

Annapolis was at war for eight years, beginning with the arrival of the "Flying Camp" in July 1776 and ending with the elaborate and expensive preparations for the defense of the bay made in 1782 and 1783. Over the whole period, the state paid out at least £1,647,750 in real (as opposed to inflated) money for soldiers' pay, bounties, food, clothing, arms, ammunition, transportation, and shelter; a charge on the population equivalent to £46.7 currency for every free white male over sixteen (in an era when over half the population had assessed wealth under £100).[8] Not all of the money

---

£590. If the same relationship between market value and assessed value holds for the whole 1783 tax list, the Dulany property that was confiscated was equivalent to 6.8 percent of the total market value of real estate in town in 1783. Data on the sale of confiscated property in Annapolis were taken from John M. Hemphill, "Notes," Gift Collection, D563, Box 13, Hall of Records, Annapolis, Md. See the 1783 Tax List, Annapolis Hundred, Anne Arundel County, Maryland Historical Society, Baltimore, Md. (hereafter cited as 1783 Tax List, Annapolis) for the assessed value of real property. There is little evidence available to make an accurate assessment of the extent of loyalist sympathies in town, nor is it possible to determine with precision how many loyalists left, but a list of "Non-Associators in [the] City of Annapolis Sept. 1775" in the Gabriel Duvall Papers, Library of Congress, Washington, D.C., provides some clues. The list contains 89 names, five of whom are noted as those who "will sign" the associators' oath. In 1775, there were about 216 males between the ages of 16 and 50 (1,280 times 16.3, the percentage of males in the same category in 1783). In other words, 39 percent of the male adult population initially were loyalists. The fact that half of the names on the list were crossed out suggests, however, that the hard core of the loyalist population was only 20 percent of this age category of white males, assuming that those crossed out eventually signed the oath.

[7]Sources for statements about people who were resident in Annapolis in 1783 are given in Biographical Summary Files, on deposit at Hall of Records, Annapolis, Md.

[8]In 1793, after going over accounts and vouchers submitted to it by each of the states, the Commissioners of the Public Debt determined that Maryland should be credited with $7,568,145.38 for money spent on the war and interest to 1793. This sum

Table 3-1 Annapolis Merchants and Their Public Roles, 1776-1783

Merchant	Year of first Ad in *Md. Gazette*	Public Offices Held
Robert Couden	1752	Assistant Indendant
John Davidson	1767	Customs Officer
		Board of Auditors
Thomas Gassaway	1769	Commissioner of the Loan Office
		Clerk in Auditor's Office
		Register of Wills, Anne Arundel County
Nathan Hammond	1759	Commissioner and
		Endorser of Bills of Credit
Thomas Harwood	1768	Treasurer of the Western Shore
Thomas B. Hodgkin	1765	Auditor of the Public Accounts
		Clerk of the General Court
Samuel H. Howard	1771	Coroner
		Purchaser of Provisions
Thomas Hyde	1760	Commissioner and
		Endorser of Bills of Credit
Joshua Johnson	1767	Commercial Agent of
		State in France
Nicholas Maccubbin	1749	
Charles Wallace	1757	Paymaster of the Troops
William Wilkins	1763	Commissioner and
		Endorser of Bills of Credit
James Williams	1770	
Joseph Williams	1770	
Lewis Neth	1781	
Joseph Eastman	1781	
John Muir	1777	Commissary of Stores
John Randall	1782	Clothier General and
		Commissary of Stores
James Tootell	1781	Army Officer

Source: Biographical Summary Files, Hall of Records, Annapolis, Md.

---

was first converted to pounds specie by dividing by 2.66, the standard conversion factor for the period. To determine how much of the sum owed was principal, a percentage was derived by dividing the total amount Congress claimed to have paid Maryland with interest ($1,075,139.38) into the principal of that amount ($66,659.02). The answer, 57.9%, was multiplied by the pound specie value of $7,568,145.38 (£2,845,167.436) to obtain £1,647,750. See Report of Commissioners of Public Debt, June 27, 1793, Volume 1, Record Group 53, National Archives, Washington, D.C. The conversion factor of 2.66 was derived from a "Summary" of the accounts submitted to the commissioners from Maryland which is in the Scharf Collection, Maryland Historical Society, Baltimore, Md. (hereafter cited as Scharf Col.). The amount the commissioners allowed Maryland is an understatement of what was actually spent. For instance, they did not allow the bulk of the Annapolis commissary's accounts, although legitimate, because sufficient receipts could not be found and the commissary had died before being able to testify. The charge on the population was computed by dividing the number of adult white males in 1782 (35,268) into the sum expended by the state. The number of adult white males was taken from "Summary Accounts of the Valuation of the Assessments in the Several Counties returned by the Commissioners of the Tax, 1782," in the Scharf Col.

was spent in Annapolis, but the war effort directly and indirectly affected the nature of economic opportunity in the community. Handling men and materiel thrust an entirely new function upon the town. Overnight Annapolis became a collection and dispatch point for commodities never processed in such bulk before and for numbers of men so large that at times the resident population was outnumbered. The dock area was alive with traffic and supplies. Hiring out a boat and services became so profitable that planters in the area found it hard to keep tenants or overseers. William Yeldhall, John Ridout's overseer, felt he could make more as the captain of his own ship and left Whitehall plantation to work for the government transporting goods and men in and out of the capital.[9] Although there were other supply depots at Frederick Town, Head of Elk, and Baltimore, Annapolis was the administrative heart of an extensive war effort that ranged from New England to South Carolina. Residents John Wilkens and Jonathan Parker, among others, maintained an express service to Congress, the army in the field, and to other places designated by the Council of Safety or its successor, the State Council.[10]

Although between 1776 and 1779 the war cost almost £500,000 (or twelve times that spent on the normal functions of government during the same period), between 1779 and the end of 1783 the cost of the war was over twice as great, or £1,160,428.2.[11] The data for the years after 1779 do not lend themselves readily to analysis by category of expenditure, but the information for the years prior to 1779 does, and probably the distribution of funds was similar throughout the last years of the war.[12]

From 1776 to 1779, £123,386 (25 percent of the total spent) went for feeding and paying soldiers. An additional £141,098 (29 percent) purchased clothes. Arms, artillery, and ammunition accounted for another 20 percent, or £97,406. Three percent went for fortifications.

---

[9] John Ridout to Colonel Horatio Sharpe, December 12, 1780, Ridout Papers, D371, Folder 100, Gift Collection, Hall of Records, Annapolis, Md. (hereafter cited as Ridout Pap.).

[10] For Parker and Wilkens, see appendix B.

[11] See table 3-2. This statement appears not to account for inflation, and thus the total actually spent in specie was probably less, but because how much of the account is inflated cannot be determined, the sums are treated as specie here and in subsequent calculations.

[12] There are extant copies of most of the accounts submitted to the commissioners appointed to settle the accounts with the states, but a large number do not have costs included. They simply list the number of goods, supplies, etc. disbursed. See, for example, "Receipts Army Accounts #1, Acc. #1380, Hall of Records, Annapolis, Md., which is summarized in "List of Accounts against the United States" in the Scharf Col.

Two percent was spent on barracks and medical care. The remainder was undifferentiated in the accounts except that 18 percent, or £91,115, was spent on the navy. If naval costs were broken down, undoubtedly they would parallel proportionately the cost of maintaining the land forces, meaning that approximately 60 percent of all funds allocated for war were spent on stores and arms, the bulk of which had to be imported from abroad (see table 3-2).

THE MILITARY PRESENCE IN ANNAPOLIS

During the war, Annapolis was a collection and dispatch point for soldiers. In April 1777, for example, the governor and council issued an order directing all persons who had enlisted in the service of the state and not joined any regiment or corps to report immediately to Annapolis.[13] An idea of the minimum number of soldiers who passed through Annapolis can be derived from the statistics of provisions issued by the Annapolis commissary, John Crissall. The graph on page 84 is based on the assumption that soldiers stayed for at least a month at a time. In fact, some remained only a few days, making it probable that the numbers fed were considerably higher at times than the monthly averages would indicate. Once, in August 1781, when the French encamped near the town, there were more soldiers

Table 3-2 Expenditures of the State of Maryland, 1776-1779

Category	Amount (£)	Percent of Total
Pay and provisions	123,386	25.04
Stores	141,098	28.63
Arms, ammunition	97,406	19.76
Navy	91,115	18.49
Fortifications	13,221	2.68
Barracks, hospital	10,690	2.15
Miscellaneous	15,920	3.25
Total	492,836	100.00
Normal governmental functions	44,707	

Source: "Sundry expenses of the State of Maryland from the commencement of the present War with Great Britain to the 1st day of January 1779, so far as accounts have been rendered into the Auditor's Office and entered on the State Books," Box 13, Executive Papers, Hall of Records, Annapolis, Md.

[13]*Archives* 16:212.

than residents, an occasion that placed severe strains on the community as it struggled to feed, clothe, nurse, and house its visitors.[14]

Estimating the number of ships and naval personnel stationed in Annapolis is virtually impossible because supplies were issued in bulk to each ship and the amount of time spent in port was not recorded, but the navy's presence only added to the demands placed on the town by the army. For one entrepreneur, renting his wharf to the navy proved one of the greatest mistakes of his career. So frequently

The Soldier and Civilian Population of Annapolis, 1776–1783.

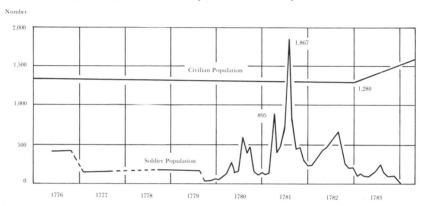

Sources: (1) the issue books of the Annapolis Commissary, MS 1146, Boxes 1, 2, and 10, Maryland Historical Society, Baltimore, Md.; (2) "Amount of Rations Delivered to Continental Troops at Annapolis Commencing the 12th of February. . . .," Vertical File, Maryland Historical Society, Baltimore, Md.; (3) "Account of Provisions Issued to the Fly^g Camp at Annapolis from 10th July till 12th Au^t, 1776," Misc. Papers Box B, Executive Papers, Hall of Records, Annapolis, Md.; (4) "Account of Provisions Received & Issued in the Victualling Office from September, 1778 to September, 1779," Box 15, Executive Papers, Hall of Records, Annapolis, Md.

[14]The ration settled by the Convention of Maryland was 1^w beef or 3/4^w pork, 1^w flour or bread per man per day; 3 pints peas at 6/– per bushel or other vegetable equivalent; 1 quart Indian meal per week; 1 gill vinegar, 1 gill molasses per man per day; 2 quarts cider, small beer, or gill of rum per day per man; 3^w candles for 100 men per week per guard; 24^w soft soap or 8^w hard soap for 100 men per week. Written inside the back cover of the Auditor General's Journal B, Book #1, Library of Congress, on deposit at the Hall of Records, Annapolis, Md. (hereafter cited as AGJB). The number of soldiers estimated to be in town during a given month was derived by taking the largest amount of rations, flour, beef, pork, etc. given for that month and dividing it by the number of days in the month. The peak in April 1781 was caused by the arrival of Lafayette and his men. In addition to the Maryland and other Continental line troops in Annapolis in September 1781, there was an unknown number of troops under Rochambeau encamped at Scott's Plantation near the town, who were fed from their own supplies. See Howard C. Rice, Jr., and Anne S. K. Brown, *The American Campaigns of Rochambeau's Army 1780, 1781, 1782, 1783* (Princeton and Providence, 1972), 2:85.

was it used and so poorly was it treated that when the contract expired the wharf and warehouse on it were in ruins. All the owner received as compensation was a large sum of practically worthless paper money.[15]

Medical Care and Housing

Although only two percent of the total war effort was spent in medical care and housing for the military, much of it was disbursed in Annapolis. The town had one of two military hospitals in the state. By 1777, it was on Statehouse Circle in the charge of Dr. Richard Tootell. In February of that year it burned, and for a time the state rented a house in town owned by the merchant James Williams, but residents were not pleased at having the sick so near. In 1780, the hospital was moved to the poorhouse a mile outside of the town limits on the road to Baltimore. There it remained for the duration of the war, while the displaced poor, less of a health hazard, were lodged in the community.[16]

When Dr. Tootell died in 1780 he was replaced by Dr. James Murray, who left a considerable body of records relating to his work. Murray's hospital at the poorhouse contained about fifty beds and had a staff of nurses to aid him.[17] The pay was not good and the work was hard, as a petition of one of the nurses points out.

Your petitioner humbly sheweth that [she] . . . has been a nurse at the hospital for about a year. She has been diligent and careful in her office . . . [and] begs for augmentation to her pay, as she only is allowed two dollars a month. She has at this present time sixteen men for to cook and take care of. . . . Since she has been a nurse she has had a great deal of trouble. She is obliged to be up day and night with some of the patients and never has been allowed so much as a little tea or coffee which she . . . hopes your honors will take . . . into consideration. . . .
P.S. She, your petitioner, out of that two dollars per month is obliged to buy brooms and the soap we wash with. . . .[18]

[15]See Edward Papenfuse and Jane McWilliams, "Appendix F: Lot Histories and Maps, National Endowment for the Humanities Grant #H69-0-178," on deposit at the Hall of Records, Annapolis, Md., Parcel 35, Section VIII (hereafter cited as Papenfuse and McWilliams, "Appendix F").

[16]*Maryland Gazette*, August 1, 1776 and February 27, 1777; *Archives*, 43:96, 581–82.

[17]In 1783, 17,598 pounds of bread and flour were issued to the hospital at Annapolis, which suggests a daily average of 48 soldiers at the hospital. "The Amount of Issues to the Hospital for one Year 1783," Box 48, Exec. Pap. For payments to nurses, see AGJB, pp. 236, 255.

[18]"To the honourable the Governer and council The Humble Petition of Alice Redman one of the nurses at the hospital. . . ." Box 15, Exec. Pap.

The hospital continued in operation even after the peace in 1783. As General Greene's army was demobilized and sent home, some of the sick soldiers were sent to Annapolis, and between January and December 1783, the hospital consumed a great number of provisions, including 17,598 pounds of bread and flour as well as 158 pounds of the soap the nurse had previously been obliged to purchase.[19]

Housing the healthy soldiers presented peculiar problems for the town. John Bullen, like his father before him, was barracksmaster for Annapolis.[20] His father's task during the French and Indian War had been relatively small compared to that facing his son. At first, troops like the "Flying Camp" tented outside the town, but in April 1777, Bullen was charged with finding more substantial housing within the city. The governor and council ordered that Bullen:

quarter such of the troops of the first and second regiments as are now in the city in such of the Houses within the same as are not occupied, in those of the first place that are least valuable and which from abuse of them, if it should happen, the least expence would be brought on the public and if he has reason to suspect persons are placed in any houses as a protection to prevent their falling within this description he is to report to this board. . . . If sufficient vacant houses within this description cannot be found to quarter the troops of those two Battalions the Quarter master is to apply for further directions.[21]

The townspeople were necessarily reluctant to house troops. They feared destruction of their homes and their fears were not un-founded. Troops housed in the jail did so much damage that it had to be torn down after the war.[22] During the course of the war, a number of people, such as the cabinetmaker Archibald Chisholm and the merchant Nicholas Maccubbin, were paid for damages done to their property.[23] Indeed, sometimes the soldiers were too much for the town, and there were neither supplies nor housing to go around. In 1782, while the state was trying to fit out barges and equip 350 sailors, General Smallwood was also in the city with newly recruited troops trying to find them housing. He wrote that because the efforts to supply the barges, food and clothing for his own men were so "shamefully scanty, that I was obliged to suffer such of the soldiers

[19]"The Amount of Issues to the Hospital for one Year 1783," Box 48, Exec. Pap.
[20]"The Province of Maryland to John Bullen . . . October 1763," Scharf Col.
[21]*Archives*, 16:195.
[22]Box 12, Folder 34, Revolutionary Papers, Hall of Records, Annapolis, Md.; and Papenfuse and McWilliams, "Appendix F," Parcel 39, Section I.
[23]December 23, 1777, Box 9, Exec. Pap.; and Intendant's Papers, 1782–1785, September 30, 1785, Hall of Records, Annapolis, Md.

who could be trusted to go home, and since the approach of the warm season they have been crowded in places substituted for Barracks which have been little better than Hog Sties, and not half sufficient to contain them."[24] A particularly acute problem, especially during the winter, was firewood. In March 1782, the council had written General Smallwood a partial explanation why they did not provide the best quarters for his men:

Within these few weeks past, we have paid an immense sum of money for houses damaged and destroyed in this City by the Soldiery, during the Winter. There was some pretence for this conduct, in the Severity of the Winter and when the Soldiers were but badly supplied with wood, but at this Season, and when wood is plentifully furnished, it is unpardonable, and yet the practice is continued in as great degree as ever.[25]

Provisions

Prior to the Revolution, Annapolis played a negligible part in the Chesapeake provision trade to Europe and the West Indies (see table 3-3). Commodities such as pork, beef, and flour, while imported for the town's consumption, were rarely exported. Cattle were slaughtered for the tanyards and may have contributed to a modest export trade some time in the past, but a large number of the hides tanned

Table 3-3 Pork and Beef Exports
from the Annapolis Trading District, 1768-1774

(in barrels)

Year	Pork	Beef
1768	34	0
1769	55	10
1770	47	10
1771	9	0
1772	23	0
1773	130	33
1774	290	17
Total	588	70
Annual average	84	10

Source: Ronald Hoffman, Analysis of the Annapolis Port Books, Manuscript in his possession.

[24]Smallwood to General Greene, 23 September 1782, Vertical File, Maryland Historical Society, Baltimore, Md. (hereafter cited as Vert. File); Smallwood to General Washington, 30 July 1782, in Thomas Balch, ed., *Papers Relating Chiefly to the Maryland Line During the Revolution* (Philadelphia, 1857), p. 190.

[25]*Archives*, 48:117.

were brought to the town from outlying plantations, and by the Revolution even that practice, along with the tanning business, was declining. Diversification was taking place to a modest degree in the region about the town, but little wheat was grown for the Annapolis export trade, and much of what the town consumed came from Frederick Town or Baltimore.[26] During the war, large quantities of foodstuffs, never handled in such bulk before, were imported to feed the troops stationed at Annapolis, to be reissued to ships defending the bay, or to be exported to the troops in the field.

From the issue books of the Annapolis commissary it is possible to determine how many provisions were consumed by soldiers at Annapolis between July 1776 and April 1784. These were only a portion of the provisions that passed through the town, according to an account covering the years 1778-1779. Between September 1778 and September 1779, the commissary in Annapolis issued 82,848 pounds of beef and pork (approximately 389 barrels), two and one half times the amount of rations given to troops in and about the town.[27]

Some of the provisions not consumed by the army probably went to the navy. For example, in February 1779, a time when the commissary was dispensing about 2,860 rations a month (about 10 barrels of pork and beef) in Annapolis, he also dispatched an additional twenty barrels of pork, ten barrels of beef, and nine barrels of bread to the *Conquor* galley stationed in Baltimore.[28]

Exactly how much the navy consumed and how much was exported to the troops in the field cannot be determined from the available evidence, but the amount at times may have been significant. In 1780, the importance of the provisions provided by the state was acknowledged by Ephraim Blaine, commissary general of the Continental Army, in a letter to Governor Lee.

I beg leave to inform your Excellency and Council that you have the warmest acknowledgments of the Commander-in-Chief for your exertions in forwarding supplies and it is greatly owing to you that I was able to feed the Army with Bread thro the Winter, and be assured I am happy of having an opportunity in all Companies of declaring how much the United States are indebted to you for the Supplies rendered.[29]

---

[26]James Dick and Stewart Company, Letter book, 1773-81, pp. 93, 152, Duke University Library, Durham, N.C.

[27]See sources for graph, p. 84.

[28]"The Conqurer Delv^d Feby 1779," Scharf Col.

[29]*Archives*, 43:506.

In September 1781, at the peak of the war effort, seventy-one boats were impressed into service to ship men and supplies from Annapolis and the Head of Elk to meet Cornwallis in Virginia.[30] The massive effort of the state at that time was acknowledged in a letter from Washington to the governor written in October: "Give me leave to return you my sincerest thanks for your exertions on the present occasion. The supplies are so liberal that they remove every apprehension of want."[31]

Even after Yorktown, provisions continued to pour into Annapolis. In the summer of 1782, over 300 new army recruits and about 350 crew members and marines for four barges were stationed in the community. Summary accounts of the commissary's office show that between February 1782 and December 1783, 1,026 barrels of flour, 510 barrels of pork, 131 barrels of bread, and 31 barrels of beef were received into the "victualing" office on the dock.[32] By that time fighting with the British was confined to a few naval engagements and what was delivered had to be combined with supplies on hand to meet the local needs; yet, the amount handled far exceeded the quantities of beef and pork exported from the whole Annapolis trading district in any year prior to the war (see table 3-3). Planters and farmers who may never have had the occasion to come to Annapolis before came with, or sent, provisions in large quantities. Practically overnight, Annapolis took on the appearance of a marketing town.

Stores

Annapolis was used to handling great quantities of drygoods, and during the war the flow into the community continued unabated as the state clothed the army and navy. Table 3-4 is an abstract of the clothes provided by the state for the duration of the war, the majority of which were given out at Annapolis by three successive commissaries of stores, John Bullen, Charles Wallace Howard, and John Muir; or in the field by John Randall, who was supplied from the town.

Making clothes created some new industry and revived an old one. Sewing shirts meant jobs for women, although prices paid may not

[30]"Account of Provisions Issued to Sundry Impressed Vessels in the Continental Service," MS 1146, Box 7, Scharf Col.

[31]Washington to the Governor and Council, October 21, 1781, Adjutant General's Papers, Hall of Records, Annapolis, Md.

[32]"Provisions Recd to the Victualling Office from 1st Feby to the 14 Nov[r] 1782," and "Provisions Rec[d] to the Victualing Office from 14 Day Nov[r] 1782 to 31 Day Dec[r] 1783," Scharf Col.

Table 3-4   An Account of Clothing Issued at Annapolis during the Revolution

	Amount		Amount
Suits of regimentals	137	Brown rolls	
Linen		Pieces	26
Hunting shirts	377	Ells	84
Coats	1,559	Yards	56
Waistcoats	394	Russia drab	
Pairs of overalls	4,667	Pieces	17
Woolen		Yards	31
Regimental coats	3,742	White linen	
Jackets with sleeves	546	Pieces	2
Waistcoats	4,497	Yards	2,107
Pairs of breeches	1,103	Sail duck	
Pairs of overalls	3,455	Pieces	1
Pairs of		Yards	10
Leather breeches	1,142	Cruder	
Stockings	8,438	Pieces	7
Shoes	15,515	Yards	470
Woolen socks	694	Swanskin in yards	9
Shirts	16,748	Plush ″	551
Hats	6,267	Thicksett ″	58
Blankets	6,125	Everlasting ″	99
Socks	1,006	Shalloon ″	150
Sheets	55	Dosolas ″	20
Beds	51	Sheeting ″	214
Mattrasses	44	Check linen ″	1,715
Knapsacks	4,062	Rowans ″	1,247
Pairs of buckles	444	Shock jaws ″	26
Knives	239	Thread	
Combs	120	Pounds	29
Woolen cloth		Slips	318
Pieces	26	Scanes	12
Yards	4,674	Pieces of Brittanies	279
Oznaburgs		Buttons	10,349
Pieces	37	Sticks of twist	330
Ells	3,221	Sticks of mohair	2
Yards	12,027	Boxes of medicine	1

Source: "Abstract of Clothing furnished by the State of Maryland for the United States, the Price thereof not fixed," Box 63, Executive Papers, Hall of Records, Annapolis, Md.

have been to everyone's satisfaction. A memorandum dated April 1778, closes with the comment: "The wimen grumble at the price of shirts—make the best bargain you can with them. . . ."[33] Supplying shoes meant new life for the tanning industry and employment for shoemakers. The state leased a tanyard from Thomas Hyde and hired several shoemakers, a development the city greeted with mixed emotions, especially when the wind was in the wrong direction.[34]

[33]Memoranda Regarding Clothing, April 24, 1778, Box 11, Exec. Pap.
[34]For rent paid to Hyde see AGJB, p. 137.

As cattle, pigs, and sheep were slaughtered for provisions, hides were left to dry before delivery to the state tanyard, a practice frowned upon by the Council of Safety and the subject of a resolution passed in 1776.

Whereas it has been represented to the Council of Safety by Physicians and others that the intolerable stench arising from slaughter houses [and because] spreading green hides to dry in the City of Annapolis may be productive of pestilential disorder and other ill consequences to the troops and others residing in the city . . . it is ordered that no butcher or other person should after the 26 July instant slaughter bullock, muttons or other kinds of meat or for the use of green hides within the limits of the city.[35]

Most stores, however, including most shoes and some hides, were not manufactured in the town, but were imported from elsewhere in the province or from abroad by merchants with public contracts.

Arms and Ammunition

No arms or ammunition were made in Annapolis. The report of the Committee on Manufactory of Arms in August 1775 argued that contractors could be found in each county, and went on to note twelve smithies in the state which were available and which could make arms. There were three in Baltimore, one in Georgetown, four in Frederick Town, one near Frederick Town, two in Hagerstown, and one in Jerusalem, but none in Annapolis. The closest was perhaps Stephen West's at Woodyard.[36] Not even the best native effort, however, could meet the demand, and throughout the war great quantities of arms and ammunition were imported. They were distributed in Annapolis by John Shaw, the noted cabinetmaker, who was appointed state armorer. Most of Shaw's records were burned in 1783, but a few surviving fragments indicate that his arsenal was commensurate with the needs of the army that passed through the town. In an inventory taken in November 1778, Shaw stated he had 1,253 arms and 1,093 bayonets on hand fit for service, not including what was on the galleys stationed at the town. Another indication of what Shaw handled comes from his records of repairing guns and making packing cases for arms and cartridges. For instance, in 1779 Shaw made 1,400 cartridge boxes and packing cases for guns, and in the fall of 1780 he refurbished 150 stand of arms.[37]

---

[35]*Archives*, 12:89.
[36]*Archives*, 13:18, 38, 209.
[37]Shaw's records were burned February 6, 1783. *Maryland Gazette*, February 6, 1783. The inventory is in *Archives* 9:312–13. The cartridge boxes are noted in AGJB, p. 165. For the arms repaired see AGJB, p. 230.

Ammunition was imported and stored at the magazine close to the city. The amount on hand varied considerably as supplies flowed in and out. In June 1777, an inventory revealed only about thirty-five barrels of good gunpowder, one barrel of damaged gunpowder, twelve muskets, twelve bayonets, twelve cartouche boxes, one tent, and an unknown quantity of lead at the magazine. Thirteen days later, however, the barge *Plater* was sent to Alexandria to pick up 120 to 130 barrels of gunpowder that had been imported from France for the use of the state, and to bring it to Annapolis.[38]

The war brought great numbers of people and vast amounts of supplies to Annapolis. It altered the town's traditional relationship with the surrounding countryside, forcing the function of marketing town upon it in such a fashion as to alienate rather than please its rural neighbors. In a letter written in May 1779 to a planter in the northern part of Anne Arundel County, several planters from the Annapolis area openly expressed their hostility to the manner in which some Annapolis residents, including the merchant Charles Wallace, went about gathering provisions.

At an alarming crisis we direct these few lines to you in hopes you will be kind enough to inform your neighbours of a plan carrying on by the Citizens of Annapolis against the country people in general. Yesterday a party to the amount of 150 armed men set out on a plundering party, went to several reputable persons houses near the head of South River and seized all the grain they could get; this day they are out on another rout in the settlement of South River on the same business; tomorrow they intend a rout on the north side of Severn & on Monday they intend a rout up the south side of Severn & to proceed to the Settlement of Elk Ridge and so to Continue their different routs until their savage appetites are satisfy'd, except a stop is put to it by some prudent measures. We think that force must force subdue, but should be glad to hear from you by express tomorrow night as the South River inhabitants will be in motion on Monday & the sooner a stop is put to those proceedings the fewer ill consequences will Ensue. The principal persons concerned in leading the mob are Chas Wallace, McHard, William Faris, Jack Chambers, the three Middletons &c and all their followers are the lower class. Their determination is to examine all corn houses, bacon lofts, &c, & where they think any person has to spare they will offer their own price & if the person refuses their price, they will put it under a guard & send it to Annapolis there to be stored until they have finished their plunder & then distribute or rather divide it amongst themselves. . . .[39]

[38]Box 7, Folders 162 and 178, Exec. Pap.
[39]"Letter to Doct^r Howard, May 8, 1779," Box 14, Exec. Pap.

Such tensions between town and country were an inevitable consequence of the war effort centered in the town, but they indicate that
Annapolis was rather precipitously becoming a marketing center for
the surrounding region, a new aspect of business in the town that
was to continue under less trying and more natural circumstances
once the war was over. For the duration of the war, however, the importance of Annapolis as a market town for the surrounding region
was overshadowed in the minds of the merchants by opportunities
provided initially by the public need and later by the revival of
private business, which emphasized interregional trading alliances
rather than principally serving people drawn to town.

ANNAPOLIS MERCHANTS
AND THE WAR: PHASE 1, 1776–1778

The new nation had no commercial allies before 1778, and exports
went circuitous routes to market. Trade was carried on at great risk,
often directly by the state, which ventured ships to the West Indies
in search of war supplies.[40] Instead of openly engaging in private
trade, over half of the Annapolis merchant community chose public
employment. If they put any capital into shipping ventures before
1778, they probably did so by purchasing shares in vessels not under
their management.

During these years, maintaining a retail outlet in Annapolis was
difficult at best. From 1777 to 1778, the Chesapeake Bay was effectively blockaded at its mouth by the British navy, and goods had to
be transported from Philadelphia or the Atlantic Ocean side of the
Eastern Shore, making them hard to get and expensive.[41] John Davidson, entrusted with settling the accounts of Wallace, Davidson and
Johnson after the partnership was dissolved in 1777, wrote Joshua
Johnson in April that in the private sector there was "a stagnation
to all kinds of business [and] a want of courts to compel payments
[which] . . . makes it difficult to settle accounts."[42] Advertisements

[40]There are a great number of records relating to state trading ventures to the West
Indies. See several "Adventures" detailed in AGJB, pp. 291, 292, 304, 311, 312, 334.

[41]Chancery Papers 2893, Hall of Records, Annapolis, Md. (cited hereafter as Chan.
Pap?).

[42]Wallace and Davidson to Joshua Johnson, April 28, 1777, Chan. Pap. 2893. According to Johnson's bill of complaint *ibid.*, he received notice of the dissolution of the
partnership when the *Maryland Gazette* of January 1777, which announced the dissolution, was handed to him some time in September or October 1777.

in the *Maryland Gazette* vividly reflect the lack of involvement in retail trade. In 1777, only two merchants advertised goods, a stark contrast to 1774, when twelve merchants advertised. In December 1777, the *Maryland Gazette* ceased publication and did not resume until April 1779, eliminating an effective means of advertising goods for sale.

Many of the richest and best customers of the merchants had fled because they were loyalists or because they wished to avoid a town so absorbed in the conduct of war.[43] If anything, the great number of military personnel that periodically flooded the town hampered retail trade. Soldiers were, in general, poor and rowdy, and in all likelihood their presence dissuaded the more affluent planters from making more than the most necessary trips to town. The soldiers themselves were not good customers until late in the war. Only after 1781, when soldiers were paid depreciation certificates and given western lands, did merchants find their business profitable. Then they were able to capitalize on the inability of the average soldier to wait until his certificates reached maturity or to afford the cost of establishing a farm on his land grant. Merchants offered him immediate credit for goods at their stores in exchange for one seventh the face value of his pay, and he accepted.[44]

Prior to 1779, public posts and public contracts offered practically the only lucrative form of employment for merchants in the town, except for an occasional cargo of goods that might be in excess of the public need and could be offered for retail sale. Between 1778 and 1779, Charles Wallace and John Davidson purchased eight cargoes of goods from France worth £1,195 sterling, a far cry from the £37,751 sterling worth of goods they had imported in the three years before the Nonimportation Agreement of 1775.[45]

How merchants in Annapolis principally employed themselves before 1779 and the nature of the opportunities open to them is illustrated by the career of Charles Wallace. As paymaster for the troops, Wallace handled considerable sums of money and, like his English counterparts who had traditionally used the office to amass fortunes, he probably took advantage of the funds at his disposal.[46] Unfortunately, if Wallace kept accounts of his private transactions with army money, they are lost, but his use of a state salt contract

---

[43]At times practically everyone was forced to evacuate, bringing business to a standstill. Wallace and Davidson to Joshua Johnson, October 4, 1779, Chan. Pap. 2893.

[44]"Smallwood's Essay on Speculation," Exec. Pap.

[45]"Statement of Goods Shipped by Joshua Johnson to W.D.J.," Chan. Pap. 2893.

[46]For the profitable use of the Paymaster of the Forces office by Henry Pelham and William Pitt, see John B. Owen, *The Rise of the Pelhams* (New York, 1971 [1957]).

was aired in a court case and indicates what he may have done with other public moneys entrusted to his care.

In 1776, Wallace agreed to supply the state with salt, a commodity in great demand because it was essential to the preservation of provisions. To implement the contract, the state advanced £5,000 in August 1777. Instead of immediately procuring salt with the money, Wallace invested it in loans to the United States and waited until the following year to honor the contract.[47] In January 1778, he provided Gillis Polk and Company with teams, harnesses, wagons, and all the apparatus necessary for a salt works to be set up in Somerset County at Sinepuxent Inlet on the Atlantic Ocean. It was a convenient arrangement. Wallace estimated the value of his contribution at £3,500, and over the next year he supplied pork, wood, and other goods worth an additional £300, charging Polk six percent interest on all money and supplies advanced. Inflation in the period probably played havoc with this particular investment, and Wallace probably made money only on the sums loaned to Congress, but by funding the salt works he satisfied part of his contract with the state and established a base on the Eastern Shore that could be used for more than the production of salt.[48]

During 1777 and 1778, when the Chesapeake Bay was blockaded by the British, Sinepuxent Inlet was used as a receiving depot for goods shipped from Europe and the West Indies or salt imported as ballast from St. Ubes, Portugal. The goods and salt were landed at places like the Polk Salt Works and freighted overland to the bay, where fast small craft would carry them to Annapolis and Baltimore. In turn, the ships at Sinepuxent would load tobacco and other cargoes for return voyages to the West Indies and Europe. In February 1778, Joshua Johnson dispatched three ships from London to St. Ubes for salt. With each he sent a double set of instructions. The first was intended for the British if the vessels were stopped by men-of-war and told the captains to take the salt to New York for the use of the British there. The second set of instructions, containing Johnson's real intentions, directed the captains to Sinepuxent Inlet (or, if the Chesapeake were open, directly to Annapolis), where the salt would be unloaded. Johnson addressed the ships to the care of his brother Thomas, the governor, who declined and turned the management over to Wallace and Davidson, who had a keen interest in acquiring the cargo as a means of meeting the terms of Wallace's

[47]Chan. Pap. 2893.

[48]*Ibid.*, and Saltworks Ledger, especially pp. 2, 17, Force Collection, Library of Congress, Washington, D.C.

salt contract with the state. It was hazardous to put a ship to sea in 1778. Only one ship belonging to Johnson, the *Nancy*, made it into the Sinepuxent Inlet, there to be burned at its moorings by a marauding British cruiser.[49]

The *Nancy* arrived at a time when the mode of supplying the war effort was entering a new stage and business prospects for Annapolis merchants in the private sector were improving. As John Davidson explained to Joshua Johnson in January 1778, on the eve of a French alliance, he and Wallace had "been neither idle nor unsuccessful in business here, tho perhaps in a line that ought not in prudence to be communicated to you, tho beneficial to our country and ourselves."[50] But the time had come to expand their operations to meet the growing demand in both the public and private sectors of the economy. In August 1778, Davidson wrote Johnson beseeching him to ship goods for sale in the Annapolis store, offering to pay him a commission if he did not choose to enter a new partnership agreement.

It is incumbent upon you to ship us goods, either on the Company or on our own particular account, to enable our living in the present time when we pay eight and ten fold prices for the necessary support of our family without the means of benefiting ourselves by selling in proportion to the extravagant terms on which we are obliged to buy. Had we been active & fortunate in the import of goods for these three years past, it would have proved more to our interest than a life of toil and Industry spent in the same line and pursuit, but as it is impossible to recall those lost opportunities, sure it is incumbent upon us to improve what yet remains of the opportunity to enrich ourselves and the means are only in your power. . . .[51]

ANNAPOLIS MERCHANTS
AND THE WAR: PHASE 2, 1779-1781

The alliance with France in February 1778 signaled a great acceleration in public spending on the war effort. In the first three years of conflict, 1776-1778, the state spent, at most, an average of £166,666 a year. Over the next five years, 1779-1783, the average annual expenditure was £232,086.[52] The expansion in the public sector was

---

[49]Chan. Pap. 2893.

[50]Wallace and Davidson to Joshua Johnson, January 23, 1778. Chan. Pap. 2893.

[51]*Ibid.*, August 14, 1778.

[52]See notes 8 and 11 above for an explanation of the real as opposed to inflated value of these figures. That for 1776-1778 undoubtedly reflects some inflation but that for

matched by improved conditions in the private sector. Except during the Southern Campaign in 1781, British ships blockading the bay were diverted to other operations in the expanded war, although British privateers continued to wreak havoc with American shipping from time to time. Embargoes were placed on commodities such as wheat, flour, bread, and other provisions necessary to the war effort, but the state encouraged the export of tobacco as a means of paying for the war and even invested directly in ships such as the *Lydia*, sent to France with tobacco to be sold for the state's benefit.[53] As a result, private business revived and Annapolis merchants cautiously returned to the retail trade.

Increased public spending was financed by taxes, loans from foreign governments and, finally, the confiscation of British-held property in Maryland. Undoubtedly, taxes could have raised most of the money required to pay for the war, and did so after the war, but taxation was also certain to breed discontent. In 1777, Charles Carroll of Carrollton put the matter well in a letter to William Carmichael, who was in France as one of the negotiators of the alliance.

We began the war without Powders, without arms, without officers, in short, in want of every thing necessary in war except Provisions; of Powder we have a good stock, but arms are still wanting and cloathing still more so; Some few good officers from France have joined our Standard, the war has already made some, and in the course of it more will be bred up; we have received 80 Brass field pieces from France, and at Philadelphia and in the Massachusets Bay they cast some every month, so that in time we shall have a formidable field artillery, But we want battering Cannon. If we can bear the expence of the war and keep up the credit of our paper money, I have little doubt of establishing our independence, but unless we obtain loans in Europe, and unless the Courts of France and Spain will assist us in supporting the credit of our paper, all our efforts I fear will prove ineffectual. We must lay heavy Taxes to defrey the charges of our several Civil establishments, and of the war. No Taxes have yet been collected; some of the New England States and this [Maryland] have begun to tax, our taxes on a moderate assessment of our property at the rate fixed by the legislature of 10/ in every hundred Pounds principal of real and personal Estate will I think bring annually into our Treasury £120,000. During the British domination you know our Taxes were very moderate, I am apprehensive the comparison of the former with the present, taxes may disgust and discourage our People, the bulk of mankind only judge by their feelings and can not see into

_____

1779–1783 does not, as it is based upon the adjusted figures for the total debt minus the sum for 1776–1778.

[53]AGJB, p. 4. Also Box 8, December 24, 1777; Box 10, January 16, 1778, January 26, 1778, February 1778; Box 11, April 3, 1778; and Box 12, August 8, 1778, all Exec. Pap.

the remote consequences of measures not immediately attended with distress and Oppression. Our People had not felt any great share of Oppression under the British government. The duties collected were but trifling, but then the right of the British Legislature to tax and bind us in all cases being once admitted, every man of understanding foresaw that the most abject slavery, and the deepest distress would, overnight follow the admission of the Right; If they had used the Right with discretion, we should have owed this forbearance more to policy than to those securities which every free People ought forever carefully to watch over and maintain, and to which all mankind are entitled by the law of nature-,

Thus men of Sense reasoned, the people saw the force of reasoning, and all Ranks joined in opposition to the usurped claim of the British Parliament, but when they came to feel the weight of taxes, that reasoning which then appeared to them so just and forcible, may not make the same impression on their minds, and they may prefer present ease to distant Evils, so the security of their liberties, to the happiness of their posterity.

It will be imprudent to tax the People to the extent of what they can even bear, and without doing it, I do not see how we shall support the war, unless some European Power should assist us with money as well as with arms, ammunition & cloathing. If Gold & Silver could be imported sufficient to discharge the annual interest of the Sums borrowed by Congress, it would be a great inducement to the monied men to lend their money to the Public, and in proportion to the sums lent the taxes must be laid; for we must not think of emitting any more bills of Credit; if large sums are lent to Congress the taxes will be less; in short, in our present difficulties, I see no other resource than what England had recourse to soon after the Revolution, Borrowing & Funding.[54]

As soon as the alliance was signed, the state of Maryland entrusted the business of borrowing to Joshua Johnson in Nantes.[55] Johnson was hampered in his efforts by Benjamin Franklin, who worked for what he perceived as the common interest rather than to the benefit of any one state. In April 1780, Johnson explained his difficulties to Carmichael, who also was finding Franklin hard to deal with.

I am surprized at what you say of Dr. F. treatment to you . . . tho I have had two much experience not to know his will . . . particularly in the management of the State of Marylands Comm[issio]n to me, he at first took me by the hand in this business & promised every assistance, threw me of[f] on

---

[54]Charles Carroll of Carrollton to William Carmichael, August 9, 1777, U.S. Congress, House, Foreign Affairs Committee, *Records of the House of Representatives Report on the Memorial of Alphonsa F. A. Blake (Carmichael Papers)*, 27th Cong. 1840, Record Group 233, National Archives, Washington, D.C. (hereafter cited as Carmichael Pap.).

[55]The resolution empowering Johnson to borrow clothing and military stores was passed in December 1777, but was not transmitted until April 1778. *Archives*, 21:14.

Dacosta Penet & Co. (who has very little Credit anywhere) and then withheld his Correspondence for Six months when he renewed it with a long list of apologies & complaints & wound them up with telling me that the Court had granted Congress a supply of Cloathing &c and that he doubted not but Maryland as one of the whole would reap the benefit of it. This stung me to the quick & in my Answer I told him that Maryland was able & ment to pay the Debts she contracted & that the State was bound to it by the powers vested in me. . . .[56]

By December 1779, it was clear to the Maryland assembly that loans to the state of sufficient magnitude were not forthcoming, and a law was passed designating Joshua Johnson, Edmund Jennings, Richard B. Lloyd, William Carmichael, and Jonathan Williams as their agents, any one of whom could go to England and "sell out the money belonging to the State in Public Funds."[57] The scheme was obviously doomed from the beginning. The British hardly could be expected to allow Maryland to sell £29,000 worth of stock in the Bank of England and then use the proceeds to continue the war.[58] The attempt was made to humor those people in the state, such as Charles Carroll, Charles Wallace, and John Davidson, who were afraid that confiscation would endanger their sterling funds still in England and impair their ability to obtain credit once the war was over.[59] When the British trustees of the bank stock refused, confiscation was inevitable and was signed into law in January 1781.[60]

Until 1781, when confiscation took place and inflation was curbed at both the national and state level, Annapolis merchants were cautious in expanding their retail trade beyond modest limits and confined themselves to the importation of small cargoes of goods for sale at their Annapolis stores. There were probably no more than nine merchants who maintained stores in town between 1777 and 1781.[61] By far the most important were Wallace and Davidson, and their activities undoubtedly reflect on a larger scale the business carried on by the other merchants.

Wallace and Davidson dealt with Joshua Johnson for four years, 1777–1780, although not in partnership. Johnson refused to enter a new partnership except on his own terms, which were an allowance

[56]April 19, 1780, Carmichael Pap.

[57]*Ibid.*, December 13, 1790.

[58]Morris L. Radoff, *Calendar of Maryland State Papers, No. 2: The Bank Stock Papers* (Annapolis, 1947), pp. xivff.

[59]Charles Carroll to Joshua Johnson, November 7, 1779, Letter Book of Charles Carroll, MS 8173, Arents Collection, New York Public Library, New York, N.Y.

[60]On confiscation see Philip A. Crowl, *Maryland During and After the Revolution* (Baltimore, 1943), Chapter 2, "The Confiscation of British Property," pp. 41–63.

[61]"Statement of Goods Shipped by Joshua Johnson to W.D.J.," Chan. Pap. 2893.

of at least £400 sterling per year for living expenses and a greater share of the profits. Wallace and Davidson thought these demands unreasonable, and wrote to their former partner:

> Suffer us to inform you that impelled by fear & drove from our houses by the Enemy has cost us more than all your claims put together & yet we thought the measure necessary, therefore tell us candidly whether you think it just & reasonable to repay as your third part of that expense, or an adequate allowance by the year in lieu of that, & such like unavoidable expenses on our part.[62]

Unable to reach an amicable settlement, Wallace and Davidson instead imported eight cargoes of goods from Johnson on a commission basis between June 1778 and October 1779, about fourteen percent of what they imported during as many months in the years before the war.[63]

The goods sent were of two types. The first type was obviously designed for the war effort and consisted of:

> oznabrigs, coarse linens and woolens, Russian drabbs & sheetings, some shoes if they can be had good and reasonable, but we mean not have fine, some hatts of the coarse middling quality . . . [and] other things you may judge reasonable there and necessary here, without meddling with the unnecessary extravagant manufactures of France.[64]

The second was quite different and reflected the growing demand for luxury items. In June 1778, Wallace and Davidson ordered "a good neat Post Chaise with harness for four hourses to be made without a box and not to exceed £100 sterling" for Captain Richard Barnes, who also requested goods for a complete suit of fine clothes.[65] Four months later, Wallace and Davidson wrote Johnson that luxury goods were still marketable if sent in discreet quantities.

> It may not be amiss to inform you that the Gay & unthinking part of our people are in point of dress as extravagant as ever you knew them & therefore your adding to the return Invoice some neat Silks, Ribbands, Gloves, Blond Laces, Cambrick, Muslin, Lawn Marseilles, Quilting, Gauze & Silkhose, will be profitable but we would have you be sparring in the quantities & judicious in the Choice of them.[66]

[62]Wallace and Davidson to Joshua Johnson, October 4, 1779, Chan. Pap. 2893.
[63]"Statement of Goods Shipped by Joshua Johnson to W.D.J.," Chan. Pap. 2893.
[64]Wallace and Davidson to Joshua Johnson, February 14, 1778, Chan. Pap. 2893.
[65]*Ibid.*, June 22, 1778, Chan. Pap. 2893.
[66]*Ibid.*, October 16, 1778, Chan. Pap. 2893.

Although the quality was not the best, a complaint that was to become universal about French goods, the profits made from the retail sale of goods could be handsome. In one letter Wallace and Davidson noted that the goods just received were disappointing, priced too high, and "would not answer here upon any such terms at anytime but the present when necessity only is the means by which we are enable to sell them."[67] Yet in another letter they reminded Johnson that "every hundred [livre of goods] you can put into our hands . . . will yet produce a thousand . . . ."[68] Perhaps, in actual fact, profits were not that high until inflation was curbed, but for one consignment received in March 1779, it is possible to measure precisely how much Wallace and Davidson made. The goods cost £5,747.60 Livre Tournois and were sold for £8,210.85, a profit of £2,463.25, or forty-three percent of the initial investment.[69]

Other than imports ordered on consignment from Joshua Johnson, Wallace and Davidson left the management of their business investments to Baltimore merchants. Before the war, Wallace, Davidson and Johnson were in the forefront of the movement to establish an import-export trade independent of London capital, and thus entered the war with a commanding lead over other native merchants engaged in the drygoods import trade. During the first phase of the war, Baltimore merchants took the lead by default, while Wallace, Davidson and Johnson and other Annapolis merchants chose to concentrate on public business. Baltimore, rather than Annapolis, became the center for most goods imported for private consumption, but in their rise to dominance in this aspect of trade, Baltimore merchants were aided and abetted by the Annapolis merchant community. Annapolis merchants sank capital into Baltimore firms and bought shares in Baltimore vessels. Even as they reentered the competition for the private sector after 1778, Annapolis merchants continued in partnership with Baltimore merchants.

The relationship of Wallace, Davidson and Johnson to the Baltimore merchant, Christopher Johnston, is an example of the ties the Annapolis merchant community had with the merchants in Baltimore. In 1776, Wallace, Davidson and Johnson purchased a brig in London, called the *Mary Carroll*. After a successful voyage to the West Indies and back, they decided to sell two thirds of the brig and entrust its management, when in America, to Johnston. Johnston was to take any freights earned on the *Mary Carroll* (renamed the *Speed-*

[67]*Ibid.*
[68]*Ibid.*, August 14, 1778, Chan. Pap. 2893.
[69]*Ibid.*, March 30, 1779, Chan. Pap. 2893.

well) and reinvest them at his own discretion in other ships or ventures. Wallace, Davidson, and Johnson sold one third of the *Speedwell* to Johnston and one third to another Baltimore merchant, Matthew Ridley. Joshua Johnson dispatched the brig to St. Ubes for a cargo of salt and from there to Johnston's care at Sinepuxent Inlet, where it arrived in July 1777. In the meantime, Wallace and Davidson loaned Christopher Johnston £1,000 to begin outfitting a second ship then being built by them at West River, called the *William*, in which Johnston had an interest. When the *Speedwell* arrived, Johnston sold a one half interest in it, paid back the loan in salt (which Charles Wallace undoubtedly used to fulfill part of his state contract), and invested the remainder of the proceeds in loading the *Speedwell* for her return voyage, and in shares of three other ships, the *William* (in which he was already a part owner), the *Rambler*, and the *Sally*. All of the ships were to be placed under Johnston's management if they made it back to Maryland, and he was to sell their cargoes in Baltimore.[70]

From the accounts Christopher Johnston rendered his partners it is possible to determine the extent of the investments made and to calculate the profits. The *William* made two successful voyages before it was stranded on the coast of Virginia. The first was to Joshua Johnson in France and cost £5,051 in May 1779, a sum equivalent to £421 when adjusted for inflation (see table 3–5 for depreciation scales as they apply to Annapolis).[71] The return cargo netted £662 deflated pounds in February 1780, or one and one half times the initial investment. The second voyage to St. Eustatia netted £421 in real money. Even when the ship was wrecked in September 1780, salvage was sold for a profit of approximately £266. Over two years a share worth £421 had yielded £1,350, more than three times the original investment. Profits were not as high from the other shares Johnston purchased or from the brig *Speedwell* (which had been renamed the *Success*). In April 1779, when the *Success* completed its last voyage under Johnston's management, the brig netted only £71. The same month, a quarter interest in the sloop *Rambler* produced £204, while the boat *Sally* yielded a net deflated return of £198. But all in all, Johnston's management of the affairs of Joshua Johnson,

[70]Joshua Johnson to Wallace and Davidson, November 11, 1778, Chan. Pap. 2893. "In the *Success* I have always esteemed you interested and in the one third part of whatever Christopher Johnston has done with the money arising from that speculation." Johnston's accounts are to be found in Chan. Pap. 2832.

[71]See also "A Scale of Depreciation by the Legislature of Maryland for the Payment of Officers or Debts," Vert. File, and "Continental Scale of Depreciation from the first of September 1777 til the 18th March 1780 Adopted by the Act of May Session 1781, 260 for 1," Vert. File.

Table 3-5 *"An Account kept at*
Annapolis in Maryland by the accurate
Mr. James Brooks, Clerk of the Council, of
the gradual depreciation of the paper currency according
to the standard of the half Johannes or Half Joe, which passed in
Maryland and Pennsylvania at Three pounds currency or eight dollars
each, the par exchange being £66 2/3 pct." *(one £ specie equals 2.667 dollars specie)*

Year	Month	Value of One Half Joe in Local Money	Number of Continental Dollars to Equal One Dollar Specie
1776	September	£ 3.07.00	
	October	3.10.00	
	November	3.15.00	
	December	4.02.00	
1777	January	4.05.00	
	February	5.00.00	
	March	5.12.00	
	April	6.00.00	
	May	6.15.00	
	June	7.00.00	
	July	7.10.00	
	August	9.00.00	
	September	10.00.00	
	October	11.05.00	
	November	12.00.00	
	December	12.00.00	
1778	January	13.10.00	
	February		5 for one
	March		6 for one
	April		6 for one
	May		6 1/2 for one
	June		7 for one
	July	10.00.00	
	August	10.00.00	
	September		4 for one
	October		4 for one
	November		4 for one
	December		5 for one
1779	January		5 for one
	February		7 1/2 for one
	March		9 for one
	April		10 for one
	May		12 for one
	June		15 for one
	July		18 for one
	August		20 for one
	September		20 for one
	October		24 for one
	November		30 for one
	December		40 for one
1780	January		45 for one
	February		50 for one
	March		60 for one

Table 3-5 (continued)

Year	Month	Value of One Half Joe in Local Money	Number of Continental Dollars to Equal One Dollar Specie
	April		70 for one
	May		55 for one
	June		60 for one
	July		60 for one
	August		65 for one
	September		75 for one
	October		80 for one
	November		85 for one
	December		90 for one
1781	January		100 for one
	January 23		115 to 120 for one
	April 9 [Philadelphia]		150 for one
	April 9 [Annapolis]		135 for one

Source: "Anecdotes of the Depreciation of Paper Currency," Maryland Volume 2, Chalmers Collection, Manuscript Division, New York Public Library, New York, N.Y.

Charles Wallace, John Davidson, and Matthew Ridley must be accounted a success. When profits were calculated in June 1779, there was a surplus of £669 on hand, bringing the total profits made to £2,019 when salvage on the *William* was completed in the fall of 1780. From a capital investment of £619.50, representing the value of the brig *Success*, and the cost of a cargo of salt, the partners reaped a gain of about £1,400, or fifty-six percent per annum.[72]

Prior to 1781, Maryland's tobacco trade was not channeled directly into French ports, but was diverted to the West Indies. In Nantes, Joshua Johnson often found himself, as he did in April of 1779, with "little or nothing to do."[73] He was dissatisfied with Christopher Johnston's management of his investments because Johnston was not sending him any business. In April 1779, Johnson entrusted his Mary-

---

[72]Chan. Pap. 2832. The cost of the cargo of salt is not known, but on another venture, Wallace, Davidson, and Johnson netted 2.9 times their investment. See Chan. Pap. 2893.

[73]Joshua Johnson to Wallace and Davidson, April 21, 1779, Box 13, Exec. Pap. Merchants in Amsterdam hoped that business would come their way. As John de Neufville & Son of Amsterdam put it in a letter written on January 29, 1781, soliciting business from John Davidson: "As a new Scene of Politics seems to be openg England having begun hostilities and issued a Manifesto against us we imagine from thence that the Trade from your State which used to be carried into St. Eustatia will now come directly this way." In a sense de Neufville & Son were correct, although effective disruption of shipping in the channel diverted most of the trade further south to France. Davidson Papers, MS 1253, Maryland Historical Society, Baltimore, Md. (hereafter cited as Davidson Pap.).

land affairs to Matthew Ridley, who was returning from France to Baltimore to establish himself as a merchant. Ridley was to terminate the partnership with Johnston and to negotiate with Wallace and Davidson about the settlement of the partnership of Wallace, Davidson and Johnson.[74] But, at this time, Johnson's former partners were unwilling to enter into a new agreement that would give him a larger share of the profits. The lack of business was discouraging, and in June 1779 Johnson wrote to Ridley, "This place [Nantes], my friend, will never do for us. The narrowness of the peoples dispositions are such that Trade can never flourish. I have taken my House for 12 months more, but I have so little prospect of Business that God only knows how I shall support my family."[75]

One of Matthew Ridley's objectives in going to Baltimore was to send Joshua Johnson tobacco and orders for goods but, as he soon found, it was not an easy task. In July 1779 Ridley wrote Johnson that:

At present the Trade to Europe is at a stand—the long voyage and great risque deters almost everybody—Eustatia Curracoa and the French Islands are their markets. This must be overdone & then I have no doubt they will begin again pushing for Europe. [Captain] Martin is gone to Holland as are some other—some to Cadiz & others going. The disposition of People seems just now for exploring new Countries & seeking new Channels of Trade.[76]

Johnson tried to pressure Ridley to get ships sent to Nantes, but to no avail. In June 1780 Ridley wrote:

You have an objection to sending a Vessell to the West Indies, the person manageing her will Send her where he pleases. You may see her one Voyage in France, the next she may go to St. Eustatia or to Holland, Gottenburgh or other places, no one will confine themselves but act as he conceives most to the advantage of the concerns generally.[77]

Ridley was optimistic, however, that the situation would change. In the same year, he wrote:

There has been & still continues in people a backwardness for European Voyages. They complain of the time spent in it. I have not doubt, however,

<hr>

[74] Joshua Johnson to Matthew Ridley, June 1, 1779, Ridley Papers, Massachusetts Historical Society, Boston, Mass. (hereafter cited as Ridley Pap.).
[75] *Ibid.*
[76] *Ibid.*, July 30, 1779, Letter Book #3, p. 4.
[77] *Ibid.*, June 9, 1780, p. 193.

in this there must be an alteration. A Continuation of low prices in the West Indies or heavy Importation from thence must oblige them to supply the country with usefull instead of luxurious articles, the usefull can only be procured in Europe. . . .[78]

Even more important than the problem of the lucrativeness of the West Indian trade was the problem of inflation. "The great reason why people will not make adventures to America is owing to the immediate depreciation of your money," Johnson wrote his brother in April 1779.[79] In Maryland, merchants were unable to secure bills of exchange because the depreciation of the currency was so rapid and, as a result, their ability to conduct business at home, let alone purchase goods from abroad, was greatly circumscribed. "The situation of everyone here [Baltimore] is nearly alike as to bills," Ridley wrote to Johnson in April 1780, "Even those who may be reckoned Men of Fortune are not able to purchase them."[80] Dollars could be converted to pounds with little difficulty, but the rate of exchange was so great that the returns fell far short of the need. Ridley observed that "the depreciation for the last six months [November 1779–April 1780] has been so amazingly rapid that no man could keep pace with it & in short I know not one man who can now buy the same quantity of Tobacco he could six months ago."[81]

It would be nearly a year before the situation improved. When inflation peaked in March 1781, the exchange rate was 578 pounds currency for one pound sterling. However, in the same month the Congress, with a great increase in loans from its allies and by insisting on taxes being paid in specie, was able to return to a specie standard, bringing inflation to an end. Now merchants were able to secure good bills of exchange from the Financier's Office in Philadelphia, drawn on commissioners in Paris or Lisbon, as payment for interest on loans made to Congress, as recompense for services rendered the war effort, or simply for cash in the form of any of the new and reliable means of exchange available since deflation.[82]

[78]*Ibid.*, Matthew Ridley to Jonathan Williams, April 23, 1780, p. 185.

[79]Joshua Johnson to Thomas Johnson, April 21, 1779, Box 13, Exec. Pap.

[80]Matthew Ridley to Joshua Johnson, April 22, 1780, Letter Book #3, p. 182, Ridley Pap.

[81]*Ibid.*, p. 181.

[82]"During the whole course of the war to the beginning of 1781, French gifts and loans had been only . . . a total of 15,400,000 livres—about $2,852,000. During the first year of his administration, Morris received from France $1,000,000 more than the sum of all French grants and loans up to that time. . . . Much of the income from France in 1781 was . . . consumed in Europe, leaving only a minor fraction to support Morris's domestic expenses." E. James Ferguson, *The Power of the Purse* (Chapel Hill, 1961), pp. 126–27. As table 3-6 points out, the loans were used to purchase goods in France through bills of exchange drawn on Paris.

At the same time that the allies were making larger sums of money available to the Congress, the French were purchasing increased amounts of supplies for their military and naval operations in the American theatre of the war with good bills of exchange drawn on Paris. The French were especially active in Maryland, buying flour and bread through agents such as J. W. Holker, who worked closely with the Baltimore merchant, Matthew Ridley.[83] At the same time, Maryland, like the national government, also was returning to the specie standard, funding its war debt with the sale of confiscated British property and taxes paid in specie or specific equivalents (i.e., goods instead of money).[84] With bills of exchange available from the French purchases of supplies and with its debt funded in hard currency, direct trade with France became a viable proposition, that was only enhanced by the British capture, in February 1781, of St. Eustatia, the most popular of the ports for Americans engaged in the trade to the West Indies.

ANNAPOLIS MERCHANTS
AND THE WAR: PHASE 3, 1781-1783

Until the spring of 1781, when the nation and Maryland returned to a specie standard, and bills of exchange, so vital to the conduct of trade, were readily available, direct trade with France was relatively unimportant to the drygood business in Annapolis and Baltimore. During the fall of 1780, however, Charles Wallace recognized that the situation was about to change. He had been a wartime partner of Robert Morris, who possibly kept him informed of developments on the national level, and was aware that Maryland's confiscation law would enhance the prospects of the state return to a specie standard. Wallace foresaw that any future that he and Annapolis might have in

---

[83]Ridley's connection with Holker is discussed by Kathryn Sullivan, *Maryland and France 1774-1789* (Philadelphia, 1936), pp. 46-47, 56, 58-83. See also a memorandum in the Ridley Pap., second series of boxes, Box 1, which outlines Ridley's dealings with Holker and probably was intended as a memorial designed to evoke compensation, perhaps from Congress, for the losses Ridley felt he had suffered because of Holker. Johnson commented on the importance of the French purchases in a letter to John Purveyance, written in May 1782. "[It] is almost a certainty that the war will be removed entirely from America [&] of course the French Troops & which [will] produce a scarcity of bills and disable you from making the Necessary Remittances." Wallace, Johnson and Muir Letter Book, 1781-1783, Manuscript Division, New York Public Library, New York, N.Y. (hereafter cited as WJM 3), p. 453. This was Joshua Johnson's letter book for the business of the firm which he maintained in Nantes, France.

[84]Crowl, *Maryland*, especially chapters 2 and 4.

the trade with France lay in a partnership with Joshua Johnson.[85] In October, Wallace wrote Johnson proposing a new firm in which Johnson would receive all the benefits that had been flatly denied him the year before: "I propose dividing the profits of this business equally with you, both here and with you. & as to the old bone of contention, I am willing to allow you what is reasonable.[86] Wallace intended to bring a new partner in on his half to keep the books and manage the Annapolis business, as John Davidson had done previously. The new partner would be John Muir, commissary of stores for the army and a former clerk in the customs house, for whom both Wallace and Johnson's brother, Thomas, had nothing but the highest regard.[87]

Joshua Johnson, like Charles Wallace, had already decided to spend less time with public affairs, recognizing that business was about to improve. In December 1780, probably before Wallace's letter arrived, Johnson wrote his friend William Carmichael that he was resigning his post as consul for Congress in Nantes and as agent for the state in France because of the uncertainty of reimbursement for public work. It was not so much that consular duties in Nantes were so difficult, but he felt that when Franklin called him to Paris to review the Silas Deane affair, "business and family," coupled with having to "live at my own expense" in Paris, were reasons enough to decline public service altogether.[88] Wallace's proposal came at an opportune time, and Johnson readily agreed. The terms of the new partnership of Wallace, Johnson and Muir were signed in June 1781, effective retroactively from January. Although no specific sum was mentioned, all partners were to be allowed to draw on the firm for "reasonable" living expenses and, in contrast to the former arrangement, there was no set time when the partnership was to cease.[89] The initial capital of the firm was relatively small, about £1,000 sterling in France and an equal amount in Annapolis, but for the commission trade little capital was needed, as the principal ingredient was the reputation each partner had for carrying on his aspect of the business.[90] Success depended upon others consigning tobacco and

---

[85]Wallace and Davidson to Joshua Johnson, January 23, 1778, Chan. Pap. 2893. In this letter they mention the fitting out of a sloop called the *Morris and Wallace*, which I assume is a reference to a joint venture with Robert Morris.

[86]Charles Wallace to Joshua Johnson, October 23, 1780, MS 281, Davidson Pap.

[87]*Ibid.*

[88]Joshua Johnson to William Carmichael, December 13, 1780, Carmichael Pap.

[89]Partnership agreement, Chan. Pap. 2893.

[90]The amount of capital each partner put into the firm is not known, but in January 1778 Wallace and Davidson proposed that Johnson send them £1,000 worth of goods in small shipments. Wallace and Davidson to Johnson, January 23, 1778, Chan. Pap. 2893.

commissioning goods; the partners intended to risk only small amounts of capital in goods for sale at the Annapolis store, and in shares of vessels. As Charles Wallace explained:

I propose that we hold but a triffling share in each Bottom, and I am firmly of the Opinion, that a great deal of money is to be made by Business of this kind and am shure we may do as much as we can cleverly manage.[91]

He and his partners were not to be disappointed.

Through the trading and investment activities of Wallace, Johnson and Muir, Annapolis played an important role in the expansion of the tobacco trade with France and in the marketing of French goods in the United States between 1781 and 1783. The nature and extent of the firm's business was markedly different from that of its predecessor, Wallace, Davidson and Johnson. Wallace, Davidson and Johnson were principally importers of goods for a retail market confined to the upper Chesapeake. They carried on a small amount of wholesale business on a commission basis, but their major emphasis was the retail trade. Their customers were the affluent in Annapolis and tobacco planters at their stores in Queen Anne and Nottingham in Prince George's County. Just prior to the war, business was expanded at Johnson's instigation to encompass the consignment tobacco trade, and the firm became exporters in addition to their import trade. At the risk of the planter, tobacco was sent to Johnson in London, who sold it for a commission. If the planter chose to convert the proceeds of his tobacco into goods instead of drawing bills of exchange, Wallace, Davidson and Johnson also profited by charging a commission and by having the use of the money until the London tradesmen were paid (usually six to twelve months after the goods were shipped).

In contrast, the first three years of Wallace, Johnson and Muir were devoted principally to the wholesale commission trade on both sides of the Atlantic. Retail sales were confined to Annapolis, and individual tobacco consignments of all but the wealthiest planters were carefully avoided. As Charles Wallace explained in his letter to Joshua Johnson proposing the new partnership: "My plan is entirely in the Commission way. I propose to take a part of every vessel of which we can have the management here and in France."[92] In America, Wallace and Muir confined themselves to the importation and distribution of goods for a commission, the export of tobacco which they

---

[91]Wallace to Joshua Johnson, October 23, 1780, MS 281, Davidson Pap.
[92]*Ibid.*

bought outright from planters, and the investment of surplus capital in shipping ventures under the management of others, from which they received cash dividends as profits if the voyages were successful. In France, Johnson became primarily a commission merchant who purchased goods for customers on a cash-in-hand basis, managed the sale of cargoes (mainly tobacco) sent by Wallace and Muir or consigned by others, and supervised the construction of ships in Nantes in which Wallace, Johnson and Muir had an interest.

Johnson's maxim was "if business don't seek us we ought to seek it."[93] When the Chesapeake was effectively blockaded again for the first ten months of 1781, he wrote Wallace and Muir:

We are sorry for the devastation and Terror spread by Cornwallace tho we think the People must suffer to make them know their Danger. . . . We attend to your objection to push business & cannot think you right if your Bay is so Block'd up that nothing can be done there. Why not go to Philadelphia.[94]

In October, before Johnson received word that his partners were paying heed to some, if not all, of his advice, he complained again:

We observe the apology you make for not exerting yourselves more & the reason assigned is the situation of affairs & your confinement to Annapolis, You will be pleased to remember that it was our JJ Stipulation that you, one or the other, shou'd go about from place to place. . . . Joney Muir is an active young man, We do not see why he cannot go to North Carolina, Virginia, Philadelphia, etc. . . .[95]

Even before the bay was relatively clear of privateers and the British lifted their blockade, Wallace and Muir did extend their investments to ships and tobacco from North Carolina and stepped up their efforts to ally themselves with Philadelphia and Baltimore merchants.[96] But the Annapolis partners refrained from going the lengths Johnson wished; they did not actively solicit consignments for Johnson that would be sent in ships in which they owned no share. Sending ships to Johnson in which Wallace, Johnson and Muir had no interest meant that the only earnings would be the commission Johnson made. When the partnership held shares in vessels, they profited from freight charges and proceeds from the sale of outgoing and

---

[93]WJM 3:135.
[94]*Ibid.*
[95]*Ibid.*, p. 212.
[96]For a geographical analysis of Joshua Johnson's correspondents, see appendix A.

return cargoes in which they owned an interest. As late as the summer of 1782, Johnson was complaining that Wallace and Muir were sending him only ships in which they owned a share, and urged them to freight vessels from others as well.[97] Although they humored him with an occasional commission from North Carolina and Virginia, they continued to concentrate on the ships in which they had invested, until peace came the next year.

The decision to invest small amounts of capital in large numbers of ships was an inevitable product of wartime trade conditions. Privateers and the British Navy took an exceedingly large number of prizes.[98] Insurance rates, which in peace were two and one half percent of the value of the ship and cargo, ranged from twenty-five to forty per cent during the war.[99] To avoid staggering losses of capital, merchants were forced to ally themselves with others and keep their investments as small as possible. The interruption of normal shipping patterns by the taking of prizes and naval blockades also forced merchants to be much more flexible in their business dealings than before the war. If Wallace, Johnson and Muir are typical, formal partnership agreements were no longer rigidly defined in terms of the length of duration and the nature of the business undertaken. They were without fixed time limits and contained only the broadest guidelines as to how the firm's affairs were to be conducted.[100] Informal partnerships with other merchants became more numerous than was ever the case in peacetime. The uncertainty as to what ports would be open and unglutted necessitated friendly alliances with merchants in the likely ports of call.

Before the war, Annapolis's strength as a market had been the concentrated demand for high-quality goods sold to an affluent clientele. But the need to sell large quantities of low-quality goods rapidly in order to free capital for reinvestment as soon as possible, meant that during the war Baltimore and Philadelphia were more logical places to import goods. In addition, Wallace and Muir, and the town of Annapolis, were deeply engaged in administering and supplying the war effort. As a result, Wallace and Muir left the management of their shares in vessels to agents and declined to move elsewhere.

---

[97]WJM 3:483. "But whilst he [Muir] remains at Annapolis it will be impossible to extend our correspondence as most what we have will be from this & that & of course must be cramped."

[98]For a list of prizes taken to Britain see Great Britain, Public Record Office, *Calendar of the Records of the High Court of Admiralty*, Vol. 27 (London, 1967).

[99]WJM 3:541, 711, 749.

[100]Partnership agreement, Chan. Pap. 2893.

The extensive nature of the contacts Wallace, Johnson and Muir established with merchants in other ports is evident from the geographical distribution of Joshua Johnson's correspondents during the years 1781 to 1783, which is presented in appendix A.[101] The bulk of the business in America was centered in Baltimore and Philadelphia, both in terms of customers who commissioned goods and in terms of where cargoes of goods in which the firm had an interest could be sold. Graphic evidence of the close working relationship Wallace, Johnson and Muir established with Philadelphia and Baltimore merchants is clear from the ownership of the two ships built at Nantes under the supervision of Joshua Johnson. The first was the *Nonesuch*, launched in 1781, in which Wallace, Johnson and Muir owned a quarter share; two Philadelphia merchants, Robert Morris and Peter Whiteside, held shares worth 5/16ths; and three Baltimore merchants, Jonathan Hudson, Archibald Buchanan, and William Hammond, the agent, owned an additional 5/16ths. The remaining 1/8th was held by the captain, Charles Wells, also of Baltimore. The second ship, the *Favourite*, was launched in 1782. Two new Baltimore merchants, Hugh Young and George Buchanan, were added to the list of those who already held shares in the *Nonesuch*.[102]

The Philadelphia Connection

The connections Wallace, Johnson and Muir formed with Philadelphia merchants began with high expectations, which were centered on the role they thought Robert Morris was to play in promoting their affairs. Morris invested in the *Nonesuch* and the *Favourite*, and agreed to recommend a suitable firm to manage the ships when they arrived in Philadelphia. In May 1782, Johnson received word that Morris was retiring from private trade to devote himself to his public employment. Johnson was dismayed and urged Morris to retain at least his interest in the two ships already built.

We are sorry to find that your public Employment is likely to prove so detrimental to your private concerns & which has determined you from entering into any new Ingagements. We are exceedingly sorry for it as it has interrupted our scheme of having three or four such ships as the Nonesuch constantly employed during the War & which would have Successfull made us a prodigious sum of money indeed.[103]

---

[101]Appendix A is drawn from WJM 3.
[102]WJM 3:60, 62, 64, 111, 129, 157, 401, 459, 490, 652, 657, 673, 682, 702, 734, 802.
[103]*Ibid.*, p. 458.

Morris recommended that Wallace, Johnson and Muir form a connection with the Philadelphia firm of Peter Whiteside & Company, but that association proved to be a disappointment. Whiteside and Company drew large amounts of bills on Johnson in France and soon was in arrears for goods shipped. To make matters worse, Whiteside & Company allied itself strongly with J. Nesbitt & Company, also of Philadelphia, which set up one of its partners in Lorient in direct competition with Johnson.[104] The major problem with Philadelphia, however, was the poor sales of goods and the careless manner in which tobacco was handled for export. By May 1782, Johnson was determined to direct vessels to the Chesapeake whenever it was possible for them to make it through. Johnson wrote a friend that the prices received for goods in Philadelphia were "so discouraging we have determined not to ship any more goods until there is a greater certainty of profit."[105] When the *Nonesuch* arrived from Philadelphia with a much damaged cargo of tobacco, Johnson was furious. He wrote to his partners:

It is damaged so much that we are ashamed almost to insist on the buyers taking it & what is still the most unsatisfying it appears damaged in the country; indeed there is an universal complaint against the Tobaccos imported from Phila & time over Buyers have come to the Resolution of never purchas'g another HHd from thence.[106]

In all, the Philadelphia connection proved a great disappointment to the firm, and although ships in which Wallace, Johnson and Muir had a share were forced to call there when conditions did not permit their going up the bay, when peace came Joshua Johnson was adamant that no further business be sent there. In January 1783, he wrote his partners that "hereafter we hope that this ship [the *Nonesuch*] will never nor anyone else that we are concerned in go to Philadelphia for from their management, we find very little come to our share."[107]

The Baltimore Connection

As Wallace, Johnson and Muir became increasingly disillusioned with the manner in which their Philadelphia friends managed the firm's business, they intensified their investments in Baltimore, turn-

---

[104]*Ibid.*, pp. 161, 177.
[105]*Ibid.*, p. 451.
[106]*Ibid.*, p. 401.
[107]*Ibid.*, p. 723.

ing to such merchants as William Hammond, who was agent for the *Nonesuch*; Jonathan Hudson, agent for the *Favourite* and the *Rochambeau*; Daniel Bowly, agent for the *Ranger*; John McClure, agent for the *York*; and John Sterrett, agent for the *Somersett* and *Felicity*.[108]

Baltimore's principal exports were wheat and flour, and in the main, Wallace, Johnson and Muir were concerned primarily with tobacco, although they did invest in other cargoes as silent partners. For instance, when the *Squirrel*, loaded with flour, disappeared on a voyage from Baltimore to St. Thomas in August 1782, Johnson lamented the "heavy" losses his firm suffered, although the port records reveal only Archibald Buchanan as owner of the ship.[109] Because the Wallace, Johnson and Muir account books for this period are missing, it is impossible to assess how much the firm allocated to wheat and flour ventures of this type; but, as they preferred cargoes that would gain them a profit on both sides of the Atlantic, undoubtedly most of their investments were made in tobacco shipped to Johnson.

Cargoes of tobacco from Baltimore are easier to associate with Wallace, Johnson and Muir than other commodities because even if Wallace, Johnson and Muir were silent partners in a venture and thus not listed as owners in the port books, ships that came to Johnson's address are noted in his letterbook. In 1782, for example, five out of the eight ships that cleared the Port of Baltimore (whose principal cargoes were tobacco) went to Joshua Johnson in Nantes, even though Wallace, Johnson and Muir were listed officially as part owners in only one case.[110]

In terms of the total volume of trade, tobacco was not a major export for Baltimore. In contrast to the eight cargoes of tobacco in 1782, there were 127 ships that cleared the harbor laden with wheat and flour.[111] It was expensive to ship tobacco from Baltimore, a fact which amazed Johnson. In May 1782, he wrote to William Hammond:

It appears extraordinary that there should be such a difference in the price of Tobacco between your City and Patuxent. The Deuce is in it if it [tobacco] costs 5 pcwt for the Carriage from thence to Balto . . . we think if that should

---

[108]*Ibid.*, pp. 734, 325–26, 661, 660, 573, 99, 133.

[109]*Ibid.*, p. 676.

[110]Naval Officer Returns for Baltimore, Record Group 36, National Archives, Washington, D.C. These returns were used by Rhoda M. Dorsey, "The Pattern of Baltimore Commerce during the Confederation Period," *Maryland Historical Magazine* 62 (1967), 119–34. I am indebted to Dr. Dorsey for the loan of the microfilm and her transcripts of the Naval Officer Returns used in this chapter.

[111]*Ibid.*

be the case, that you would do well to let her [the *Nonesuch*] run down to Patuxent & take in her cargo. It will be a great saving to the concern.[112]

But Hammond, like other of the agents with whom Wallace, Johnson and Muir dealt, preferred to have the tobacco shipped to Baltimore so that as soon as goods were unloaded, tobacco could be put on board for the return voyage, instead of delaying the sailing by a side trip to Patuxent.

Until Wallace and Muir were willing and able to return to currying the favor of Patuxent planters and establish stores in the area, most of the tobacco the firm shipped came from Philadelphia, Baltimore, and, occasionally, Annapolis. As they became increasingly dissatisfied with Philadelphia because of the damage done to the tobacco before it left port, Wallace and Muir depended primarily on Baltimore exports. They would buy up tobacco in the country and ship it by small bay craft or overland to Baltimore, or sometimes Annapolis, relying on the planters to come to them for goods or to go without. In October 1782, Johnson received a letter from Dr. Edward Johnson of Lower Marlboro, lamenting the distress of planters and asking Wallace, Johnson and Muir to establish a store in the town. Johnson's only reply was that the firm had "a very considerable quantity of tobacco on hand & can not procure shipping to send it out in."[113] The old consignment business and customers on the Patuxent would have to wait until peace would allow trade to drift back into its old channels. Until then, Baltimore and, to a much lesser extent, Annapolis, would have to do as a source of goods for planters and as a place to which tobacco would be shipped for export to market.

Wallace, Johnson and Muir's principal reason for maintaining an alliance with Baltimore merchants, aside from a desire to load their ships quickly with tobacco, was to provide as many of the Baltimore retailers as they could with goods wholesale. Although no full study of the Baltimore merchant community and the volume of retail trade it handled has been made, some indication of how much of that trade Wallace, Johnson and Muir supplied is suggested by the fact that Johnson corresponded with almost half of those identified by one researcher as the seventy-six most prominent wartime Baltimore merchants.[114] Typical of the cargoes Johnson sent from Nantes was that of the *Nonesuch*, which made her second voyage to Philadelphia in

[112]WJM 3:460.

[113]*Ibid.*, p. 622.

[114]John J. Motley, "The Merchants of Baltimore During the American Revolution" (unpublished seminar paper, presented to History 458: Seminar, The American Revolution, Georgetown University, May 19, 1969).

April 1782. The ship was sent to the care of the agent, William Hammond, who had to go to Philadelphia to take charge of unloading and distributing the cargo. Aside from goods shipped on freight by other merchants in France, there were twenty-seven orders sent by Johnson, eleven of which came from Baltimore, twelve from Philadelphia, three from Annapolis, and one from Virginia.[115] Johnson also sent orders on ships that he did not manage in France. Although the port records covering the period August through December 1782 show no ships entering Baltimore directly from Nantes, all four arrivals from Lorient carried goods from Johnson to Baltimore merchants.[116]

The associations with Baltimore merchants were not without their shortcomings. Customers like Charles Carroll of Carrollton complained bitterly about the exorbitant cost of goods shipped first to Philadelphia and then to Baltimore, and finally to his plantation at Doughregan Manor or his townhouse in Annapolis. In 1781, when Carroll's goods aboard the *Nonesuch* arrived in Philadelphia and then were pillaged on their way to Baltimore, Carroll was incensed.

The exhorbitant freight the owners of vessels importing from Europe extort from the importers will discourage all future importations . . . . The freight of my goods pr the Nonesuch including charges on them from Philadelphia to this port [Annapolis] amounts to £112.19.9 specie which from the want of cash I am obliged to discharge by a bill of Exchange, at the exchange of six shillings specie for every 5 livres.[117]

In effect, Carroll was forced to pay not only a freight he thought unreasonable, but also had to accept an exchange rate that increased those shipping costs an additional twenty-four percent. If planter customers were unhappy, Johnson was uneasy about some of the alliances his partners 'had made with the Baltimore merchants. He became annoyed with the Smiths when he found they were dealing with his competitors in Lorient and Nantes.[118] He was much concerned when Hugh Young was greatly in arrears for overdrafts; Wallace, Johnson and Muir had lent Young £3,000 to load tobacco to Johnson's address, but instead the money was used to do business elsewhere.[119] Archibald Buchanan also drew heavily on the firm to build and outfit ships, only

---

[115]WJM 3:401.

[116]Naval Officer Returns for Baltimore, Record Group 36, National Archives, Washington, D.C.

[117]Charles Carroll to Johnson, October 30, 1781, Letter Book of Charles Carroll, MS 8173, Arents Collection, New York Public Library, New York, N.Y.

[118]WJM 3:383.

[119]*Ibid.*, p. 573.

to charter them to people who were not associated with Wallace, Johnson and Muir.[120] Tensions were only exaggerated as peace approached, because Wallace, Johnson and Muir feared competition from Baltimore for tobacco.[121]

In spite of reservations about some of their erstwhile Baltimore allies, the war prompted a working relationship with a few merchants that Johnson hoped would survive the war. He expected "Billy" Hammond and Captain Wells would continue working with him and his Annapolis partners.[122] The only difference would be that Wallace, Johnson and Muir would assume direct control of their own affairs, taking charge of all vessels in which they had a share and not leaving the management to Baltimore friends.[123] Once peace came, the consignment tobacco trade would revive. Planters would be more willing to assume the cost of transporting tobacco than under the abnormal shipping conditions of war. To cultivate this trade, Wallace, Johnson and Muir would have to depend on their own efforts at finding clients on the Potomac and Patuxent Rivers and had no need of help from Baltimore. If Wallace, Johnson and Muir purchased tobacco it would be cheaper if it were not shipped to Baltimore first, and this, too, militated against the need for a friend in Baltimore to handle tobacco exports. After the war, Baltimore would be useful primarily as a market for goods and as a source of tobacco consignments from friendly merchants who had contacts with planters at Elk Ridge or the other major tobacco-producing areas of northern Anne Arundel, Baltimore, and Harford counties. With no further public duties to perform, Wallace and Muir could concentrate on expanding their tobacco business and on handling all the cargoes of goods that Johnson could send.

Johnson in France

While Wallace and Muir were active in promoting commercial alliances in Philadelphia and in the Chesapeake, Joshua Johnson quickly established himself as one of the major American merchants in France. There were four major ports on the west coast of France

---

[120]*Ibid.*, pp. 181, 211.

[121]*Ibid.*, p. 710. Johnson was aware that peace would make great changes in the nature and control of business in Baltimore. He wrote to William Hammond in January 1783 that "We are a good deal puzled to know how matters will turn on this revolution [peace] a great many of your present great men we apprehend will soon sink into obscurity & who will be replaced by an amazing influx of foreigners. . . ." *Ibid.*, p. 723.

[122]*Ibid.*, p. 750.

[123]*Ibid.*, pp. 647–49. With peace, Johnson argued, it would be "more profitable than taking parts, besides we are subject to the tempers of the Capts & Owners, whom have almost teazed us out of our Lives."

that had the facilities to handle the American trade: Nantes, Lorient, Bordeaux, and La Rochelle.[124] Johnson was confident that Nantes would become the most important of the four. He sent a map of France to a prospective customer, suggesting that, "by casting your eye over it you will immediately see that the extensiveness of this River [the Loire] makes it the only port for the American Trade as we draw the linen and wollin manufactures of the North by water carriage & even those of Flanders and Switzerland."[125]

Although correct about the minimal roles Bordeaux and La Rochelle would play in the wartime American trade, Johnson misjudged the nature of the competition from Lorient. There American merchants with ties to Philadelphia, such as Nesbitt & Company, proved effective in channeling at least as much trade their way as went to Nantes. Lorient merchants even had the audacity to invade Johnson's territory. When a ship addressed to Nesbitt & Company arrived at Nantes, Nesbitt came to Nantes to sell the cargo, instead of turning it over to Johnson (whom the owners of the ship had listed as their second choice as agent if Nesbitt declined), and splitting the commission.[126] Johnson countered by trying to establish strong connections with a Philadelphia firm, John Purveyance & Company, in order to persuade the Philadelphia shopkeepers and the owners of Philadelphia-managed vessels to send their business to him instead of to Lorient. In September 1781, Johnson wrote his partners that he thought it was most desirable for them to

form a connection with Mr. John Purveyance of Philadelphia, & that we find [it] more necessary every day—the noises from thence Established at L'Orient has become most jealous of us & doing everything in their power to circumvent us. Indeed we thought Whiteside [another Philadelphia merchant] the proper person for us, but we now find he is too highly connected with the house of Nesbitt & Co ever to render us much service. If Purveyance is totally unengaged to theirs & would be active in our Employ . . . he could render in Essential Services & we could be in turn most useful to him here.[127]

Johnson proposed that Purveyance purchase a brig that could carry 150 to 200 hogsheads of tobacco, in which Wallace, Johnson and Muir, Purveyance, Purveyance's brother in Baltimore, and Hugh Young of Baltimore would each hold an eighth share. Purveyance

---

[124]Jean Meyer, *L'Armement nantais dans la deuxième moitié du XVIIIe siècle* (Paris, 1969), p. 452.
[125]WJM 3:262.
[126]*Ibid.*, p. 212.
[127]*Ibid.*, p. 211.

would sell the remaining shares to good friends in Philadelphia. "If we could effect this plan," Johnson concluded, "and Mr. Purveyance will go about amongst the shopkeepers, we should have more orders than will fill her with back freight."[128] Wallace and Muir followed Johnson's advice and made an arrangement with Purveyance, but the competition from Lorient remained keen. No quantitative study has been made of the distribution of American trade among the French ports, but Johnson's correspondence suggests that throughout 1781 and 1782 the bulk of the American trade was fairly evenly divided between Nantes and Lorient. The number of American ships in each port constantly fluctuated; first one would have more and then the other, but the race was always close. For instance, in July 1782, when nine ships were reported in Lorient, there were only seven in Nantes, but within a short time two more arrived to Johnson's care and redressed the balance.[129]

There was no competition from La Rochelle.[130] Competition from Bordeaux was of minor importance, because of its poor location for obtaining goods (other than wine) suitable to the American market, and because its merchants were notorious for their inept handling of American commissions. As Johnson explained to a correspondent who was unfortunate enough to have sent a ship that called at Bordeaux instead of Nantes: "When the People of Bordeaux gets anything in their hands it is impossible to Get it from them. Had this ship fortunately arrived here . . . you should have had the account long since."[131] To handle any ships that might arrive at Bordeaux to his address, Johnson sent one of his clerks, Thomas Ridout, a former Annapolis resident and half brother of one of the town's leading loyalist sympathizers, John Ridout. When Thomas Ridout decided to stay and establish himself as a commission merchant in Bordeaux, Johnson feared little in the way of competition and even sent him small commissions to execute. As Ridout himself was to point out later, he soon found there was little trade for him to manage and his chief income, insufficient as it was, came from acting as an insurance broker for American merchants elsewhere. In reminiscences written in the 1780s, Ridout described his Bordeaux sojourn:

[Johnson] not having much confidence in the house of French & Lynch, who had hitherto done his business there, . . . desired me to go to Bordeaux and transact the business and dispatch the vessel. I did so, notwithstanding the

128*Ibid.*
129*Ibid.*, pp. 526, 530.
130La Rochelle is not mentioned at all as a competing port in WJM 3.
131*Ibid.*, pp. 31–32.

impediments cast in my way by Mr. Lynch. I no soon[er] got her ready for sailing that Mr. Johnson ordered me to purchase 4000 [livre] worth of goods, and to ship them on board as an adventure for his and my account. . . . I did not receive even the least return for the services I had rendered, and the adventure we had made together . . . having been sold without benefit, I never received anything for it.

I made, whilst the War continued, some adventures to America. Some were lost, of which I recovered the Insurance, others arriving, I did not receive any remittance for three years afterwards. I made several insurances, or rather got them effected for some people at Nantes, but as on the Recovery of Insurance in settling with the Underwriters, they paid me in their own notes at a long date. I made my remittances at a great disadvantage and loss, and I found that what little commissions I had made were very far from being sufficient to support me.[132]

While Johnson's main competition from other French ports came from Lorient, he also faced competition from other American merchants in Nantes, the chief of whom was Jonathan Williams, the son of a Boston merchant. Although French firms in Nantes such as Penet & Company were active securing public contracts for clothing for states such as Virginia, American merchants such as Johnson and Williams conducted most of the private business with America, a pattern true in the other ports as well. Initially, Johnson and Williams, who had been neighbors in Nantes since 1778, were on friendly terms, but in October 1781, when Williams was commissioned to load a ship Johnson felt was rightfully his, the relationship became strained and did not improve for the duration of the war.[133]

Apart from his major competitor, Williams, Johnson also was faced with the arrival, after 1781, of a few new American merchants from New England who came to take advantage of the growing wartime commerce of Nantes. To some extent, Johnson brought the challenge on himself. As prices for tobacco reached a record high, he encouraged his New England correspondents to send ships to the Chesapeake to load cargoes of tobacco and bring them to Nantes. In March 1781, he wrote to Henry Mitchell of Boston suggesting that armed vessels from New England could obtain forty to fifty percent freight for tobacco in Maryland, and offered to have Wallace and Muir load them.[134] When, in the spring of 1782, rumors of twenty ships from New England heading toward the Chesapeake for tobacco temporarily caused tobacco prices in Nantes to fall, Johnson was as-

[132]"Reminiscences of Thomas Ridout," *Maryland Historical Magazine* 20 (1925), 230–31.
[133]WJM 3:212.
[134]*Ibid.*, pp. 40–41.

tonished and refused to believe his informant.[135] When a few New England ships actually began to arrive, he was even more dismayed to find that the cargoes had not been loaded by his partners and were consigned to the captains who gave their business to New Englanders. Johnson fumed to a Baltimore correspondent: "Captain Boardman, like all other N. England men placed a preference in an unexperienced young man from that country. In one word my good friend, these people are only fit to do business together."[136] In other letters, Johnson did his best to convince planters and merchants that it was an expensive folly to trust tobacco to the New Englanders. Again using his experience with Boardman, Johnson wrote of the encounter to a Virginia planter. Boardman had come to Johnson on the recommendation of the planter which gave Johnson

an opportunity of tendering him our services, but he like most others of his *country*, wanted to squeeze down the Merchant out of his commission which was a sufficient cause of our parting. His Business he has put into the hands of a *Mr. Watson* of his *country* who has sold at 20% less . . . than what we sold Mr. Tandy's tobacco in the same ship. This may answer the Capt. purpose but never can that of the Owner.[137]

Although greatly annoyed by the New England competition, Johnson was convinced that their sales record would "teach shipowners how to trust them hereafter,"[138] and by the fall of 1782, his prediction appeared to be correct, as the number of New England ships bearing tobacco to Nantes declined dramatically at a time when the number of ships addressed to Johnson's care was greater than ever before. Even at the peak of the New England arrivals in the summer of 1782, Johnson had as many ships as he could effectively handle; and, on balance for the year, he and Jonathan Williams shared the distinction of managing the overwhelming majority of ships that came to Nantes, a combined total of twenty-one.[139]

In general, Johnson purchased goods for customers only if they had some form of credit balance with him. As can be seen from the chart of goods he sent in 1781, most of his customers paid in bills of exchange drawn on Paris or maintained a credit balance by sending cargoes of tobacco which Johnson sold on commission (see table 3-6). After 1781, bills of exchange were available in quantity because of

[135]*Ibid.*, p. 318.
[136]*Ibid.*, p. 459.
[137]*Ibid.*, p. 441.
[138]*Ibid.*, p. 582.
[139]L. Rouzeau, "Aperçus du rôle de Nantes dans la guerre d'independence d'Amerique (1775–1783)," *Annales de Bretagne* 74 (1967), 271.

Table 3-6 A Typical Cargo of Goods Shipped by Joshua Johnson from Nantes

Ship: *Lady Lee*, 8 guns
Captain: Robert Dashiell
Date Sailed: March 1781

Customer	Amount (in Livre Tournois)	Form of Prepayment
Charles Carroll of Carrollton	1,804.09	Account current (funds in Johnson's hands)
E. Kerr	5,110.10	Bills drawn on Commissioners in Paris
D. Crawford	452.17	Draft on Fearon & Co.
J. Dowson	132.13	Charles Carroll of Carrollton draft on W. D. & J.
John Davidson	6,336.09	Bills drawn on Commissioners in Paris
S. Forde	599.11	Bills drawn on Commissioners in Paris
W. Graham	1,754.01	Bills drawn on Commissioners in Paris
J. Gardner	660.00	Bills drawn on Commissioners in Paris
J. Hopkins	157.19	Account current (funds in Johnson's hands)
T. & B. Harwood	4,539.13	Bills drawn on Commissioners in Paris
T. Harwood	120.00	Bills drawn on Commissioners in Paris
D. Harris	718.06	Bills drawn on Commissioners in Paris
W. Lyles	228.11	Account current
F. Leek	682.05	Bill on John Roberts & Sons, London
E. Lloyd	233.10	Account
J. Muir	4,445.00	To debit
G. Mason	5,431.00	?
J. Robinson	1,875.16	Bills drawn on Commissioners in Paris
Reed & Forde	3,449.15	Bills drawn on Commissioners in Madrid
W. Taylor	1,534.00	M. Holker on Leray de Chamont
J. Sterrett	1,198.13	Bills drawn on Commissioners in Paris
J. Smith	3,777.10	Bills drawn on Commissioners in Paris
S. Smith	2,622.14	Account current, balances account
J. Swan	4,500+	Holker on Chamont
Eastman & Neth	454.13	Tobacco sales
Joseph Williams	1,124.11	Tobacco sales
W. Hanna	914.05	J. Callahan on Hanbury & Co.
A. & I. Vanbibber	1,171.06	Account Current
James Williams	199.09	Philip Key on W. D. & J.
W. Wilkens	274.03	Gerrard Hopkins on W. D. & J.
W. J. & Muir	6,300.00	Sent on joint account with J. Nesbitt
W. J. & Muir	9,604.12	First goods of new partnership
John Muir and William Wilkens	13,574.09	Profits of the *Lady Lee* to them as agents
Hammond & Hudson	21,628.19	Charterers of the *Lady Lee*
J. Nesbitt	6,000.00	Darmond's bill on Partier

Source: Data culled from Wallace, Johnson and Muir Letter Book, 1781–1783, Manuscript Division, New York Public Library, New York, N.Y.

the dramatic increase in foreign loans to the Congress and because of the French purchase of supplies and provisions for their army and navy in America. Johnson tried to ship goods in the amount of money or credit the customer had in France. To avoid heavy losses to his partners and his biggest customers in the event of capture by privateers or natural loss at sea, he divided the shipments among several bottoms, but even then he tried to dispatch goods as soon as possible after money or cargoes had been received.[140] Both he and his partners wished to keep their capital and the money of their customers turning. When remittances were slow for some goods he had sent on consignment to Philadelphia, Johnson wrote: "for your future Regulations we have to inform you that we had rather submit to a less profit than lay out our money because we mean to be continually turning it."[141]

Wallace, Johnson and Muir were reluctant to grant credit to anyone, and on several occasions Johnson turned down requests to send goods before payment was made.[142] In some instances, when Johnson was trying to lure a customer he knew could afford to pay, he would send a small shipment on consignment, but in the main he abided by his rule to keep capital "turning."[143] This tendency is clear from the generally small number and size of debts owed Johnson by January 1783, when he was settling up his accounts and preparing to move from France (see table 3-7). The major exceptions to Johnson's rule were the credits he extended to one Philadelphia firm, Peter Whiteside & Company, and two Baltimore merchants, Hugh Young and Archibald Buchanan. The first two exceptions were made because Wallace, Johnson and Muir wanted to strengthen their ties with Whiteside and Young in the expectation that they, in turn, would cultivate the wholesale market among retailers in Philadelphia and Baltimore. In neither case was the hope justified, and the mistake was felt keenly by the firm. When Peter Whiteside wrote to encourage Johnson to go even further and speculate with him in bills of exchange, allowing him to draw when the exchange rate was high and remitting when it was low, Johnson balked and wrote a strong letter noting the risk involved, and asserting that he needed his money to pay debts, something that Whiteside should be doing as well. At that

[140]WJM 3:81, 151, 287.
[141]*Ibid.*, p. 20.
[142]*Ibid.*, pp. 81, 151, 605.
[143]*Ibid.*, p. 20; also see table 3-6. In a letter to Wallace and Muir, Johnson argued that it was a good idea for him to send small consignments to reputable merchants because they "may lead to Transactions extensive & mutually advantageous." WJM 3:49.

Table 3-7 Debts Owed to Wallace, Johnson and Muir in France, 1783
(1 livre tournois equals 10d sterling)

Name	Residence	Amount (in Livres Tournois)	Percent of Total
Whiteside & Wharton	Philadelphia	68,209.10	22.5
Archibald Buchanan	Baltimore	48,949.09	16.1
Jonathan Hudson	Baltimore	34,460.17	11.3
Ramsay & Cox	Philadelphia	31,360.06	10.3
Isaac Wickoff	Philadelphia	24,330.10	8.0
McLure & Young	Baltimore	16,066.00	5.3
Blair McClenachon	Philadelphia	14,282.11	4.7
Charles Wallace	Annapolis	12,802.09	4.2
Capt. William Graham	Philadelphia	10,267.05	3.4
Samuel & Robert Purviance	Baltimore	7,598.19	
William Neill	Baltimore	6,744.13	
Morris & Woodward	Philadelphia	4,596.01	
Footman & Carmick	Philadelphia	4,468.10	
John McClure	Baltimore	4,235.10	
John Davidson	Annapolis	2,610.00	
Capt. John McKirdy	Baltimore	1,731.02	
Williams & Muir	Annapolis	1,641.12	
Stephen Steward & Son	Baltimore	1,616.07	
Capt. Samuel Mansfield	Baltimore	1,613.10	
Isaac & Abraham Van Bibber	Baltimore	1,575.00	
McClure & Russell	Baltimore	1,307.04	
William Stevenson	Chester	1,036.00	
John Coulter	Fells Point	498.12	
Capt. James Tibbett	Baltimore	383.09	
Elizabeth Sprigg	West River	357.11	
Hugh Young	Baltimore	238.14	
John and Samuel Davidson	Annapolis	238.08	
Richard Sprigg	Anne Arundel County	191.10	
Capt. William Middleton	Annapolis	121.18	
Capt. Nicholas Martin	West River	119.14	
Benjamin Rumsey	Joppa	90.00	
Samuel Sharpe	Talbot County	31.14	
Philip Key	Chaptico	13.00	
Capt. Samuel Maynard	Herring Bay	13.05	
George Gartner	Baltimore	10.10	
Robert Dennis	Snow Hill	6.04	
Total in livres		303,803.00	
Total in pounds sterling		13,291.07	

Percentage of total debt owed by people owing
over 10,000 livres tournois   85.8

Source: Wallace, Johnson and Muir Letter Book, 1781–1783, Manuscript Division, New York Public Library, New York, N.Y., pp. 734, 785ff.

point, Whiteside owed Johnson about 68,000 livres.[144] By the end of the war, Hugh Young owed over 100,000 livres, and Johnson was anxious for a ship of his to arrive in France, either with payment or so that he could seize it as collateral.[145] The difficulties with Archibald Buchanan were somewhat different from those with the other two major debtors. Buchanan was a fast friend; his two brothers were captains that Wallace, Davidson and Johnson and Wallace, Johnson and Muir had employed regularly and who were considered among the best in the business. Wallace, Johnson and Muir advanced Buchanan money to build ships, and although he exasperated them at times by chartering the ships out to others instead of letting the firm have them, the major problem with Buchanan was a succession of bad luck. Ships he built were overturned by squalls in the bay and foundered on the coast of France. His losses were heavy and his ability to pay back loans was severely constricted. Johnson fussed and fumed but found it possible to forgive. In the same letter in which he complained bitterly about Peter Whiteside & Company addressing three parcels of tobacco to others, even though they had drawn great sums on Wallace, Johnson and Muir, Johnson also expressed his dissatisfaction with Buchanan. Although he can find no excuse for the Philadelphia firm, he draws back from outright condemnation of Buchanan, asserting that, in spite of his faults, "you know we love this Man."[146]

Neither Johnson nor his customers were pleased with the goods he sent from France. They were costlier than and much inferior to English goods. Johnson wrote that the woolens of Britain were "so much Superior . . . besides we find from experience that these [French woolens] will not suit the American market at any rate."[147] Cheap cloth for Negroes was not to be had anywhere, nor did Johnson believe that "any country can furnish on equal terms with England."[148] When a customer asked for pattern cards showing the designs of French cloth, Johnson wrote that none was to be had because "the Manufacturers of this country are not quite So clever at these matters as they are in England."[149] But war made it impossible to get English goods, except from an occasional prize or through neutral ports such as St. Eustatia. The competition for prizes was keen, often making

[144]*Ibid.*, pp. 468–69.
[145]*Ibid.*, p. 710.
[146]*Ibid.*, p. 561.
[147]*Ibid.*, p. 424.
[148]*Ibid.*, p. 439.
[149]*Ibid.*, p. 75.

their purchase by Americans highly speculative ventures because the initial cost was so high.[150] The capture of St. Eustatia in February 1781 effectively put a stop to the trade in English goods through the most prominent of the West Indian ports.[151] The entry of the Dutch into the war against Britain also channeled the linen trade through France. As Johnson explained to an American customer in February 1781, "As the Dutch war has cut entirely your intercourse with Holland, we see no route [linen] can come so cheap as by way of the Loire."[152] Yet the duties imposed as the linen was moved through the French provinces to Nantes greatly increased the cost to the customer, further adding to his dissatisfaction with buying goods from France.[153] Most American merchants in France were convinced that the dry-goods trade with France was a temporary phenomenon created by the necessities of war and that the trade would return to its old channel once peace came. As Johnson wrote to one of his correspondents in Maryland: "We shall also send you the cloth you ask for unless peace should be made. In that case it would only be picking your pocketts as you will be able to get English so much cheaper."[154] As long as the war continued, however, there was an excellent demand for French goods because there was nowhere else goods could be purchased, and until peace came, Johnson was busy filling orders.

In addition to dispatching cargoes of goods, Johnson also was active selling tobacco that came to his address. With its disruption of shipping, its dislocation of manpower so essential to such a labor-intensive crop as tobacco, and its encouragement to planters to allocate their resources to meeting the army's provisions needs, war greatly restricted the supply of tobacco at a time when the demand in Europe was as great as ever. Tobacco prices in France were higher than they had ever been in England. In 1774, prices for tobacco in London peaked at six pence sterling per pound, although the mean price for the year was around three pence.[155] In March 1781, Johnson wrote that "Since the commencement of hostilities by the English on the Dutch all kinds of American Productions has increased but particularly tobacco,"[156] and over the next two years, Maryland to-

---

[150]*Ibid.*, p. 58.

[151]*Ibid.*, p. 37. The French recaptured some of the tobacco and temporarily glutted the market until the Farmers General bought the bulk of it. *Ibid.*, pp. 65, 76, 91.

[152]*Ibid.*, p. 23.

[153]*Ibid.*, p. 43.

[154]*Ibid.*, pp. 678–79.

[155]Wallace, Davidson, and Johnson, Ship Entry Book, 1774–1776, Acc. #4544, Private Account Books, Hall of Records, Annapolis, Md.

[156]*Ibid.*, p. 19.

bacco rose from about 9.7 to as much as 10.5 pence sterling per pound.[157] It might even have gone higher. Some merchants in America speculated that it would and were engrossing, but by December 1782, European farmers were growing tobacco to meet the great demand, and peace the following year ended any hopes that even 10.5 pence would prevail.[158] Once the war was over, direct tobacco trade with France for the quality reexport market in Holland and Germany was no longer viable. As Johnson observed in a letter to a Philadelphia merchant who was predicting exports to France would increase with peace:

We observe with attention what you say about a considerable export of tobaccoes taking place from the different States to this country on peace taking place. We differ exceedingly with you in opinion & can almost venture to assert that you will find you are mistaken. The Vexation, difficulties & Pleague in doing business in this country will make every Trader give England & Holland the preference. . . . [The first market for Maryland tobacco is Holland.] They take all our imports & give us good prices.[159]

If it was difficult to conduct the business of selling tobacco in France during the war, much of the profit was devoured by shipping costs and the high price of insurance. In December 1782, when Maryland tobacco was selling at 100 livres per hundredweight or 10.5 pence sterling per pound, the freight and insurance consumed seventy-five to eighty livres per hundredweight, or 75 to 80 percent of the selling price.[160] In London, no more than 64 percent of the net proceeds from tobacco sales went for similar charges in 1774.[161] Freight went from a peacetime norm of £7 per four hogsheads (or approximately 7 percent of the selling price when tobacco sold at six pence sterling per pound) to 40 and 50 percent of the selling price.[162] Insurance, which in peacetime was approximately two and one half percent of the value of the ship and cargo, soared to 40 percent.[163]

The high price of tobacco in France did compensate for some of these increased costs. Charges on a three pence per pound sale in

[157]*Ibid.*, pp. 19ff. The sterling value is derived from the standard exchange rate of 1 livre equals 10-1/2 d. sterling.

[158]*Ibid.*, p. 278.

[159]*Ibid.*, p. 582.

[160]*Ibid.*, pp. 693–94.

[161]James F. Shepherd and Gary M. Walton, *Shipping, Maritime Trade and the Economic Development of Colonial North America* (New York, 1972), p. 57.

[162]*Ibid.*, p. 192, and WJM 3:40–41.

[163]WJM 3:518. In one instance, Johnson could only get insurance at 45 percent. See *ibid.*, p. 655.

1774 meant a net profit of 1.08 pence, while charges on a 10.5 pence per pound sale in 1782 meant a net profit of 2.1 pence per pound and, of course, the amount of the commission a merchant earned was proportionately higher. But the cost of maintaining ships in the tobacco trade in 1782 offset much of this advantage.[164] In wartime the *Favourite* had fifteen guns and was manned by one hundred men who demanded high wages. In peacetime twenty men were needed at most, and there were no guns. The space filled by sailors and armament could be used for tobacco.[165]

If there were profits to be made in the trade with France, they came primarily from the sale of French goods in America at exorbitant prices. For instance, in Baltimore goods sold at 2.74 times their invoice value, which included freight and insurance charges.[166] Cargoes of tobacco paid for the cost of the goods and their freight, and they provided cash to keep the exports in goods flowing; but as soon as the market for those goods evaporated, there would be no rationale for continuing to send quality tobacco to France. The French Farmers General would continue to buy tobacco in bulk regardless of quality at the lowest possible price and such a market would be supplied, as it had been before the war, by merchants in Scotland and London. The quality market would return to London, where tobacco could be sold at good prices to Holland and Germany, and where goods suitable to the American market could be obtained at lower prices and with considerably less difficulty.[167]

Although there were distinct disadvantages to being an American merchant in France, there is no question that the profits to be made from the wartime trade were greater than anything that might have been expected in peacetime. When the *Nonesuch* returned from her maiden voyage with a cargo of tobacco that represented the cost and profits of the goods that Johnson had sent out in her, Johnson remarked that even in spite of the damage done to the tobacco, "She has made us a great voyage & cleared more than we can do in half a year's hard work at 5% commission,"[168] How much Wallace, Johnson and Muir made is not possible to determine with any accuracy, as

---

[164]Shepherd and Walton, *Shipping*, p. 192, and WJM 3:40-41.

[165]WJM 3:401. Johnson proposed to take off the *Favourite*'s guns and add a deck which would allow her to carry 100 hogsheads more.

[166]*Ibid.*, p. 204.

[167]*Ibid.*, p. 597. "It is not here as it is in London when a person wants goods you have nothing to do but put your purchase in to the hands of the warehouse keepers and they will be assorted. Know! [sic] you must attend the purchase of every ounce of Pins & which takes up imensity of time."

[168]*Ibid.*, pp. 381-84.

their books for the period are lost; but in contrast to the small amount of capital, £3,000 sterling, that was invested in 1771 when Wallace, Davidson and Johnson was formed, Joshua Johnson was estimating that profits would be about £4,400 sterling in 1781 and £10,000 sterling in 1782.[169]

If short-term profits were to be made from the drygoods trade with France during the war, the French sojourn of American merchants also had a beneficial effect on long-term profits. The cost of doing business in France was so great that merchants "threw money away" if they continued to charge commissions at the prewar level of two and one half percent. More time had to be spent in preparing goods that were costlier than English goods, yet inferior in quality. Credit terms were so short that merchants had to pay interest more often and at higher rates than they had in London.[170] In a very short time, the normal commission rose to five percent and stayed at that level throughout the war. When peace came, no effort was made to return to the old two and one half percent. Merchants were content to charge more, and apparently customers who had become habituated to five percent made no effective complaints.

During the war, Wallace, Johnson and Muir concentrated on the wholesale market, importing goods for others on commission and purchasing tobacco in the country to sell at their own risk in France as a hedge against wartime inflation.[171] It was a mode of business quite different from the prewar years, when they primarily shipped goods on their own account and to planters who had consigned tobacco to them. Before the war, Johnson strongly resisted buying goods for others and was at odds with his partners over their extending credit for goods to such firms as Richard Tilghman Earle on the Eastern Shore.[172] In 1781, Johnson served more customers in many more places than he had in all the years in London, when he was in partnership with Wallace and Davidson, and heavily extended credit to Philadelphia and Baltimore merchants (see tables 3-6 and 3-7).

By December 1782 Johnson, like most Americans, expected peace, although when the Preliminaries were signed, he was taken by surprise. He wrote on December 20, 1782 that, "It was done before anyone knew of word of it. It has therefore derainged all of us & at present there is nothing to be done."[173] With peace in sight, Johnson

[169]*Ibid.*, pp. 212, 481.
[170]*Ibid.*, pp. 151, 424.
[171]*Ibid.*, p. 668.
[172]WDJ 1:135-37.
[173]WJM 3:676.

and his partners longed to get back to the old method of doing business, concentrating on tobacco consignments and supplying their stores in Maryland with goods. Johnson advised his partners to "exchange all the goods you have by you for good Patuxent tobacco," because French goods "will not bring first cost."[174] He began writing circular letters to all the old consignment customers, urging them to send him tobacco in London, where he intended moving in the spring of 1783.[175] To a Portsmouth, New Hampshire customer he wrote, "The return of Peace has caused a revolution in the American business here & we find that our Countrymen are looking back to England for her manufactories. . . ."[176] To further the consignment business, Johnson wrote his partners that they ought to have Stephen Steward, David Weems, and Archibald Buchanan each build a ship to "load this fall," and advised them to purchase Thomas Rutland's ship, putting her up for freight immediately. Johnson expected Rutland's ship to get £12 per ton freight, but even if it was not "a very profitable ship . . . it is an object to be the first."[177]

Johnson also recognized that it was important for the firm to ally itself with the best possible captains because the captain's relationship with the planters often made the difference as to how fast a ship could be loaded and dispatched. During the war, captains were simply shepherds of cargoes quickly provided for them at ports of call. As Johnson had remarked in the fall of 1782, "The times now seems altered and instead of the shippers paying homage to the Captains they are in turn obliged to solicit of the merchants."[178] When peace came, captains were once again in great demand, and Johnson had no reason to regret the kindness he had extended to several captains throughout the war.

For at least a year prior to his departure for London, Johnson had been sending capital to his bankers there, Prescott, Grotes & Company.[179] He was confident that, with funds in London and his partners active in securing consignments of tobacco, he would have more than enough business to handle and little opposition from old competitors. To a James River planter he wrote, "We have very little to apprehend from the opposition of all the old houses combined together as our countrymen cannot so soon forget [their] conduct

[174]*Ibid.*, p. 401.
[175]*Ibid.*, pp. 794ff.
[176]*Ibid.*, p. 762.
[177]*Ibid.*, p. 713.
[178]*Ibid.*, p. 601.
[179]*Ibid.*, pp. 241, 291.

through out this business."[180] Commerce would not be exactly the same as it had been before the war, however. The experience of wartime trade, which necessitated close cooperation among merchants in other ports, broadened the vision of Chesapeake merchants such as Wallace, Johnson and Muir. The war caused major realignments in the conduct and capitalization of the tobacco trade that were not abandoned even as trade reverted to its old channels. In the prewar years, Wallace, Johnson and Muir would never have considered pooling capital with Philadelphia firms in order to engage in more effective competition for the Maryland tobacco trade. After the war, when Peter Whiteside & Company proposed a new alliance and offered stock in their Philadelphia bank, Wallace, Johnson and Muir were eager to accept.[181] Although, contrary to Johnson's enthuasiastic prediction, London capital reentered the race for Maryland tobacco, its prewar dominance of the market, so ably challenged by the profits from the Annapolis retail trade, was never regained. Commercial alliances of merchants from Philadelphia to Richmond (in which Wallace, Johnson and Muir initially played a key role) were to prove too competitive.

If the war greatly affected the nature of business relationships and promoted, as Robert East has suggested, a tendency toward the centralization of capital in such large urban centers as Philadelphia and Baltimore, it also wrought great changes in the prospects for the economic development of Annapolis.[182] On the one hand, the horizons of the business community were greatly enlarged in terms of the potential for interregional trading alliances; on the other hand, mercantile opportunity within the confines of Annapolis became greatly restricted. The conditions that made Annapolis the best market in Maryland for quality luxury goods and contributed to the rise of an entrepreneurial merchant class before 1776 were dissipated by war, the emergence of Baltimore, and finally, in the 1790s, by a severe depression of several years' duration in the tobacco trade. With the coming of peace, the merchants of Annapolis and their fellow townspeople were forced to cope with a change in the nature of opportunity that undoubtedly few had imagined possible and which greatly altered the course of their lives.

[180]*Ibid.*, p. 780.
[181]See chapter 5.
[182]Robert A. East, *Business Enterprise in the American Revolutionary Era* (New York, 1938), p. 231.

CHAPTER 4

THE ADJUSTMENT TO PEACE: GREAT EXPECTATIONS AND CONSTRICTING OPPORTUNITY 1783–1793

PEACE brought prospects of unparalleled prosperity for Annapolis. The community now had two functions aside from being a center of local, state, and (temporarily) national government: it was emerging as a market for the surrounding countryside, and it was flourishing as a center of international trade. Its merchants sought to promote both developments, although commerce far overshadowed the market place in the years immediately after hostilities ended. Optimism about the future of international commerce grew out of expectations that merchants would continue to gain in their efforts to dominate the tobacco export trade and out of a belief that demand for imported goods would continue to rise. The initial success of Wallace, Johnson and Muir encouraged such views. After the war, they rapidly expanded their involvement in the tobacco trade and, in 1786, became agents for Robert Morris in a tobacco contract with the French that guaranteed a market for 20,000 hogsheads of tobacco a year until 1788 for the firm and its suppliers.[1]

But many factors militated against continued growth in Wallace, Johnson and Muir's business and against the town's prospering. Although Annapolis capital and mercantile enterprise contributed to the rise of Baltimore, Alexandria, and other urban centers of trade, the very existence of these towns tended to draw off customers and divert the capital so essential to sustaining growth in Annapolis. As Baltimore increased in size, it became the social center of the state and its increasingly independent merchant community competed for tobacco as well as dominating the grain trade. At the same time, the planter elite, to whom firms such as Wallace, Johnson and Muir catered, came less and less to rely on direct importation of goods to meet their needs, and, as a result, no longer found it necessary to commit the bulk of their tobacco to those firms that

[1]See chapter 5.

had supplied goods from London on a commission basis. Such long-term adverse changes as these were also accompanied by other developments that exacerbated even further the fortunes of the town. The depression in 1785 and 1786, which was brought about by an enormous influx of goods sent from London on generous credit terms, accentuated and perhaps even hastened decline. So did the removal, in 1789, of Wallace, Johnson and Muir from trade, which was in the end brought about by an irresolvable quarrel between the Annapolis partners and Joshua Johnson. Wallace, Johnson and Muir stood at the apex of the Annapolis business community, supplying as wholesalers many other businesses in town with goods. No other local firm was in a position to replace it; but even if one had been, the general economic revival that was under way by 1788 was of short duration for the tobacco trade. The European wars of the 1790s, with their devastating disruption of the continental market for all but the best Maryland tobacco, would have crushed any new enterprise in the same way that it defeated merchants in other ports such as Georgetown, Piscattaway, and Port Tobacco.[2]

The impact of economic decline on opportunity and the manner in which the community reacted to the sudden collapse of a world in which expansion had been the rule for at least a generation present questions of behavior and how to analyze that behavior that rarely are considered by early American historians. Early American history generally is written as a success story, and the effects of success are relatively easy to measure. To assay the nature and consequences of decline on a community is more difficult. Evidence is scattered. When people are less successful, they are less apt to leave records, the exception being merchants who, when forced into bankruptcy or acrimonious disputes over partnerships, often take their cases to courts with civil and equity jurisdiction. In order to

[2]For the impact of the European wars on American commerce see Anna Cornelia Clauder, *American Commerce as Affected by the Wars of the French Revolution and Napoleon, 1793–1812* (Philadelphia, 1932). Several bleak years for tobacco exports in the 1790s forced merchants with limited capital out of business and encouraged planters to move or diversify. When the tobacco trade revived in the first decades of the nineteenth century, Baltimore merchants had the capital to encourage the carriage of tobacco there for reexport to Europe, and the once-flourishing trading towns along the Potomac and Patuxent were left to decay. See "Baltimore," *North American Review* 46 (1826), 99–137; Joseph Scott, *A Geographical Description of the States of Maryland and Delaware . . .* (Philadelphia, 1807), p. 128; and Reverend John R. Biddle, "Historical Geography of Bladensburg, Maryland" (master's thesis, Catholic University, 1954). The standard work on trade conditions in the 1780s and the general course of business in the Revolutionary era is Robert East, *Business Enterprise in the American Revolutionary Era* (New York, 1938). See his chapter 11, "Economic Developments in the 1780's," pp. 239–62, for a discussion of the depression of 1785–1786.

place the mercantile community in perspective, however, it is necessary to view it in the context of the community as a whole. Fortunately, sufficient biographical detail on 181 of 216 property owners,
bachelors, and paupers resident in Annapolis in 1783 is available to
provide some indication of the general patterns of economic behavior
in the postwar decade.[3]

Table 4-1 is a summary of the distribution of heads of households
among occupations in 1783. Understandably, government and occupations related to serving the needs of the wealthy predominated.

[3]Names drawn from the tax list for 1783 were the starting point for the career
studies used in this chapter. See "A Return of Property in Annapolis Hundred
as Valued by Francis Fairbrother for the Year 1783," Maryland Historical Society,
Baltimore, Maryland (hereafter cited as 1783 Tax List, Annapolis). For each name on
the list an exhaustive search of the extant records was made in an effort to reconstruct
the elements of the individual's career. The work on the biographies was begun
under the auspices of an NEH grant #H69-0-178, which I directed. For a discussion
of methodology see "Final Report, National Endowment for the Humanities Grant
#H69-0-178: "Southern Urban Society after the Revolution: Annapolis, Maryland
1782-1786," on deposit at the Hall of Records, Annapolis, Maryland. The analysis
of the data compiled by my staff and me, and much additional research, especially
with respect to the careers of merchants and storekeepers, was done subsequent to
the NEH project, but without the preliminary work sponsored by the NEH grant, this
chapter could not have been written.

The 1783 tax list undoubtedly is comprehensive in its coverage of all employed
adults and paupers in Annapolis at the time it was compiled. Anyone with real or
personal property was listed by name. Bachelors without property were named and
taxed. Paupers were included to fulfill the secondary function of the tax list, which
was to be a census. Perhaps the quality of other 1783 tax lists varied according to
who drew them up, but there is no question that the one for Annapolis was carefully
and expertly done. The assessor, Francis Fairbrother, had been a long-time resident
and had gained great expertise at appraisal through the compilation of numerous
estate inventories. Where he can be verified, Fairbrother is invariably correct. A
study of land use in the town failed to turn up any leaseholder or landowner that he
had missed. See the three-volume study by Edward Papenfuse and Jane McWilliams,
"Appendix F: Lot Histories and Maps National Endowment for the Humanities
Grant #H69-0-178," on deposit at the Hall of Records, Annapolis, Maryland (hereafter cited as Papenfuse and McWilliams, "Appendix F"). On the 1782 tax list,
John Ball is credited with the same amount of plate that he had in his inventory when
he died in 1783, which suggests that Fairbrother was a careful observer when it came
to personal property as well.

In the following pages only quotations and statements not relating to the careers
of townspeople are documented. General statements about opportunity, mobility,
and wealth accumulation within occupational groupings and basic facts about individual careers are derived from data housed in biographical files on deposit at the
Hall of Records, Annapolis, Maryland. Reference should be made to these working
files for any questions relating to the details of career analysis in this chapter. A
general description of the sources used in reconstructing the careers of the townspeople is given in the bibliography at the end of the book. In addition, appendix B
provides: (a) an occupational index to the biographical files at the Hall of Records
which are maintained in alphabetical order by name on the 1783 tax list; (b) an
alphabetical listing of the 1783 tax list with a summary of the tax data; and (c) a rank-
ing of the 1783 tax list by total assessable wealth, which was used in constructing
table 4-4.

Table 4-1 Occupations in Annapolis, 1783

Occupation	Number	Percent of Sample
Professionals and government employees		
Doctor	3	1.39
Gentleman-planter	13	6.02
Lawyer	8	3.70
Merchant-public servant	5	2.31
Minister	1	.46
Scrivener and clerk	12	5.56
Total	42	19.44
Merchants and storekeepers		
Merchants	18	8.33
Storekeepers	13	6.02
Total	31	14.35
Craftsmen		
Blacksmith	2	.93
Blockmaker	1	.46
Bricklayer	1	.46
Cabinetmaker	2	.93
Carpenter	5	2.31
Coachmaker	3	1.39
Painter-glazer	1	.46
Pumpmaker	1	.46
Printer	2	.93
Shipcarpenter	1	.46
Shoemaker	9	4.16
Silversmith	3	1.39
Staymaker	1	.46
Surveyor	1	.46
Tailor	5	2.31
Tanner	1	.46
Watchmaker	4	1.85
Wheelwright	1	.46
Total	44	20.37
Service occupations		
Baker	2	.93
Barber	4	1.85
Butcher	2	.93
Ferrykeeper	1	.46
Ship captain and mariner	17	7.87
Tavern, inn, and boardinghouse keeper	23	10.64
Total	49	22.69
Laborers and unknown		
Laborer	5	2.31
Unknown	27	12.50
Total	32	14.81
Widows and spinsters	18	8.33
Grand total	216	100.00

Source: See chapter 4, note 3.

Government was the mainstay of the community in 1783, and most livelihoods in one way or another depended upon it. In 1786, when efforts were made to remove the capital to Baltimore, a great outcry was raised and an exchange appeared in the newspapers which detailed the disastrous consequences townspeople perceived would befall them if the proponents of removal succeeded. Alexander Contee Hanson, a noted Annapolis lawyer, pleaded that the town would become a village filled with unemployed clerks, merchants, and tavern keepers.[4] He exaggerated, but about 20 percent of the heads of households in town had government-related jobs, while the merchants, storekeepers, and tavern owners (another 25 percent), derived much of their business from government employees and people who came to town for court days and the sitting of the General Assembly. In a letter to the editor of the *Maryland Journal and Baltimore Advertiser*, written in 1787, Hanson argued for a higher salary and provided an analysis of his yearly expenditures to demonstrate the need (see table 4-2).[5] Undoubtedly, Hanson padded his account to fit his purpose, but the list does provide some indication of how at least one government employee allocated his resources to meet the daily cost of living. Hanson's salary was £500 currency per annum and he claimed that, exclusive of out-of-town expenditures, he spent over £600, 70 percent of which went to local storekeepers for foodstuffs and clothing. As long as Annapolis remained the capital, there was at least one segment of the market upon which the mercantile community could depend; and, in 1783, there was considerable cause for optimism that even more government employees soon would make their appearance with the arrival of the Continental Congress there in the fall.[6]

Industry played a very minor role in the fortunes of the town. Tanning and leather-related trades accounted for the occupations of about 5 percent of the heads of households. Commerce drew ship captains and mariners. Nearly 9 percent of the heads of households were engaged in maritime activities, although shipbuilding and related industries, such as ropemaking, had long since declined. The rest of the townspeople were evenly distributed among a wide

---

[4][Hanson, Alexander Contee], *Considerations on the Proposed Removal of the Seat of Government, Addressed to the Citizens of Maryland, by Aristides* (Annapolis, 1786). Hanson's pamphlet first appeared in *Maryland Journal and Baltimore Advertiser*, no. 804, in reply to an article by "the Farmer" in the same paper, nos. 800 and 803. The debate was continued by "Phocian" and "Aristophanes" in *The Maryland Gazette: or The Baltimore Advertiser* for February 7, 1786.

[5]*Maryland Journal and Baltimore Advertiser*, April 6, 1787.

[6]For a discussion of why the Congress came to Annapolis, see Joyce W. McDonald, "The Congress and the Community," Part III, Appendix B, "Final Report National Endowment for the Humanities Grant #H69-0-178," Hall of Records, Annapolis, Md.

Table 4-2 "An Estimate of the Annual
expences of a family in Annapolis, consisting of ten
persons (half of whom are servants) keeping two horses and one milch cow"

House rent	£ 75.00.0
Pork, 1600 lb @37/6	30.00.0
Beef & other butcher meat, 1200 lb @6d	30.00.0
Poultry, fish, fruit, vegetables	30.00.0
Tea, coffee, salt, spice, etc.	25.00.0
Loaf sugar, 180 lb @1/2	10.10.0
Brown sugar, 150 lb @8d	5.00.0
Superfine flour, 10 bbls @40/-	20.00.0
Indian corn, 20 bbls @15/-	15.00.0
Oats, 180 bus @3/-	27.00.0
Hay, 2 tons @£6	12.00.0
Firewood, 50 cords @20/-	
including carting, cording, etc.	50.00.0
Candles, 140 lb @15d	8.15.0
Spirits to represent table liquors, every kind,	
30 gallons @6/8	10.00.0
Wine of every kind, 50 gallons @12/-	30.00.0
Butter, 150 lb @15d	9.07.6
Hire and cloathing of 5 servants	60.00.0
Medicines, physicians, etc.	15.00.0
Cloathing of family, 5 persons to appear decently, no less than	120.00.0
Expence of attending twice a year on the Eastern Shore	37.07.6
No allowance for casualties or for what is called Pocket Money	c. 80.00.0
Total	£700.00.0

Source: Maryland Journal and Baltimore Advertiser, April 6, 1787.

variety of trades and services, as can be seen from table 4-1. For the most part, their livelihood depended upon the patronage of the affluent, and they would be greatly affected by any constriction in the flow of money into the town.

THE DISTRIBUTION OF
WEALTH AMONG OCCUPATIONS AND THE
POTENTIAL FOR UPWARD ECONOMIC MOBILITY IN 1783

At any point in the history of a community the careers of heads of households would be in various stages of completion. Grouping people according to their assessed wealth and then examining the careers of those within defined ranges of wealth would provide no solution to the problem of age disparity. A man who had less than £50 of property might be embarked on a career that would place him among the most wealthy. In order to convey a sense of the hierarchy of potential wealth among occupations and to cope with the problem of age, the taxable wealth of individuals within each occupational category was averaged, and the occupations were ranked according to average wealth (see table 4-3). In this way, the economic status of a given occupation was defined and the potential for vertical mobility between occupations could be assessed. In addition, other types of mobility could be related to economic status. The evidence gathered about the careers of people in town made it possible to weigh the ability of a man to improve upon the career of his father, as well as to determine his ability to acquire wealth and status in Annapolis in the years prior to 1783. The central assumption is made that, within each occupational grouping, opportunities were roughly equal and the prospects of success for those who were beginning their careers in 1783 were as great as those that had confronted people whose careers were at a peak in 1783. The nature of opportunity changed after 1783, of course, but the consequences of that change are best measured in terms of what might have been, based upon past performance: the only terms in which people in any age can gauge their accomplishments.

Occupations with Average Assessed Wealth
above £500

Gentlemen-planters, lawyers, and merchants were the only people to fall into this category of wealth. In numbers they made up only 20 percent of the heads of households, but they controlled 49 percent of the assessed wealth of the town held by residents. Government employment was an important source of income for many of the wealthy, although it was not an initial means to wealth. Appointments to lucrative posts came after careers were established or for people who were born with wealth and status. The offices provided additional revenue or a way to improve upon existing resources. Many gentlemen-planters were resident in town because they were public servants, although families such as the Lloyds and the Carrolls built townhouses during the age of affluence as part of their social obligations and as a means of displaying their wealth.[7]

As Aubrey C. Land has pointed out, planting was not sufficient for the accumulation of wealth.[8] Most planters who prospered were also merchants or professionals, and it was normal to find the occupations

---

[7]See chapter 1 for a discussion of townhouse building in Annapolis before the Revolution.

[8]Aubrey C. Land, "Economic Base and Social Structure: The Northern Chesapeake in the Eighteenth Century," *Journal of Economic History* 25 (1965), 639–54, and Land, "Economic Behavior in a Planting Society: The Eighteenth-Century Chesapeake," *Journal of Southern History* 33 (1967), 469–85.

Table 4-3 Occupations and Wealth in Annapolis, 1783

Wealth/Occupation	Number	Percent of Sample	Percent of Total Wealth	Average Taxable Wealth	Total Taxable Wealth
Above £500:					
Gentleman-planter	13	6.02	16.28	847.19	11,013.50
Merchant	23	10.64	23.98	707.24	16,226.50
Lawyer	8	3.70	8.32	703.38	5,627.00
£400 to £500					
Printer	2	.93	1.37	462.00	924.00
Carpenter	5	2.31	3.23	437.20	2,186.00
Watchmaker	4	1.85	2.57	434.44	1,737.75
Doctor	3	1.39	1.89	426.50	1,279.50
£300 to £400					
Baker	2	.93	1.17	397.00	794.00
Cabinetmaker	2	.93	1.14	386.50	773.00
Storekeeper	13	6.02	6.70	349.46	4,543.00
Blacksmith	2	.93	.94	317.75	635.50
Surveyor	1	.46	.46	310.00	310.00
Tavern, inn, and boardinghouse keeper	23	10.64	10.48	308.37	7,091.75
£200 to £300					
Blockmaker	1	.46	.35	238.00	238.00
Butcher	2	.93	.64	218.00	436.00
Tailor	5	2.31	1.51	203.95	1,019.75
Silversmith	3	1.39	.90	203.17	609.50
Ship captain and mariner	17	7.87	5.04	200.47	3,408.00
£100 to £200					
Barber	4	1.85	1.09	183.87	735.50
Widows and spinsters	18	8.33	4.47	168.14	3,026.50
Scrivener and clerk	12	5.56	2.45	137.96	1,655.50
Tanner	1	.46	.20	132.75	132.75
Shoemaker	9	4.16	1.57	117.67	1,059.00
Coachmaker	3	1.39	.51	115.00	345.00
Shipcarpenter	1	.46	.16	110.00	110.00
Under £100					
Painter-glazer	1	.46	.13	86.50	86.50
Pumpmaker	1	.46	.10	66.00	66.00
Staymaker	1	.46	.08	53.00	53.00
(Unknown)	27	12.50	1.91	47.74	1,289.00
Laborer	5	2.31	.28	38.20	191.00
Ferrykeeper	1	.46	.05	34.00	34.00
Minister	1	.46	.03	20.00	20.00
Bricklayer	1	.46	.00	00.00	00.00
Wheelwright	2	.46	.00	00.00	00.00
Total	216	100.00	100.00		£67,656.50

Source: See chapter 4, note 3.

combined. Merchants, too, combined business with public service. Holding office did not seem to provide any great advantage to merchants in the accumulation of assessable wealth. Merchants who held public office were worth on the average £5 less than merchants who did not; but office-holding may have had other attributes obscured by the tax rolls. John Davidson, collector of the port of Annapolis, undoubtedly knew subtle ways of helping his business in defiance of the laws of trade.[9] Thomas Harwood, treasurer of the Western Shore, probably was able to make more judicious investments in public securities than most men. Robert Couden, although retired as a merchant by 1783, assumed the post of assistant to the intendant of the revenue, and then apparently speculated in the finances of the state as silent partner with another merchant, James Tootell.[10]

The designation "gentleman-planter" was a mark of status and appears to have been the goal of anyone who acquired wealth. Invariably the pattern followed by merchants and others who became wealthy was to purchase a plantation and to behave as a gentleman. Charles Wallace is but one example of several. He was successful in business, purchased a plantation, renovated a townhouse, attended the races, and was appointed to the governor's council. Yet aspiring after status and obtaining it were two different propositions. As his nephew and heir put it, even though Wallace was a "useful citizen" during the Revolution and, as a result, was appointed to the governor's council, "There were great distinctions of rank and class [in society] . . . and tho he associated with some of the most prominent [gentlemen] such as Governors Johnson and Paca . . . he was not quite a patrician."[11] It is difficult in most cases to weigh how successful people were in achieving social status, but mobility in terms of acquiring sufficient wealth to behave like gentlemen can be assessed. If a man was not born into wealth, yet achieved it, he was obviously mobile.

[9]In July, 1771, Joshua Johnson wrote to his then partner John Davidson, telling him that he had found a way to slip a few bottles of "good old speritt" past the London custom officials, playfully reminding Davidson that he probably was not unfamiliar with how it was done. As Johnson put it, "but Jonny you know we have studied the art of smugling." Wallace, Davidson, and Johnson Letter Books, 1:8, Hall of Records, Annapolis, Md. (hereafter cited as WDJ 1).

[10]See biographical files of Robert Couden and James Tootell, Hall of Records, Annapolis, Md.

[11]Charles Wallace Hanson, manuscript introduction to the collected works of Alexander Contee Hanson; the introduction appears in a volume entitled "Pamphlets by Alexander Contee Hanson," Rare Book Collection, Maryland Historical Society, Baltimore, Md.

Few of the gentlemen-planter class in Annapolis came from humble backgrounds. Out of thirteen, only William Campbell, whose origins are obscure; Allen Quynn, who parlayed a shoemaker's trade in Annapolis into a fortune; and John Ridout, immigrant secretary to former Governor Sharpe, were not born into prominent planter families. Of the eight lawyers who were heads of household in 1783, only two came from relatively poor homes. The rest were drawn from old and established planter families. In general, opportunity as a lawyer in Annapolis was confined to those with proper social connections, although those who practiced in the town taught an unknown number of less prominent lawyers who came to serve their apprenticeship and returned to practice in county courts elsewhere in the state. The prominence of the legal profession in Annapolis in 1783 can be gauged by the achievement of two of the eight lawyers, Samuel Chase and Gabriel Duvall, who became Supreme Court justices, and by the reputation Governor Paca had for instructing aspiring laywers. As one visitor noted in September of 1783:

Annapolis is a nursery of the long robe. Its lawyers would do honour to any bar in Europe. The Governor, who is of this profession, has instituted a society composed of students of the law, who meet at his house, at stated periods, to discuss law questions and questions in political economy. He proposes the subject, sits as President, and gives judgment, in conjunction with his council, the Chancellor, the lawyers and the Judges of the General Court. When the debates are finished the company sup with the governor. . . .[12]

If the ranks of resident planters and lawyers were largely closed to people not born into social status or wealth, the case was quite different for merchants. Mobility was the rule rather than the exception. Over half of the merchants (twelve, or 52 percent of the sample) came from poor families, unable to help their sons with capital to launch their mercantile careers. Ten of these were forced to begin their income-producing lives as apprentices or clerks in other less remunerative occupations than trade.

Of the twenty-three merchants resident in town in 1783, only six came from wealthy planter families who could have provided them with sufficient funds to begin as merchants. One, or possibly two, came with capital supplied from England. William Brown, partner in the British firm of Perkins, Buchanan and Brown, which had a store in Annapolis, came to town on the eve of the Revolution in order to safeguard the firm's property and remained in town, supported by goods

[12]*Maryland Journal and Baltimore Advertiser*, September 30, 1783.

and cash from home. Thomas Wilson also may have had similar backing early in his career. Five Annapolis merchants came from merchant families; although in only two cases, those of James Mackubin and Joseph Dowson, did family fortune and business help their careers. Mackubin inherited a going concern and valuable Annapolis real estate from his father. Dowson emigrated from London to be a clerk in his brother's Baltimore store and established himself in Annapolis with aid from his uncle, Charles Wallace. In contrast, James and Joseph Williams received little from their Uncle Thomas in the way of capital or goods, even though they took over his small Annapolis store and clientele. Although Isaac Hyde was a merchant at one time, he left his son, Thomas, a penniless orphan, destined to begin his career at a tender age as an apprentice shoemaker.

Of the five immigrants who became merchants (including William Brown and Joseph Dowson), at least two came with little money. John Davidson and John Muir left Scotland to begin their Annapolis careers as clerks in the naval office. Lewis Neth, a German who came by way of Philadelphia and was able to establish himself immediately as a merchant on his arrival in Annapolis, probably came with capital. But his onetime partner, Joseph Eastman, was of obscure origins and probably started his career with as little fortune as his kinsmen, the Williams brothers. None of the remaining six native-born merchants was fortunate to have a family that could aid him financially. Three were the sons of poor planters; Absalom Ridgely and Thomas B. Hodgkin moved to town to begin their careers as small storekeepers, and John Randall came as an apprentice carpenter. Charles Wallace, William Wilkins, Jr., and James Tootell were born in Annapolis. Wallace's parents were too poor to be noted in the public record beyond mention of his birth, and he was apprenticed at an early age to be a staymaker. James Tootell's father was a saddler, and William Wilkins, Sr. kept an inn.

In terms of upward economic mobility the past experience of the Annapolis merchant community must have been encouraging to anyone who considered entering a mercantile career in 1783. Subsequently conditions would change dramatically, and opportunity for all occupations, but especially for merchants, would be severely curtailed. In the meantime, however, there was occasion for the optimism about the future which pervaded the merchant class.

Occupations with Average Assessed Wealth
between £400 and £500

The three doctors came from similar backgrounds. Two had been trained in Scotland and had fathers who were prosperous doctors themselves. The oldest, Dr. Scott, had come to Maryland in the entourage of a former governor and had capitalized on his close connection with such a socially prominent individual. In medicine, it would appear, opportunity was limited to an established professional class which perpetuated itself.

Opportunities for printers had been effectively blocked for all but the Green family since the reestablishment of the *Maryland Gazette* in 1745. Carpenters, if their prospects can be measured by the success of Joshua Frazier, were highly mobile and were able to acquire considerable property. The building of townhouses and public buildings went on at an accelerated rate in the years between the French and Indian War and the Revolution, and carpenters such as Frazier profited from the demand for their services. Watchmakers prospered as well, but the key to their prosperity lay in diversification. The most affluent, William Whetcroft, also doubled as a storekeeper.

Occupations with Average Assessed Wealth between £300 and £400

Almost 20 percent of the heads of households had occupations with average taxable wealth between £300 and £400. It is quite likely that bakers were so prosperous because of the opportunities afforded by war. Frederick Grammar came to Annapolis in 1777, two years after emigrating to Philadelphia from Wurttemberg, Germany. For the remainder of the war, he supplied bread for the troops and, by 1783, had amassed considerable property. Both cabinetmakers were well established by 1783, and their careers suggest the opportunities offered by their craft. John Shaw emigrated from Glasgow and, with Archibald Chisholm, established a reputation as a skilled cabinetmaker. Chisholm had married well and was about to retire to his plantation, while Shaw still was prospering in 1783. In addition to cabinets, he was also the local undertaker, an occupation not unusual for his craft.

The evident success of the two blacksmiths is not difficult to understand; their services were in constant demand. Simon Retallick combined smithing with ironmongery and used his skill on townhouses and public buildings. Isaac Harris made enough money in his trade to invest in a ship, the *Betsy*, which he dispatched with a cargo of foodstuffs to Edenton, North Carolina in 1773. Although the ship was lost on the voyage, Harris had insured it and recovered £230 sterling of its £256 value.[13]

[13]WDJ 1:180, 220.

There was only one surveyor in town in 1783 and his presence is more an indication of the subsequent development of the town than of opportunity before 1783. William Brown, the surveyor, came to Annapolis in 1783 after a long career as a carpenter, tavern keeper, and ferryman in Londontown. Between 1783 and his death, he was to be employed by two people who were developing vacant land in town in expectation of future growth.

Almost 11 percent of the heads of households were tavern and inn-keepers. Six were widows, although most of them are more appropriately designated "boardinghouse keepers." The widow innkeepers were themselves an opportunity for some aspiring males. Robert Clarke married a widow who was established in business and thus became an innkeeper, and others may have done the same. A few of the innkeepers had other occupations, and many had been employed in other jobs before obtaining their "ordinary" license. Bakers, mariners, and shipcarpenters opened inns. In 1783, the most successful were Gilbert Middleton and George Mann. Middleton's father had begun the business and combined it with renting boats and providing a ferry service. Gilbert was trained as a shipcarpenter, but took over the family business when his father died in 1770. George Mann's career suggests the opportunities open for an enterprising innkeeper. He arrived in town soon after the Revolution began, purchased (on credit) the confiscated townhouse of a prominent Tory, and opened a hotel which catered to a distinguished clientele, including Washington and Lafayette.

On the whole, however, no innkeeper came from a socially prominent family and no great fortune was made through innkeeping. The innkeeper's world at its best included the genteel, such as those who stayed at Mann's, but it usually entailed catering to the middle and lower classes of society. James West never made money at anything he did, although his father may have been a prosperous planter. James chose to open a tavern and whiled away his time at cards or tried to prevent damage as his customers brawled. Much has been written about Annapolis society of the type that centered at Mann's[14] but life at West's was probably more typical and is vividly described by one of his disgruntled patrons in a deposition taken in 1780:

On the Night of the 14th Instant (Thursday) I had occasion, and did call (between 8 and 9 o'clock, to the best of my recollection) at the House of James West, in order to pay some Money to a Gentleman, who I promised to

[14]For example, see Walter B. Norris, *Annapolis: Its Colonial and Naval Story* (New York, 1925).

meet there. When I got there, I went into the Room, where Company usually sit, but not finding the person I looked for, nor any one there, I applied to a Servant who had just come from the back part of the House or kitchen, to know if any Company was in the House, and in particular the person I wanted, who answered in the affirmative; that all the Company were in the front room, and had removed there, to prevent the noise disturbing Mrs. West (who lay upstairs). I then returned back, knocked at the front room door, opened it, and asked, if my Company was intrusive, which was answered in the Negative, and I walked in, — The Company, to wit, James West, Thomas Pryse, Thomas Grahame, Robert Thorpe and William Ball, were at Cards. I told Robert Thorpe, I wanted to speak to him, and comply with my promise; after which, I was asked to join in their Cardparty. This I comply'd with, merely to pass away the night. M. Thorpe, left the Company, about 10. Clock, to go to bed, we still play'd on.

I could perceive, that from the time I came into the room Thomas Pryse viewed me with a jealous and scornful Eye, seemed very sullen, and contradicted almost every word I say'd, intending thereby, to insult me, and bring on a quarrel, which I evaded, by not outwardly taking any notice of his particular behaviour to me; this conduct of mine seemed to raise his choler the more, and not having an immediate opportunity of gratifying his wish, he was forced to stifle his resentment, until an event of that kind took place, which he took every opportunity of bringing to the issue that afterwards happened, by a repetition of contradictions and scurilous language. To the best of my recollection, the only provoking word or sentence I made use of, was, that as I did not consider him upon an equality with me, (which he might see, by my behaviour and indifference towards him) I would not take any notice of what he say'd. He immediately got up, called me a damned Rascal, *"That he long wish'd, for an opportunity, to flog me."* Struck me a most violent blow on the side of the head, which knocked me down, and whilst down, gave me several violent blows, on the Head, body and breast and another blow on the upper lip, which cut it very much, drag'd me about the room, with one hand, whilst he beat me, with the other, tore my Coat and Waistcoat and used me in a most cruel and inhuman manner. The treatment, has been the means of my being confined for three days to my Room, (one entire day to my bed) with my Head and face sore and swelled, and my mouth cut and swelled very much, a high fever on me, and unable to eat or retain on my Stomach, that sustenance which nature craved, from the pains in my Head, arms and Sides and the disorder in my Stomach, created from the cruelty of this usage.

Not yet content, he pursued me out of the Room, and whilst I was talking with James West upon the steps, outside the street Door, attacked me a second time (with this Prelude), *"you damned Rascal, I'm not done with you yet,"* and immediately struck me again on the Head. I then say'd, this is really cowardly. Pryse you will not fight me upon equal terms, explaining, *"with Pistols,"* he say'd he would fight me, with one hand meaning, *"he would box me with one hand, the other to be tyed"*; to this I agreed, provided he would come out upon the Common. We then left West's House, accompanied by Thomas Grahame, when we three proceeded up the alley (that divides Doctor

Steward's House and Pryse's backyard) towards the Common, for the purpose of aforesaid; but so far, was an equal method of fighting from his intention, that he again attacked and struck me on the side of the Head, which staggered me so much, that with difficulty I prevented myself from falling, which if it had been the case, I confidently believe he would have murdered me. — One of my Hands being disabled, and having nothing in the other to defend myself with. I found a necessity in endeavouring to make my escape in the best manner I could, for had I attempted to fight, it must have been at a double disadvantage. I therefore made an effort, to run up the Street which he prevented, by crashing me, and at same time, made a blow at me, which providencially missed. I then was forced to take another course, and by a stratagem endeavour to make a retreat, which after a great deal of difficulty and fear and many other blows made at me, I effected.

When I had got up the Street, nearly as far as John Randall's I stopp'd and overheard Pryse talking very loud and distinct to Grahame, and after some invectives and of scurilous language thrown out by him, at my expense, he say'd, *"Damn him, if he would not whip me, wherever he could find me,"* which clearly shows (Together with what has before been mentioned, *"I have long wish'd for an opportunity to flog you"*) malice propence in the highest degree.

James West, William Ball and Thomas Grahame can prove the first assault, and the cause thereof.

James West can prove the second assault and Thomas Grahame can prove the last assault.

But as these three assaults will be construed with one assault, happening on the same Night, I would wish to have the whole proved, in which case, the Jury will give higher Damages ——

Wm. Vereker[15]

Before 1783, tavern keeping offered the opportunity of above-average wealth, but little prospect of greater achievement. Many people from other occupations could and would become innkeepers, but the movement from innkeeping to even greater wealth and status was unlikely.

If a man wanted to better his economic status and he started with little or no capital, the most productive path to wealth was storekeeping. Smithing and cabinetmaking took skills that men in adulthood would have difficulty in mastering. Inn- and tavern keeping offered a modest return, but no likelihood of enormous gain. To most people, storekeeping probably seemed a stage on the way to even greater wealth as merchants. Most Annapolis merchants who entered trade without much capital began as storekeepers. Over half (52 per-

[15]Miscellaneous Court Papers, Anne Arundel County, 1785, Hall of Records, Annapolis, Md. Although the case came before the court in 1785, the events were alleged to have taken place in September 1780.

cent) of the merchant community in 1783 launched their mercantile careers modestly, importing small amounts of wet goods, drygoods, and groceries for retail sale. As capital was accumulated from the profits on retail sales, storekeepers branched out into the export trade, by investing in tobacco and grain; and into the wholesale import business by purchasing cargoes of rum, wine, and more drygoods than they could sell in their stores.

There were thirteen storekeepers in Annapolis in 1783 who, at that point in their lives, were confining themselves almost exclusively to the retail trade.[16] Their profile is similar to the twelve merchants who began with little capital, although less is known about their origins than is the case with the merchants. Five apparently came from small planter families or were small planters themselves before becoming storekeepers. One of these, Nicholas Maccubbin, was apprenticed by his father to be a shoemaker and, even when he opened a store, used the title "cordwainer" to distinguish himself from a number of other Nicholas Maccubbins living in the area. Storekeeping was not perceived as a difficult task, and some planters even saw it as a means of providing for their old age. In 1777, William Maccubbin agreed to exchange his 175 acres for £1,000 current money and a house to be built on a lot in Londontown near Annapolis. A friend explained that Maccubbin was lame and needed a new occupation. The money would pay the debts and enable him to purchase a good supply of items to sell at his new house. He would have "nothing to do but go from his fireside to the counter" and could "get his living in a much easier way" than planting.[17] Although Maccubbin died before he could test his theory, a number of Annapolis residents were attracted to storekeeping by the easy terms on which goods were offered for sale. Only a portion of the wholesale price needed to be paid; the rest was due in installments and could be paid as the goods were sold.[18]

Being a successful storekeeper, of course, was not as easy as Maccubbin envisioned it, but it was an occupation in which a shrewd man could parlay a small capital investment into a modest fortune. When

---

[16]A storekeeper is defined as a member of the lowest class of retail merchants. People on the 1783 tax list were placed in this category if they met any of the following criteria: they called themselves storekeepers and thus did not think of themselves as merchants; the nature of their advertisements and other measures (such as court cases in which they sued for debts owed) suggested only a small retail business; they sold groceries or other commodities as their principal business and only occasionally offered drygoods for sale; they purchased their stock of drygoods locally, rather than ordering spring and fall cargoes from abroad.

[17]Chancery Records, 13:473ff., Hall of Records, Annapolis, Md.

[18]For example, see the Biggs and Eastman accounts in the Ridout Papers, Gift Collection, Hall of Records, Annapolis, Md. (hereafter cited as Ridout Pap.), D371.

it is considered that less than a quarter (23.77 percent) of all the households in Maryland in 1783 had more than £300 in assessable property (see table 4-4), and that storekeepers could hope for even greater economic achievement as merchants, small planters and others who were able to enter into trade were justified in perceiving Annapolis or any other center of commerce as a place of great opportunity.[19]

At least two who were storekeepers in Annapolis in 1783 were immigrants: Jacob Hurst, "the peddler," and Joseph Clarke, although the latter combined storekeeping with a profession as an architect and was able to supplement his capital from his other work. The remainder probably were born in or near the town, although the origins of two, Thomas Graham and Jonathan Pinkney, are not certain. John Wilmot was the son of a schoolmaster. John Johnson's father was a peruke maker. Archibald Golder's father was a cabinetmaker who died of mushroom poisoning when Archibald was a young boy. Only William Hyde began his store with substantial backing from his father, Thomas Hyde. All the others launched their careers much more modestly, although by 1783 at least one had gained status and fortune as a public official. Thomas Gassaway, who was born into a small planter family and started as a sales clerk for Perkins, Buchanan and Brown in their Annapolis store, was appointed register of wills

Table 4-4 The Distribution of Wealth in Annapolis and Six Maryland Counties, Derived from the Assessment of 1783

Assessed Value (£)	Annapolis Households	Percent	Sample County Households	Percent
Pauper	13	6.0	1,052	11.5
10-49	46	21.3	2,409	26.4
50-99	31	14.3	1,307	14.3
100-149	17	7.9	883	9.7
150-199	10	4.6	604	6.6
200-299	30	13.9	712	7.8
300-399	11	5.1	512	5.6
400-499	14	6.5	331	3.6
500-999	30	13.9	751	8.2
Above 1000	14	6.5	579	6.3
Total	216	100.0	9,140	100.0

Source: Analysis of 1783 assessments for Annapolis Hundred and six counties: Harford, Caroline, Charles, Calvert, Somerset, Talbot.

[19]Gregory A. Stiverson compiled the county information in table 4-4, and it appears in similar form in Edward C. Papenfuse and Gregory A. Stiverson, "General Smallwood's Recruits: The Peacetime Career of the Revolutionary War Private," *William and Mary Quarterly* 30 (January, 1973), 117-32.

for Anne Arundel County in 1780, and held the much-sought-after post until his death in 1787.

In 1783, storekeepers had every reason to expect that, with a little good fortune and a great deal of hard work, even greater prosperity was within their grasp. As a group, they were in the upper one-third of the resident wealthholders in town and legitimately could assume that ultimately they would become even wealthier as they altered the character of their business enough to call themselves merchants. It was not entirely their fault that they soon found themselves mistaken.

Occupations with Average Assessed Wealth between £200 and £300

Tailors and silversmiths catered to the wealthy and made a comfortable living, as their position in table 4–3 demonstrates. As long as the wealthy clientele remained in Annapolis, there would be opportunity for anyone skilled in these crafts. However, two of the five tailors were the sons of carpenters, and thus downwardly mobile in terms of what their fathers had done. One of the three silversmiths was following the trade of his father, while another was the son of an impoverished gentleman-planter. With shipbuilding on the decline, blockmaking was not in much demand. The two butchers were from obscure backgrounds, and no one who entered this trade was known to have been occupationally mobile.

Ship captains and mariners were numerous in 1783; they comprised nearly 8 percent of the heads of households. Their origins are obscure for the most part, as they came to town from other parts of the state. Only two were born in Annapolis, the sons of a mariner-turned-innkeeper. One career can be traced to a previous employment as a planter. The subsequent careers of at least two suggest that the movement from planting to the sea and vice versa was not difficult. Such evidence adds weight to the argument that small planters found it relatively easy to move into town and become mariners, innkeepers, and storekeepers. It was not unusual for a retired ship captain to open a tavern or boardinghouse, as Captain Beriah Mayberry and John Sands had done. But opportunity for ship captains to move into the retail trade in Annapolis apparently had declined. In the 1730s and 1740s, Captain Patrick Creagh and Captain Robert Gordon had stores (see chapter 1). But in 1783, only one former captain, Joseph Dowson, who was the nephew of Charles Wallace, was a storekeeper. Ship captains and mariners could aspire to keeping a modest inn, but probably not much more. To become an innkeeper would make the ship captain more upwardly mobile than others in the £200 to £300 average wealth category; the move from ship captain to innkeeper meant an increase in average wealth of 50 percent. Storekeepers were in the same wealth category as innkeepers, but could rightfully aspire to becoming merchants, an occupation worth on the average twice as much as simply keeping store.

Occupations with Average Assessed Wealth between £100 and £200

Almost a quarter of the heads of households (22.22 percent) had occupations with an average worth between £100 and £200. Barbers were the wealthiest in this grouping. Their trade depended upon the patronage of the affluent. One barber, William Logan, was able to diversify, but he was an exception and no other barber did as well. Before the war Logan, a native of Annapolis, invested in a brickyard and built a wharf. He might have been even more mobile than he was by 1783, had he not overextended himself.

A large number of people were clerks in government offices. Within the occupation there were notable extremes in wealth, which suggests that while there was significant opportunity for some, for the majority a below-average income could be expected. Those clerks who were most successful were from established planter families and held clerkships that had social status as well as sizeable incomes. Examples are the clerkship of the county court, held by Nicholas Harwood, and the registership in chancery, held by Samuel Harvey Howard. Nevertheless, there was some hope that a person of lower social (but not economic) status might get a lucrative clerkship. By 1783, John Callahan, the son of a tailor, had become clerk of the land office.

Another large segment of people with average wealth expectations of between £100 and £200 were the shoemakers. During the Revolution, many had employment because of the demand for shoes for soldiers. The state ran its own tanyard and, undoubtedly, the leather was farmed out to local shoemakers. But the accumulation of greater average wealth than already achieved probably was not likely, even when the market for shoes was at its best. Nicholas Maccubbin was an exception, going from cordwainer to storeowner, and he probably did so with capital gained from the planting he carried on in addition to his trade. Allen Quynn and Thomas Hyde had been shoemakers once, but their fortunes were made initially through investments in the tanning industry which, with the exception of the wartime revival, was of declining importance to the economy of the Annapolis area.

Occupations with Average Assessed Wealth below £100

If the unknowns are included as probable laborers, almost one fifth (18.03 percent) of the heads of households had jobs worth less than £100. The one staymaker might look to Charles Wallace as an example. Wallace rose from that trade to become a wealthy merchant, and perhaps Vachel Yeates expected to do as well. But on the whole, the chances for economic success of people in the below £100 category were not great.

The total number of laborers (32) at first seems small, even if the unknowns are included. Such a small population would be strange if it were not for the fact that slaves formed an important part of the labor force. In 1783, there were 449 slaves within the town proper. Some were used as house and domestic servants. Charles Carroll, the richest man in town, had nineteen slaves as servants.[20] Other slaves performed manual labor, such as working on the dock and carting goods.[21] Little can be said about the laborers. The richest, Vestal Meeke, was an unsuccessful planter who drifted to town in search of work. Only one laborer or "mechanic," Jubb Fowler, is known to have moved upward on the economic scale. By 1783, he was best defined as a clerk, although he continued to describe himself as a mechanic.

On the whole, as might be expected, people in this average wealth category were the least economically mobile and had the least prospect or expectation of rising above their lot. No laborer on the 1783 tax list moved from poverty to wealth in Annapolis, although it is possible that some of their more prosperous fellow citizens came from laboring families. Many Annapolitans from obscure origins had obtained wealth by 1783 but what their fathers did for a living will never be known because of the lack of records.

In terms of the potential for wealth accumulation as well as the prospects of vertical economic mobility, merchants and storekeepers in Annapolis in 1783 were at an advantage over their fellow townspeople. Although all occupations, except those with the least average wealth, had benefited from the prosperity prior to 1783, the merchant community, in conjunction with their wealthy planter and lawyer patrons, formed the economic elite of the town. Merchants represented the epitome of economic mobility. The jump from storekeeper to merchant was not large and was seemingly the most fruitful path to wealth for anyone in an occupation of an average wealth potential under £400. People from a great variety of occupations turned to storekeeping in their efforts to acquire fortune, and store-

[20]See appendix B, Part 2.
[21]For example, see "James Brice's Accounts as Treasurer of the Corporation of Annapolis," Hall of Records, Annapolis, Md. (hereafter cited as Brice Account Book), p. 6. An entry for December 29, 1785, reads "To Same [James Brice] paid negro labourer assisting in piling scantling."

keepers had legitimate reasons for hoping that the expansion of their business would lead to the ranks of the prosperous merchant elite.

For a decade prior to 1775, the Annapolis business community thrived on the spending habits of wealthy and near-wealthy customers. The war ushered in a new form of market growth created by the demands of the war effort that, in a number of ways, enhanced business further. It is no wonder that in 1783 the townspeople, but especially the merchants and storekeepers, were optimistic about the future, and briefly their hopes were to meet with some justification.

THE POSTWAR ECONOMY

The postwar period, 1783 to 1793, was a time of dramatic change for Annapolis. In the first half of the decade, the town expanded rapidly, but after 1788 population growth halted, commerce declined, and the town completed the transition from a commercial center and seasonal home for the wealthy to a quiet market town and way station for the traveler. Between 1783 and 1788, people were optimistic about the future of the town. Congress's short stay there in the fall of 1783 and the spring of 1784 only added to the general prosperity, although the depression of 1785 and 1786 served to dampen enthusiasm. Heavy investments were made in trade. Waterside lots were laid out and leased, a market house built and stalls rented, and docks improved in the expectation of continued growth. Even a tobacco inspection warehouse was erected on the dock, in hopes of enhancing Annapolis's position in the collecting and reexporting of tobacco, a role that the town had not played since the early decades of the century.[22]

The new interest in developing the dock area and building a market house stands in stark contrast to the attitude of the community in the prewar years. In 1766, a controversy raged over how money allocated for the building of a wharf was spent. The exchange is humorous for the lengths to which people went to avoid blame. One writer commented that anyone was "welcome to call it a blundering misapplication of public money, but not a breech of Public Trust."[23] The debate over why the wharf was not built is important for at least

---

[22]For an analysis of the development of the dock area see Papenfuse and McWilliams, "Appendix F," Parcels 38 and 39. On the relative unimportance of tobacco exports from the town, see chapter 1. The new tobacco inspection warehouse on the dock is mentioned in the *Maryland Gazette*, August 5, 1784, and March 20, 1788.

[23]See John Brice's reply to the grand jury in the *Maryland Gazette*, May 5, 1766. In 1772, another attempt was made at improving the dock by raising money through a lottery, but to no avail. *Maryland Gazette*, June 4, 1772.

two reasons: it demonstrates that at no time before the 1780s did the town feel it necessary to expend public money (other than that raised as painlessly as possible through a lottery) for the improvement of port facilities, and it makes clear that Annapolis's function as a marketing center for the produce of the surrounding countryside was still rudimentary. When the existing excuse for a market house was pulled down in 1763, only temporary, disreputable-looking structures took its place until 1783, when a group of merchants donated land and organized a public subscription campaign to build a market house and dock which were then completed over the next five years.[24] At the same time, land prices for privately held property on the dock jumped astronomically, although the owners preferred developmental leasing to outright sale.[25] After the Revolution, merchants and other townspeople worked together to build better facilities for trade. In an area that had been the marshy site of a decaying shipbuilding industry and a few taverns and inns, respectable stores and substantial private wharfs arose, in addition to the public docks.[26] These developments testify to the town's enthusiasm and hopes for the future, but it was not long before signs of overcommitment became painfully apparent.

By 1786, the prospects of further growth in Annapolis began to dim, although they were not completely extinguished. Taxes were high, money was in short supply, and the market was glutted with goods.[27] Elements in the legislature even attempted to have the capital moved to Baltimore.[28] Former Governor Sharpe tried to be optimistic. If the government were moved, he wrote, Annapolis still had an asset in its harbor which, unlike Baltimore, was free from ice during most of the winter. As long as trade was brisk, the growth of Baltimore would be paralleled by growth in Annapolis because both were tied to trade.[29] The capital was not moved and Baltimore expanded rapidly, but Annapolis failed to grow as Sharpe predicted, a fact evident from census records and custom house receipts. Demographically, the town's white population ceased expanding around 1790, declined somewhat by 1800, and changed hardly at all for the decade 1800 to 1810 (see table 4-5).[30]

[24]Brice Account Book, pp. 6, 21, 33.

[25]Papenfuse and McWilliams, "Appendix F," Parcels 38 and 39.

[26]*Ibid.*

[27]For a good general description of the economic and political situation in Maryland in this period, see Philip A. Crowl, *Maryland during and after the Revolution: A Political and Economic Study* (Baltimore, 1943), especially chapter 4, "The Struggle for Paper Money and Debtor Relief, 1785-1787," pp. 83-110.

[28]See note 4 above.

[29]Horatio Sharpe to Dr. Upton Scott, May 1, 1786, #130, Ridout Pap.

[30]The white population of Annapolis probably reached a peak before 1790 which it did not equal again until after 1820. The tax list of 1783 gives the white and slave

Table 4-5 *Population of Annapolis, 1783-1830*

Category	1783	1790	1800	1810	1820	1830
White	831	[1380]	1293	1294	1363	1587
Slave	449	(670)	646	558	505	578
Free Black	?	[120]	273	333	392	458
Total	1280	[2170]	2212	2185	2260	2623

Sources: Figures in brackets are based on the rate of decline for the whole county between 1790 and 1800, projected backward from the 1800 census for Annapolis. Data for 1800, 1810, 1820, and 1830 are from the original census schedules for those years for Annapolis, in the National Archives, Washington, D.C.

Custom house records make it possible to say fairly precisely that in 1793 the town ceased even the pretense of being a center of international trade. Between 1783 and 1785, Annapolis's share of the total duties paid there and at Baltimore rose from 6.4 percent to 18 percent, but, by 1791, it had dropped to .01 percent. After 1793, the collection of duties in Annapolis declined dramatically. Between 1790 and 1792, receipts averaged $2,471.43; between 1793 and 1796, they averaged $105.78.[31] In 1793, John Davidson resigned as collector of the port. Alexander Hamilton expressed regret at losing Davidson, but could not offer more salary and attributed the decline in commission revenue to the "restriction of Commerce," which he had no doubt would be permanent.[32] In the same year, the leading tavern keeper in town found that he could lease his business only on condition that the seat of government would not be moved to Baltimore, in which event the lease was to become void.[33] Owners of other property had difficulty in leasing, while those who did lease often were unable to collect or were forced to reduce rents. One merchant agreed to buy

populations of Annapolis Hundred. No evidence of free blacks could be found for that date, and, as most manumissions came after that date, there probably were none. Between 1800 and 1810, the number of males between 16 and 26 declined from 173 to 134, while the total white population remained stable, suggesting that younger sons were leaving the town.

[31] The percentages are based upon Naval Office Accounts in the Scharf Collection, Maryland Historical Society, Baltimore, Md. (hereafter cited as Scharf Col.), and a paper called "State of Duties 1785" in the Pforzheimer Collection, Hall of Records, Annapolis, Md. The duties received by the Annapolis collectors after adoption of the constitution are recorded in "Accounts Current, Annapolis. . .," in Record Group 36, National Archives, Washington, D.C. The receipts as presented in the reports of Alexander Hamilton give a slightly different picture, but, between 1791 and 1792, the percentage of the total trade from Annapolis and Baltimore derived solely from Annapolis slipped from 1 percent to .2 percent. *The Papers of Alexander Hamilton* (New York, 1961-), 13:38-39, and 15:482-83.

[32] Alexander Hamilton to John Davidson, March 13, 1793, Record Group 56, Microfilm #178, roll 36, frame 124, National Archives, Washington, D.C.

[33] Anne Arundel County Deeds, N. H. 7, p. 534, Hall of Records, Annapolis, Md.

waterfront property in 1787 and then refused to complete the contract in the 1790s because the value of property had depreciated. If the "city of Annapolis had flourished in commerce as was expected," the agreement would have been fair, the merchant argued, but as this was no longer the case, he pleaded with the court to nullify the contract, and the court agreed.[34]

By 1789, undoubtedly most people sensed that an era of business expansion had ended. In August of that year, a storekeeper in town wrote to a friend in Philadelphia:

I have no news to give you from this place, everything being at a stand. I in my store don't receive more than from two to three dollars per day. Annapolis is diminishing fast, no expectation of Congress there, presently we shall have houses at our own price. Citizens leaving it every day! I had this in contemplation but the enormous sum due me since my commencement in business has prevented me doing myself that pleasure £445 due in 9 mo[nths]s and can not receive one Shilling, . . .[35]

ECONOMIC DECLINE
AND THE COMMUNITY OF 1783

In an age of exceptional geographical mobility, the tenacity of those who were identifiable residents of Annapolis in 1783 is remarkable. Almost two thirds chose to remain in town until the end of their careers, in spite of constricting opportunity and a narrowing of wealth expectations (see table 4-6). Only 19 percent definitely moved, although probably another 16.2 percent for whom no information is available also can be counted among the migrants. As might be expected, those who had the most to lose or the most to gain found it easiest to leave. Of the seventy-five who moved, twenty-three (31 percent) had occupations of an average taxable wealth of over £300, while twenty-five (33 percent) had an average taxable wealth of under £100.

In terms of how it affected opportunity for the rest of the community, the departure of the wealthy had consequences far greater than numbers would suggest. Although only thirteen out of forty-four of those in the average wealth category of over £500 left, their move was symbolic of fundamental changes taking place in the patterns of

[34]Chancery Papers, Hall of Records, Annapolis, Md. (hereafter cited as Chan. Pap.), 5798.
[35]David Geddes to John White, August 21, 1789, Executive Papers, Box G, Hall of Records, Annapolis, Md. (hereafter cited as Exec. Pap.).

Table 4-6 *Geographical Mobility and
Insolvency among 1783 Residents of Annapolis*

Wealth/Occupation	Moved		Remained		Unknown
	Solvent	Insolvent	Solvent	Insolvent	
Above £500					
Gentleman-planter	5		8		
Merchant	3	1	18	1	
Lawyer	4		4		
£400 to £500					
Printer			2		
Carpenter			3	1	1
Watchmaker			3		1
Doctor	1		2		
£300 to £400					
Baker			2		
Cabinetmaker			2		
Storekeeper	1	1	8	3	
Blacksmith	1		1		
Surveyor			1		
Tavern, inn, and boardinghouse keeper	6		15	2	
£200 to £300					
Blockmaker			1		
Butcher			2		
Tailor	1		2	2	
Silversmith	3				
Ship captain and mariner	5	1	8		3
£100 to £200					
Barber			1	2	1
Widows and spinsters			15	1	2
Scrivener and clerk	3		7	2	
Tanner			1		
Shoemaker	2	1	4	1	1
Coachmaker			2		1
Shipcarpenter			1		
Under £100					
Painter-glazer			1		
Pumpmaker			1		
Staymaker			1		
(Unknown)			5	1	21
Laborer	1				4
Ferrykeeper			1		
Minister	1				
Bricklayer				1	
Wheelwright				1	
Total	37	4	122	18	35
Percent of sample	17.13	1.85	56.48	8.33	16.20
	Moved: 18.98		Remained: 64.81		

Source: See chapter 4, note 3.

where social events were held and where wealth was displayed. During the 1790s, Baltimore fast displaced Annapolis as the center of capital and gracious living. Old planter wealth vied with new mercantile fortunes for luxury goods and townhouses in Baltimore in a manner familiar to Annapolitans who remembered the decade before the Revolution. Some clung to the old ways and were reluctant to relinquish their Annapolis homes. Charles Carroll did not stop living in Annapolis until the 1820s. In the meantime, he solved the problem of maintaining social responsibilities by building a townhouse in Baltimore, and dividing his time among the two cities and his plantation.[36]

Although the Duc de la Rochefoucault-Liancourt greatly exaggerated the extent of the population decline (see table 4-5), in 1797 he correctly pointed to the migration of wealth to Baltimore and the visible remains of Annapolis's once great hopes for continued growth.

Annapolis . . . since the Revolution retains the name of the metropolis of the state and continues to be the seat of Government, but Baltimore has drawn all commerce from it. The Capitalists go and reside at Baltimore . . . the Population of the Town diminishes every year. There is a church large enough to contain three times the number of inhabitants . . . At the time it was built [1786] there was no suspicion of the present depopulation of the city which does not contain more than 2000 inhabitants.[37]

The decline in commerce and the removal of the wealthy to Baltimore least affected those who held government posts or who were in government-related professions. Of the eight lawyers on the tax list, only Samuel Chase is known to have left because he felt his clientele was not large enough. In January of 1786, John Ridout wrote that Chase

---

[36]Ellen Hart Smith, *Charles Carroll of Carrollton* (Cambridge, 1942), p. 299. The wealthy began leaving after 1786, but probably not before. John Ridout had no qualms about being able to rent his elegant townhouses until 1786 when there was a move on the part of "a pretty strong party . . . to remove the seat of Government to Baltimore." The threat of removal gave Ridout a feeling of "uneasiness on account of my houses in this place and makes me regret that I ever built them." January 28, 1786, #128, Ridout Pap.

In 1782, Annapolis was still very much the city of wealth and the social center of the state. In August of that year, Baron Ludwig Von Closen visited the town and observed that "the wealthiest personages in the State . . . have preferred to reside in Annapolis; hence the city contains a charming society and some very pretty women, very well bred, rather well dressed, and fond of entertainment." Evelyn M. Acomb, translator and editor, *The Revolutionary Journal of Baron Ludwig Von Closen, 1780–1783* (Chapel Hill, 1958), p. 220.

[37]Duc de la Rochefoucault-Liancourt, *Travels Through the United States of North America in the Years, 1795, 1796, 1797* (London, 1800), 3:259, 579.

has determined to remove with his family to Baltimore, . . . persuaded that he can make much more money by his profession in that place than he can here, and living as he does with so large a family to support, it is absolutely necessary he should by some means or other get a great deal.[38]

If lawyers moved they did so for reasons of political advancement or to retire. Gabriel Duvall quit a lucrative practice in Annapolis for an executive appointment in Washington as comptroller of the Treasury. William Paca gave up his practice to return to his Eastern Shore plantation after serving a term as governor.

Scriveners and clerks who came from prominent families and filled prestigious posts such as county clerk or clerk of the council were usually not touched by the changes in the economy of the town. Once appointed to a post they stayed; Nicholas Harwood recorded Anne Arundel County deeds for twenty-five years. To some, a clerkship in the town continued to offer status and fortune. John Callahan, the tailor's son, rose to commissioner of the land office, acquired the title of "Esquire," and died a wealthy man by the standards of his neighbors. Others moved in search of better jobs. Three found the new city of Washington a place where their talents were in demand. For example, John Knapp worked in the office of the comptroller of the Treasury until his death in 1820. Even among clerks, however, adversity was felt. Two became insolvent, although for what reasons the existing records do not say. In the case of Joshua Dorsey it may have been speculation in confiscated property. In 1783, he was clerk of the office of confiscated estates. There is no evidence of when George Rankin failed. He had been clerk of the general court and at times wrote for the executive council, but he was dead by 1788, leaving no property and a wife who was forced to declare herself insolvent.

Ship captains and mariners were also among the least affected by Annapolis's decline. Nine, or 53 percent, left town, probably for employment in Baltimore or Georgetown. Only one, Nicholas Valliant, became insolvent. Even if ship captains left the sea, a number were able to change occupations with obvious ease. The Middleton brothers, William, Gilbert, and Joseph, began their careers as mariners and shipcarpenters. Gilbert took over his father's inn and hired out boats with himself as pilot. By 1790, he had moved to Baltimore, where he opened a boardinghouse. Joseph and William served on the barges during part of the war and shipped goods on their own boats for the remainder. By 1787, Joseph had given up the

---

[38] John Ridout to Horatio Sharpe, January 28, 1786, #128, Ridout Pap.

Church Circle, *ca.* 1794. Photocopy by M. E. Warren, Annapolis.

sea for farming. By 1800, William had done the same, and had become such a model farmer that the noted Maryland agronomist,
John Beale Bordley, praised him highly.[39] William's estate demonstrated that he adapted well to his new occupation. Even after
$5,000 worth of debts had been paid, his heirs received $3,131.90.[40]

In contrast to government and maritime occupations, job opportunity in the building trades suffered severely from the failure of the
wealthy to invest in new townhouses after the Revolution. There was
little in the way of private construction in Annapolis after the war
until the first decades of the nineteenth century. For a time, be-

[39]William B. Marye, "Place Names of Baltimore and Harford Counties," *Maryland
Historical Magazine* 53 (1958), 56–58.
[40]Chan. Pap. 88.

tween 1785 and 1793, public funds provided some work. A church and college were built, a market house was raised, and the state house was renovated and capped with a new dome. The church, built between 1786 and 1788, cost £4,976. The market house cost £550 and was completed between 1785 and 1790. The state house and St. John's College, both finished by 1793, probably did not require much more than £11,000.[41] At most, £16,346 (an annual average of £1,816) was expended on public construction in Annapolis during the nine-year period. In contrast, over three times that amount (£5,737 per annum) was spent on private townhouses in the ten years before the war, not to mention the cost of the state house, built between 1771 and 1774.[42] When most public projects all but ceased after 1794, the situation became even worse for people in the building trades and it remained that way for at least two decades.[43] Only if some other employment, preferably government, was available were those in the building trades able to accumulate wealth after 1783. For example, William Tuck, the sole painter and glazer in town in 1783, worked on the Brice House in the 1760s and probably on other townhouses as well. By the 1780s, he had saved enough to establish himself in business as an ordinary keeper, and became tax collector and sheriff for Annapolis, posts he held for a number of years. When Tuck died in 1815, he had personal property alone worth $1,500, approximately seven times his total assessed wealth of thirty-two years before.

Other craftsmen and those who provided services for the wealthy also were adversely affected by economic decline. Barbers floundered with the absence of the rich. Of the four in Annapolis in 1783, William Logan became insolvent in 1788, followed by James Reed in 1791. One was geographically mobile. One appears in the probate

---

[41]For the church see the *Maryland Gazette*, March 23, 1786, and Chan. Pap. 2942. For the market house see Brice Account Book. £3,500 was allocated for St. John's, but by 1789 only £1,500 had been collected. *Maryland Gazette*, July 6, 1786 and February 19, 1789. The state house cost "approximately the same as . . . the original" according to Morris Radoff, *Buildings of the State of Maryland at Annapolis* (Annapolis, 1954), p. 94. The "original" cost £7,500 sterling from 1771 to 1777, *ibid.*, p. 82, but as the source Dr. Radoff cites is the Indendant's ledger, which was kept in currency, I have used £7,500 currency in this calculation. That there was little evidence of any major private construction is clear from Papenfuse and McWilliams, "Appendix F." A singular exception was an imposing three-story edifice erected on the dock by the baker Frederick Grammar, which was completed sometime around 1791. See Papenfuse and McWilliams, "Appendix F," Parcel 35, Section V. Employing the formula explained in chapter 1, note 35, Grammar's building probably cost £2,230 currency to construct.

[42]See chapter 1 and note 41 above.

[43]A jail was built in Annapolis between 1794 and 1800 for c. £1,500. See Radoff, *Buildings*, pp. 29–40, and *Maryland Gazette*, February 27, 1794, and January 30, 1800.

"Bladen's Folly," St. John's College in the 1850s. Detail from a Sachse print, Maryland Hall of Records, Gift Collection. Photocopy by M. E. Warren, Annapolis.

records. The other two died in such poverty as to escape the notice of the register of wills. Insolvency for Logan was the end of what began as a promising career. Before the Revolution, he built a wharf and probably was about to enter trade. During the war, he made the mistake of leasing the wharf to the navy and the ships destroyed it. In addition, the government paid him in depreciated currency for both rent and repairs, and he never recovered the full

State House in the 1850s. Detail from a Sachse print, Maryland Hall of Records, Gift Collection. Photocopy by M. E. Warren, Annapolis.

value of his losses. In the end, he was reduced to hawking patent medicines and scraping together a living as best he could.

Tailors had difficulties. Of the four tailors and one seamstress on the 1783 tax list, two of the tailors became insolvent, and one died without leaving any personal estate. The future for a shoemaker or cordwainer in Annapolis in the 1790s was equally dim. Two of those resident in 1783 were able to reestablish themselves in new occupations: William Maw became a planter and Jonathan Willshire had the dubious distinction of leaving shoemaking for the life of a chimney sweep. Three, including Maw, left town for a new start elsewhere. The remainder stayed behind and died with little or no property.

After the war, few cabinetmakers appeared in Annapolis. Chisholm married well and retired to the splendor of his wife's estate. The demands for Shaw's work continued, but his income rested to a great extent on government contracts. He made hay scales for the city, repaired the fire engines, and finished the public necessary, more commonly known as the "temple." When he died in 1829 at the age of eighty-four, it was rightfully said that he had lived a full life. It might have been added that he had made the most of opportunity in the years since emigrating from Scotland, but that he was the last of his occupation to be so successful in Annapolis.

Silversmiths and engravers fared better in Annapolis before 1783 than after. All three who were in town in 1783 sought opportunity elsewhere. Thomas Sparrow went to Washington. When Baltimore became the place to have townhouses, both John Chalmers and Charles Hogg followed their clientele, although only Chalmers achieved rank and status. Hogg disappears from the records. Watchmakers, in contrast to silversmiths, remained in spite of the loss of wealthy patronage, probably because they had always been diversified. William Whetcroft involved himself in a variety of business ventures in the 1770s and 1780s, but fell on hard times by his death in 1799 because of overextension in trade. The others did better in spite of a limited market for clocks, and supplemented their incomes as retailers or ordinary keepers.

Of the people classified as tavern, inn, or boardinghouse keepers, only two failed. Six left town. Services for the traveler could be turned to a profit in the early 1780s by those who remained in business, but after 1790 even the most prosperous ordinary keepers were not able to cope with a shrinking number of patrons. When George Mann wanted to retire in 1793, he had great difficulty in leasing his inn because of the concern over the future of the town. After his death in 1795, the rapid turnover in those who owned or leased his business further emphasized the innkeeper's plight.

The prospects confronting those women who kept boardinghouses were not much better. It took Mrs. Howard almost thirteen years to collect on the bills left by some Tory patrons just prior to the Revolution.[44] Business improved with the arrival of the Continental Congress

---

[44]See Mary Howard's accounts against the confiscated estates of Daniel Dulany of Daniel, Daniel Dulany of Walter, Lloyd Dulany, and Governor Eden, Scharf Col.

in the fall of 1783, but declined drastically when Congress left in the spring. In June of 1784, Robert Moale wrote from one boardinghouse in Annapolis:

We have but a thin House since the Departure of Congress and I expect a much thinner as A Weisenthall and ? have some notions of spending the summer in Baltimore so that J.M. D and ML will compose the family, a great change from 16 or Seventeen and fear it will be the means of breaking up the Boarding house.[45]

Still, there continued to be a limited demand for boardinghouses after 1784. When St. John's College was founded in 1785, some women, such as the widow of the merchant James Tootell, took in students for a monthly fee.

Although everyone in Annapolis was affected to some degree by the halt in economic growth, the greatest impact was on those with greatest expectations: merchants and storekeepers. Merchants entering business during and after the war were not as numerous and did not flourish to the degree that their predecessors did. Temporarily, they were able to capitalize on demobilization. Merchants were in a particularly advantageous position to speculate in government certificates issued to soldiers in compensation for the times they had been paid in practically worthless depreciated currency. Between 1781 and 1791, certificates in the amount of £294,661 specie were issued to Maryland soldiers who could not afford to wait for them to mature and were forced to sell them to merchants at an average rate of one-seventh of their value. A memorandum on speculation written by General Smallwood some time around 1783 demonstrates the extent to which Annapolis merchants took advantage of the soldiers. John Randall, Joseph Dowson, James Mackubin, and James Tootell, along with the clockmaker-merchant William Whetcroft and the storekeeper Joseph Clarke, held £2,097 worth of the £2,476 of certificates Smallwood listed. The certificates had cost them only £167 in specie, £14 in the new Maryland currency, and £120 in goods, a total of £301.[46]

The opportunity for such speculation was curtailed greatly after 1783 by the efforts of people like Smallwood to get a fairer rate of exchange for the soldiers. In addition, the optimism of merchants in the immediate postwar years was further eroded by a market that became glutted with goods and the growing lack of wealthy customers. In 1783, a letter advising a government clerk to become a

---

[45]Robert Moale to Walter Stone, June 17, 1784, Stone Papers, Library of Congress, Washington, D.C. (hereafter cited as Stone Pap.).
[46]"Smallwood's Essay on Speculation," Exec. Pap.

storekeeper contained a note of urgency. If the clerk were to take the advice he should do it quickly and get "fixed before the cloud of Murchants foreign and domestic arrive. . . ."[47] During the same year, a former proprietary officeholder, John Ridout, was casting about for something to enable him to live more agreeably to his "inclinations" and the "desire" of his family.[48] He decided to import goods as a wholesaler. The adventure was a disaster from the beginning. No one would buy the merchandise. Fortunately for him, he was able to thrust the burden of responsibility onto the London tradesman who consigned the goods originally and onto the storekeeper who contracted to sell the goods at retail in Annapolis. The accounts were still being settled ten years later, and everyone, including Ridout, suffered.

The worst failure was Thomas Rutland. He went bankrupt in 1785, owing over £20,000 sterling to his British creditors. John Petty, one of the creditors, came to Annapolis in an attempt to recoup his losses. For five years he kept store in the town while opening other retail outlets on both the eastern and western shores of the bay. Finding it hopeless, he gathered all his remaining stock at Baltimore, chartered a boat to Georgia, and opened two stores there.[49] Another who overextended himself in Annapolis and attempted to start anew elsewhere was Joseph Dowson. He moved to Cambridge in Dorchester County, but found his debts insurmountable and died there insolvent in 1790.

Merchants, both those who began their careers in the prewar years and those who started after the war, had difficult times in the declining years of the late 1780s. Four left town. One of the Davidson brothers moved to Georgetown, a rapidly growing center for the export of tobacco, while his brother remained in Annapolis. Thomas B. Hodgkin moved to Baltimore and James Ringgold moved to Chestertown on the Eastern Shore. Of those who stayed in Annapolis, all but Thomas Rutland managed to survive the setbacks, although the prospects of enormous profits were greatly diminished. Opportunities open to merchants speculating in tobacco and acting as commission merchants on goods were especially curtailed. To survive in the same line of business, the merchant became principally a storekeeper, purchasing his goods wholesale, probably from Baltimore merchants. Gone were the days of direct import-export trade with London firms. A merchant with enough capital might continue to

---

[47]M. J. Stone to Walter Stone, May 3, 1783, Stone Pap.
[48]June 22, 1783, #114, Ridout Pap.
[49]Chan. Pap. 3943 and 5884.

prosper as a storekeeper, as did James Mackubin, who retired in relative affluence in 1806, or as a banker, like John Muir or Charles Wallace, but a role as business entrepreneur engaged in direct foreign trade was no longer possible.

Those who did not engage directly in foreign trade and were storekeepers in 1783 also suffered from the belief that Annapolis would flourish as a commercial center. Four out of a total of thirteen storekeepers had gone bankrupt by 1788, chiefly because they had overstocked and could not sell their goods in time to meet the payments due the wholesaler. One who went bankrupt left town to recoup his losses. William Biggs took up farming in Kent County and died eleven years after insolvency with an inventory worth almost twice as much as his taxable property in 1783, and land worth an additional £300. The other three storekeepers who became insolvent remained in Annapolis. William Hyde, with backing from his father, possibly could have recouped his fortune, but he died in 1786 of wounds incurred during the war. Thomas Graham managed to open an ordinary in the 1790s, but he died with an estate worth £1.9.6. John Wilmot came from a family that had been chronic failures for four generations. His grandfather and father were insolvent, and when he went bankrupt, his wife regained the family lands only to have their son lose them again.

The majority of storekeepers were not as fortunate as Biggs was in adversity, but neither were they such failures as Wilmot. Most made more modest adjustments to the economic situation of the late 1780s and early 1790s. Only Joseph Clarke left town to become an architect in the new city of Washington, and he was replaced by his brother, Stephen, who kept a store in Annapolis for the rest of his life. The remaining eight (62 percent of the sample) continued as storekeepers in Annapolis until retirement or their deaths.

Baltimore was only forty miles away and jobs were plentiful there, but faced with a sudden change in the town's fortunes, two thirds of the adults who were resident in Annapolis in 1783 chose to remain. Why they did so is difficult to gauge. Perhaps they found the adjustment to living in the less hectic world of a small market town compatible with their perception of how life ought to be. Family ties, inability to accept declining opportunity until it was too late in their careers, a willingness to accept less, perhaps even sheer laziness, may also have been factors in their decision to stay. Whatever the reasons, those who remained accepted their fate with a calmness that became, if not proverbial, at least a subject of humor.

In the years after 1783, merchants and storekeepers, along with most other Annapolitans, accommodated themselves to the decline in the town's fortunes with varying degrees of success. Those who, in 1783, were overly optimistic about the future of the community often overextended themselves and were unable to recoup their losses. Others adjusted by catering to the needs of a less affluent community and the surrounding region, investing any excess capital in basically agrarian enterprises rather than international trade. As the merchants and storekeepers died or retired, they were replaced by storekeepers who undoubtedly never held any of the vision of a prosperous future that had once been a part of the normal expectations of the generation of 1783. The following chapters will examine the pattern of adjustment made by the merchants of 1783 and use the experience of Wallace, Johnson and Muir to demonstrate the basic changes in the nature of mercantile activity and opportunity that took place not only in Annapolis but throughout the upper Chesapeake in the first quarter century of the new republic.

CHAPTER 5

THE END OF AN ERA: THE DISINTEGRATION OF WALLACE, JOHNSON AND MUIR, 1783–1790

T HE commercial history of Annapolis in the post-Revolutionary era is closely tied to that of its most important mercantile house, Wallace, Johnson and Muir. In the spring of 1783, at the age of fifty-six, when many men might think of retirement, Charles Wallace was eager to plunge deeper into trade.[1] His success in the tobacco consignment business before the war with Joshua Johnson and John Davidson, and the profits he, Johnson, and Muir had made as commission merchants during the war encouraged Wallace to think in grand terms about his role in the reorganization of the Maryland tobacco trade at the advent of peace. The total, if temporary, absence of British capital from the consignment tobacco trade appeared to provide an opening too attractive to ignore and, with Johnson's credit well established in London, Wallace, Johnson and Muir could also strive to supply on commission a goods-hungry retail merchant clientele.

The consignment trade had languished under the uncertain conditions imposed by wartime disruption of shipping. What tobacco was exported went as the collective purchase of merchants and adventurers who sought to spread their capital among as many ships as possible to reduce the risk of loss. The import trade was conducted in the same manner, and Wallace, Johnson and Muir's role had been as a broker for customers scattered from New England to North Carolina, securing goods through their partner in France, and charging a commission on each of the small shipments he made.[2] When peace came, Wallace, Johnson and Muir turned their energies to reestablishing themselves in the consignment tobacco trade and to serving customers in an area that geographically was more concentrated, although they did not abandon the ties with merchants in Baltimore

---

[1]Wallace was born in Annapolis in April 1727, the son of John and Anne Wallace. St. Anne's Parish Register, 1:79, Hall of Records, Annapolis, Md. Although the evidence as to when merchants usually retired is difficult to obtain for this period, the median age for death for the merchant community of 1783 was 61, while the mean was 60. Sample: 26 careers.

[2]See appendix A.

and Philadelphia that had been established during the war and, indeed, borrowed money to finance their postwar enterprises from a Philadelphia bank in which they also held shares.[3]

THE POSTWAR EXPANSION
OF WALLACE, JOHNSON AND MUIR, 1783–1786

Returning to the consignment trade and loading Wallace, Johnson and Muir's ships meant reopening stores that had been discontinued during the war and pushing into areas that had once been dominated by British merchants. Partnerships were formed with local American retail merchants: with Boteler and Bowie at Nottingham and with Tyler and Duckett at Queen Anne.[4] In addition, a new store was established at St. Leonard's Creek in Calvert County, an area where their old competitor, the London merchant William Molleson, had been active before the war. After 1783, Molleson and other British merchants were frantically occupied with collecting their prewar debts, by no means a safe or fruitful occupation until 1787, when the courts began to honor their claims and lawyers felt safe in prosecuting their debtors.[5]

William Cooke, a Loyalist who returned to Maryland to practice law after the Revolution, later explained the circumstances that prevailed between 1783 and 1787.

When the Peace took place in 1783 an especial law passed in this state which excluded me from practicing as an attorney or council until 1787—the Law then expired, and I first appeared in Court in May term that year. What pass'd before I do not certainly know, but I have heard and believe that, such prejudice and popular clamour where [sic] excited against some Lawyers who had brought suits for British Creditors, and in one Instance such violence was used that the attornees were compelled to discontinue . . . the suits that were brought and were deterred from bringing others very generally.[6]

---

[3] Wallace, Johnson and Muir Letter Book, 1784–1785, MS 1180, Maryland Historical Society, Baltimore, Md. (hereafter cited as WJM 4), pp. 300, 356.

[4] For Tyler & Duckett see WJM 4:146, 249, 292, 300. For Boteler, Bowie, & Co. see *ibid.*, pp. 109, 158, 219–20, 264–65, 297. For the location of places mentioned in this chapter, see the map by Dennis Griffith (Philadelphia, 1794), p. 171.

[5] For a discussion of Molleson's efforts at debt collection see Chancery Papers 8513, Hall of Records, Annapolis, Md. (hereafter cited as Chan. Pap.), and Great Britain, Public Record Office, Audit Office Papers (hereafter cited as PRO, AO), 13/40, 13/32.

[6] Great Britain, Public Record Office, Treasury Papers, September 15, 1805 (hereafter cited as PRO, T), 79/34.

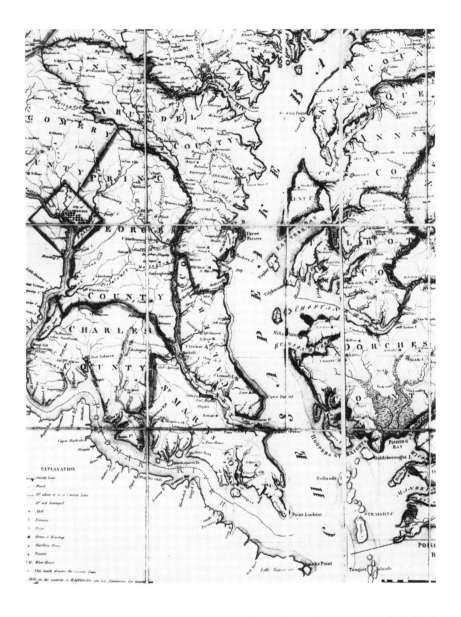

Detail from a Map of Maryland by Dennis Griffith, 1794. Maryland Hall of Records, Map Collection. Photocopy by M. E. Warren, Annapolis.

When Cooke began to practice law in 1787, only one suit brought by a British creditor was pending before the courts. Cooke was "immediately retained by all the British Creditors, and brought a great number of suits."[7] When a case Cooke prosecuted in 1787, Russell vs. Harwood, established the validity of a proof of security on a debt (such as a man's bond) and henceforth caused the enforcement of all such debts so secured, the collection of prewar debts and debts in general became more regular.[8]

In the meantime, between 1783 and 1787 local American merchants such as Joseph Wilkenson and John Turner, with the aid of Wallace, Johnson and Muir, drew off the old customers of British merchants such as Molleson. The agreement among Wallace, Johnson and Muir, Wilkenson, and Turner was tripartite, and probably is similar to those entered into with Boteler and Bowie and Tyler and Duckett. Wallace, Johnson and Muir agreed to import from their "house in London and to furnish goods wares and Merchandizes to be vended and disposed of in Calvert County"—one third part at the risk and benefit of Wilkenson, one third part at the risk and benefit of Turner, and the remaining one third part at the risk and benefit of Wallace, Johnson and Muir.[9]

To encourage planters to ship their tobacco, in addition to offering credit at their stores, Wallace, Johnson and Muir employed riding captains or "tobacco beggars" to go about the countryside soliciting business. All were captains who spent part of their employment commanding the vessels of the firm and the rest convincing the planters they could be trusted with tobacco. Captain Thomas worked the Eastern Shore; Captains Magruder, Bradstreet, and Maynard worked the Western Shore. The usual practice was for a riding captain to bring a ship out from London early in the spring and spend the summer loading it and subsequent ships until the fall, when he returned to London with one of the last cargoes for the year.[10] As part of the payment for his work he was allotted the privilege of the proceeds of any lumber he carried on the trip to London. At one point, when Johnson neglected Magruder by not providing him with a ship, Wallace and Muir explained how it hindered their operations:

Perhaps when you are told that we lost another hundred Hhds Tobacco by your not chartering a Ship for Magruder to succeed the Nantes & that we have

[7]*Ibid.*
[8]*Ibid.*
[9]Chan. Pap. 5594.
[10]On riding captains see WJM 4:64, 69, 221, and Joshua Johnson's Letter Book, 1785–1788, Library of Congress, Washington, D.C. (hereafter cited as WJM 5), pp. 49, 280, 286.

been obliged to pay Capt. H. Magruder 150 guineas in lieu of privileges, you will wish you had looked out better. . . . We believe in no Trade but the London trade, Capts are allowed the privileges of the Lumber, & therefore we cannot conceive you could not have Chartered a Ship, securing the Lumber to Magruder, which would have saved us the payment of the . . . 150 guineas. A number of Ships will be wanted next year, they must be chartered ones, for it will never do to purchase as many as will be requisite, & you must Labour to secure the Lumber to our Riding Capts, or at least a part of it, otherwise you will fix such Expenses on your business as it will not bear. Magruder is to be back here by the first of April, he is a most Valuable man, he is a Genteel fellow & knows the people well, & is respected by them & puts them in practice, he is by far the best Tobo beggar within our knowledge, & is close attached to our Interest, he must have a ship Next year.[11]

Although Johnson was not always as pleased with the performance of the riding captains as Wallace and Muir were, because of the expense they incurred, he did acknowledge a debt to Captain Bradstreet. When Bradstreet died, Johnson was quick to note his special talent and the need to replace him with someone equally as competent.

Indeed we shall miss Poor Bradstreet, but if you change Johns from the Nonesuch to the Potomack, he must be about the old quarter where Brad-street used to go & where few other Capts ever visited, the upland Tobacco is not only the best but the people are more wealthy & can do without advances or drawing, better than those can below, but be he whom you may that you make your Captain there, he ought to be eternally on Horseback & driving about.[12]

To oversee their operations on each of the major rivers and streams feeding into the Chesapeake and to load their ships at the principal landings, Wallace, Johnson and Muir depended upon partners such as Boteler and Bowie and upon salaried employees (see table 5-1). The latter usually were planters prominent in the area who also main-tained stores supplied by Wallace, Johnson and Muir. Col. William Deakins in Georgetown, William D. Beall in Bladensburg (both in Prince George's County), and Joseph Wilkenson in Huntingtown, Calvert County, used their local influence to persuade neighbors to ship on consignment.[13] When influence alone failed, Wallace, Johnson and Muir would provide their agents with cash to pay consigning planters an advance on what the tobacco would bring in the London market. The planter got the advantage of seeking the highest possible price for his tobacco through consignment while having some cash in

[11]WJM 4:164.
[12]WJM 5:60.
[13]For Deakins, Beall, and Wilkenson as retail cargo customers, see table 5-4.

Table 5-1 The Agents of Wallace, Johnson and Muir, 1785

Location	River	Name
Maryland, Western Shore		
Upper Marlboro	Patuxent	Thomas Sprigg Bowie
		Thomas Clarke
Queen Anne	Patuxent	Tyler & Duckett
Pig Point	Patuxent	Thomas Tillard
Nottingham	Patuxent	Boteler & Bowie
Hunting Town	Patuxent	Joseph Wilkenson
Georgetown	Potomac	Col. William Deakins
Bladensburgh	Potomac	William Dent Beall
Port Tobacco	Potomac	John Hoskins Stone
Elk Ridge	Patapsco	John Sterrett
Maryland, Eastern Shore		
Talbot Court House (Easton)	Tred Haven Creek	Nichols, Kerr & Chamberlain
Virginia		
Urbanna	Rappahanock	Overton Cosby
	York	Matthew Anderson

Source: Wallace, Johnson and Muir Letter Book, 1784–1785, MS 1180, Maryland Historical Society, Baltimore, Md., pp. 215–16, and a name index in the same.

hand to satisfy his immediate needs. The agents, in addition to promoting consignment among the planters, also assumed the responsibility for finding shipping. Col. William Deakins, with the blessing of Wallace, Johnson and Muir, chartered the ship *Hazard* in 1785 to carry their tobacco from Georgetown. Only after the ship had been loaded did Wallace, Johnson and Muir bother to inquire about the terms of the charter.[14] They relied heavily upon the good faith of their agents to do their jobs well and, in the main, they were not disappointed.

To carry their exports to market, Wallace, Johnson and Muir both owned and chartered ships. In 1785, they employed fifteen, five of which were their own (see table 5-2). The ships would dock at one or two landings during the course of their stay in Maryland, which usually lasted about three months. Small craft would bring the cargo to the ship's side from as far away as the Eastern Shore. Samuel Handy at Snow Hill in Worcester County regularly sent his tobacco to Wallace, Johnson and Muir's ships at Lower Marlboro and Nottingham.[15] Ideally, as one ship was loaded another would take its place, so that in the course of a year about three ships could be filled at landings designated by the firm.[16]

[14]WJM 4:211.

[15]*Ibid.*, pp. 129–30.

[16]See table 5-2. Wallace, Johnson and Muir actually maintained seven ships on the Potomac and four on the Patuxent but at different landings.

Table 5-2 Wallace, Johnson and Muir's Shipping and Exports, 1785

Name	Captain	Ownership	Cargo Tobacco (hhd)	Cargo Wheat (bus)	Naval District Where Entered And Cleared	Naval District Where Loaded	Arrived	Departed	Destination	Arrived
Maryland										
Hazard	New	Chartered in Maryland	?		North Potomac?	Potomac	c. 1/85	c. 3/85	London	?
Iris	Cole	Chartered in Maryland		9,602	Georgetown	Georgetown	c. 1/85	c. 3/85	Lisbon	?
Liberty	Reed	WJM		11,600	Georgetown	Georgetown	1/8/85	3/3/85	Falmouth	?
Potomack	Bradstreet	WJM	450		Georgetown	Georgetown	4/23/85	6/29/85	London	8/10/85
Alice & Jane		Chartered in Maryland	495		North Potomac?	Potomac	c. 5/85	c. 8/85	London	9/85
Mary	Bodfield	Chartered in London	400		North Potomac	Potomac	c. 8/85	c. 11/85	London	12/85
Nantes	Wallace	WJM and Weems	c. 300		Annapolis	Potomac	c. 8/85	?	London	?
Nantes	Maynard	WJM and Weems	c. 314		Annapolis	Patuxent	1/26/85	5/1/85	London	?
Chance	Stafford	Chartered in London	250		Patuxent	Patuxent	3/85	c. 6/1/85	London	?
Sally	Hunter	Chartered in Maryland	486		Annapolis	Patuxent	5/24/85	7/13/85	London	8/31/85
Commerce	Hill	Chartered in Maryland	305		Baltimore	Patuxent	c. 7/85	8/17/85	London	9/24/85
Nonesuch	Johns	WJM	379		Baltimore	Patapsco	c. 8/85	11/16/85	London	2/11/86
Antelope	Traverse	Chartered	198		Baltimore	?	8/85	9/21/85	London	11/85
Maryland total			3577+	21,202						
Virginia										
Liberty (renamed York)	Outram	WJM	260		York River	York River	12/84	5/85	London	?
Independence	Wells	Chartered in Maryland	600		York River	York River	4/85	6/27/85	London	9/28/85
Washington		Chartered?	?		York River	York River	c.5/25/85	?	London	12/11/85

Source: Wallace, Johnson and Muir Letter Book, 1784–1785, MS 1180, Maryland Historical Society, Baltimore, Md. and Joshua Johnson's Letter Book, 1785–1788, Library of Congress, Washington, D.C.

In addition to the promotion of the consignment trade in Maryland, Wallace, Johnson and Muir expanded their operations into Virginia at York River, where they followed the same pattern of organization established up the bay. They invested in the firm of William Anderson and Company, purchasing ten shares worth between £800 and £1,000 sterling.[17] They employed William Cosby as their agent and the Outrams, father and son, as their riding captains.[18] Because of the distance and their relative unfamiliarity with the planters on that river, they also frequently sent down their "principal clerk," Francis Charlton, who had been trained in Nantes by Joshua Johnson and who came to help in the American side of the business in the spring of 1783, shortly before Johnson left for London.[19] The Virginia venture was not Wallace, Johnson and Muir's main interest and, for a variety of reasons, they became increasingly disillusioned with trying to conduct the consignment business there. They did not know the planters well, riding captains proved incompetent, and the market for Virginia tobacco was not as good as that for Maryland. At most, they kept three ships in the Virginia trade, which Johnson felt was more than adequate considering the return, and concentrated the bulk of their shipping in Maryland.[20]

The amount of tobacco produced in Maryland of a quality that made consignment profitable was limited by the amount of good tobacco soil available and by the market for other cash crops, such as wheat, that encouraged diversification and the transfer of planter capital from tobcco into grain. Before the war, the quality tobacco trade as represented by the quantity shipped to London, was approximately 70 percent of the tobacco crop, or approximately 22,000 hogsheads in 1774.[21] How much of the tobacco grown in 1785 was of a quality that would make consignment profitable is difficult to ascertain, but it probably was not more than 16,306 hogsheads. In that year, the total amount of all grades of tobacco produced in Maryland was approximately 19,300 hogsheads (see table 5–3).[22] From Baltimore

[17]WJM 5:105, 107.

[18]WJM 4:69, 163.

[19]Wallace, Johnson and Muir Letter Book, 1781–1783, Manuscript Division, New York Public Library, New York, N.Y. (hereafter cited as WJM 3), p. 778; and WJM 4:122, 127.

[20]WJM 5:24.

[21]In 1774 Maryland exported 31,295 hogsheads, of which approximately 21,907 were destined for sale in London. See Charles A. Barker, *The Background of the Revolution in Maryland* (New Haven, 1940), p. 381, for tobacco exports, and chapter 2, note 1, for the analysis of quality versus inferior grade exports before the Revolution.

[22]Table 5–3 is drawn from Naval Office returns scattered in several collections at the Hall of Records, Annapolis, Md., the Maryland Historical Society, Baltimore, Md., and in the *American State Papers, Class IV, Commerce and Navigation*, Vols. 1 and 2

Table 5-3 Tobacco Exports from the
Several Naval Districts of Maryland, 1768-1792   (in hhds)

Naval Office	1768	1770	1772	1774	1784	1785
North Potomac						[1,355]
Patuxent						2,233
Annapolis						[1,100]
Baltimore					15,958	11,712
Georgetown						2,911
Total	24,080	23,705	33,495	31,295		[19,291]
Total quality				[21,907]		[16,306]

Naval Office	1786	1787	1788	1790	1791	1792
North Potomac	1,492			[1,817]		
Patuxent	1,275	3,345	3,541	5,705		
Annapolis	1,293			[1,816]		
Baltimore	9,971			8,184		
Georgetown	5,152		7,072	7,135		
Total	19,812			24,657	25,019	28,292
Total quality	[16,806]			[16,473]		

Source: See chapter 5, notes 21 and 22. Brackets denote estimates.

2,985 hogsheads were exported to France, implying that at least that quantity could be classified as inferior tobacco. Shipping returns for the other naval districts in 1785 have not survived except in summary form, as presented in table 5-3, and it is not possible to determine how many more hogsheads went directly from them to France, but even on the basis of 16,306 hogsheads of quality tobacco exported in 1785, Wallace, Johnson and Muir did well in light of the performance of their predecessor firm, Wallace, Davidson, and Johnson. In their brief careers as consignment merchants before the war, Wallace, Davidson, and Johnson exported an average of 2,186 hogsheads a year, or about 10 percent of Maryland's quality tobacco exports to

(Washington, D.C., 1831-1862). At the Hall of Records I used the Naval Office returns and the uncatalogued manifests and returns for Baltimore and Georgetown. In the latter I discovered a summary account for 1786 which is the source for that column on this table. At the Maryland Historical Society the bulk of the Naval Officer Accounts I used are now in MS 1668, which is a separate collection taken from MS 1999, the Scharf Papers. Numbers in brackets are estimates. The data for 1790 are taken from "A List of the Number of hhds of Tobacco inspected and shipped from the several Warehouses in the State of Maryland, 1790," MS 1999, Scharf Collection, Maryland Historical Society, Baltimore, Md. (hereafter cited as Scharf Col.), and from the Archives of Maryland, Vol. 72 (Baltimore, 1972), 157-58, 160, 205 (hereafter cited as Archives). The 1784 and 1785 returns for Baltimore were compiled from "Baltimore Entrances and Clearances, 1782-1824," Record Group 36, National Archives, Washington, D.C. (hereafter cited as RG 36, NARS).

London in 1774.[23] After the war, Wallace, Johnson and Muir did much better. By 1785, they were exporting at least 3,577 hogsheads (see table 5-2), or 21.9 percent of the market, assuming it was 16,306 hogsheads.

In addition to tobacco, Wallace, Johnson and Muir also entered the wheat trade. The encouragement given by the supply needs of the war effort to diversification and the cultivation of grain crops was sustained after the Revolution by a demand for wheat in Europe that continued unabated until at least 1786. Wheat was grown principally on lands least suitable to the production of quality tobacco, which meant that on the Western Shore wheat replaced poorer grades of tobacco most extensively along the Potomac. In addition, many wheat farmers in Frederick County found access to the Potomac easier than the Patapsco and were encouraged to ship their crops out of Georgetown instead of Baltimore. How much wheat was moved by craft to be milled in Baltimore is not known, but the export wheat trade from the Potomac was dominated by Wallace, Johnson and Muir who, through their agent, Col. William Deakins, loaded their ships at Georgetown. The wheat Deakins obtained was consigned in part by him as partial payment for goods imported for him by Wallace, Johnson and Muir. A portion of each cargo also belonged outright to Wallace, Johnson and Muir, who purchased it or received it in payment of debts. The rest was a form of remittance by cargo customers who had ordered goods on credit from Johnson in London. For instance, in 1785, of the 11,600 bushels exported on the *Liberty*, cargo customers in Frederick Town, Georgetown, Alexandria, and Annapolis shipped 11,000, and Wallace, Johnson and Muir only 600. The wheat went at the risk of the shipper to wherever Johnson judged was the best market. In the case of the *Liberty*, its ultimate destination was France, after touching at Falmouth for orders; but it might have been Lisbon or even Liverpool if a short domestic crop opened the port to foreign grain.[24]

Wallace, Johnson and Muir kept only two vessels employed in the export of wheat. During 1785 and 1786, they carried about 40,000 bushels from Georgetown, approximately half of all the wheat exported from Maryland exclusive of Baltimore, and twice as much as shipped from Baltimore proper.[25] Undoubtedly Wallace, Johnson and

[23]See table 2-8*b*.

[24]See WJM 4:260 for a list of customers who shipped wheat with Wallace, Johnson and Muir. Sim & Smith were in Frederick, Maryland. For a comment on rising bread and wheat prices in France see WJM 5:25. For additional references to Wallace, Johnson and Muir's wheat trade see WJM 4:5, 59, 68, 83, 220, 259, and WJM 5:1, 5.

[25]In 1786, Wallace, Johnson and Muir exported approximately 22,000 bushels of wheat on the *Liberty* and the *Essex & Samuel*. According to a summary of "Exports at

Muir would have been happy to have shipped more if their cargo customers had been willing to oblige, but circumstances dictated otherwise.

The "cargo customers," as Wallace, Johnson and Muir called them, were the new American merchants who tried to take the place of the Scots in the poorer tobacco-growing regions, or were merchants of the type that had been supplied by British middlemen prior to the war. In the first years of their partnership, Wallace, Davidson, and Johnson had been reluctant to engage in the cargo trade, and had not been at all satisfied with their first major excursion into the business, which they made in 1772, on behalf of Richard Tilghman Earle and Company on the Eastern Shore.[26] In 1774, they again trusted a couple of firms, but by the time of the Revolution, the total amount of goods shipped to cargo customers did not exceed £4,000 sterling.[27] After the war, Wallace, Johnson and Muir operated on the assumption that the demand for goods would not be met by British tradesmen, who would be frightened of advancing credit to merchants they did not know, and that the firm would be free to play the role of middleman, little doubting that remittances from customers would be forthcoming on time.[28]

To secure cargo customers meant coping with competition from Baltimore. As John Ridout explained in a letter to former Governor Sharpe, written in June 1783, most goods were first imported into Baltimore, where they were sold wholesale to merchants throughout the state.[29] But Wallace, Johnson and Muir were not deterred and soon had contracts with merchants on both the Eastern and Western shores (see table 5-4).[30] The agreements were often verbal and the terms usually were not recorded, but in the case of an Eastern Shore firm, John Voorhees and Company, of Georgetown, Kent County, a written contract survives. On December 16, 1783, Wallace and Muir agreed

---

the Several Districts within the State of Maryland in the year 1786," uncatalogued manifests for Georgetown and Baltimore, fifth deck, Hall of Records, Annapolis, Md., 41,991 bushels of wheat were exported, of which only 6,426 cleared from Baltimore.

[26]Wallace, Davidson, and Johnson Letter Book, Vol. 1, Hall of Records, Annapolis, Md. (hereafter cited as WDJ 1), pp. 121–22.

[27]See table 2-5.

[28]WJM 3:180. Johnson was not oblivious to the large amount of goods being readied for shipment to America in the spring of 1783. In March, he wrote to Captain William Graham of Philadelphia that "Everyone Seems mad about making shipments in goods for America all expecting to make their fortunes," *ibid.*, p. 756, but he felt the push could not last and that those with capital would prevail in the end.

[29]Ridout Papers, Gift Collection, D371, Hall of Records, Annapolis, Md. (hereafter cited as Ridout Pap.), No. 114.

[30]Nichols, Kerr & Chamberlain is the only customer on table 5-4 from the Eastern Shore. The rest were concentrated along the Potomac and Patuxent rivers, with a few like Hammond & Wells, Andrew Buchanan, John Sterrett, and the Ridleys from Baltimore. The only Annapolis customer noted is James MacKubin.

Table 5-4 Wallace, Johnson and Muir's
Known Cargo Customers and Their Debts, 1785-1786

(in £ sterling)

Name of Cargo Customer	Date of Account Current	Amount
Thomas Lee	10/17/85	2,259.17.11
William & Henry Lyles	10/17/85	2,284.05.04
Col. Charles Ridgely	10/17/85	1,279.06.01
Charles Ridgely of Jno.	10/17/85	172.04.01
John Fitzgerald	10/17/85	4,501.02.07
William Dent Beall	10/20/85	3,316.01.10
Samuel Davidson	10/20/85	4,592.15.07
Henry Hardy	10/20/85	1,580.04.10
O'Neill & Waring	10/20/85	2,879.13.10
John Hoskins Stone	10/20/85	6,757.12.07
Thomas, William, & Horatio Claggett	12/85	59.11.00
William Hammond	12/85	1,747.13.07
Hammond & Wells	12/85	337.05.05
Thomas Smith & Sons	12/85	2,002.07.10
Forbes & Turner	12/85	934.19.01
John Forbes	12/85	3,479.09.10
Robert Bowie	12/85	2,631.08.09
John Thomas Boucher	12/85	4,012.09.06
Andrew Buchanan	12/85	1,481.19.06
Sim & Smith	12/85	3,606.00.09
Beall & Lamar	1/86	115.16.10
William Murdock Beall	1/86	925.07.10
James Smith	1/86	2,375.14.00
Col. William Deakins, Jr.	1/86	6,762.15.09
John Sterrett	4/86	142.18.06
Alexander Ogg	7/86	301.13.07
Nichols, Kerr & Chamberlain	7/86	4,999.07.02
James MacKubin	7/86	2,141.10.01
Total		67,683.11.08

Source: Joshua Johnson's Letter Book, 1785-1788, Library of Congress, Washington, D.C., pp. 22, 23, 37, 41, 72, 99.

with James Pearce, Voorhees's partner, to supply goods from London for five percent plus the invoice cost of the goods, to be paid for in good bills of exchange twelve months from the date of invoice. Pearce was to pay 5 percent interest on all sums past due, and Wallace and Muir were to allow 5 percent interest on all sums remitted before the twelve months expired. Voorhees's first shipment arrived in July 1784, and within a year he had received £6,594.14 sterling in goods, on which he owed an additional £546.11.0 sterling in commission. Voorhees was but one of a great number of cargo customers.[31] Between

[31]Chan. Pap. 4174.

1785 and the summer of 1786, Wallace, Johnson and Muir extended £67,683.11.08 sterling worth of credit to twenty-eight known firms in Maryland and Virginia (see table 5-4), £20,043.25 more than the total sterling value of all the goods Wallace, Davidson and Johnson had shipped between 1771 and 1775.[32] By itself the debt of the known cargo customers in 1785 and 1786 was an enormous one for the firm to incur with their London tradesmen and, when the books were settled, proved to be only a portion of the total actually owed. If the cargo customers failed to honor their agreements in time, the consequences were likely to be severe.

Extending credit to cargo customers was, initially at least, a relatively painless means of expanding business, but in the consignment trade competition for the limited supply of quality tobacco was fierce. Purchase of tobacco in the country had always been a deterrent to planters contemplating consignment. Before the Revolution, Scottish merchants used long credit and cheap goods to enter a market and defeat their competitors; and London firms, such as John Buchanan and Son, directed their agents to purchase when consignments were not to be had.[33] After the Revolution, the inability of British merchants to collect debts until 1787 made them wary of venturing capital for purchases of tobacco. In their place, Baltimore merchants, and to a lesser extent merchants in other Maryland ports, such as Thomas Rutland of Annapolis, became the principal purchasers in the immediate postwar years. Baltimore merchants, such as Robert Gilmor, Oliver and Simm, and the Pattersons, shipped directly to Amsterdam and the Low Countries now that the British navigation acts were no longer applicable to the American export trade.[34]

Absolutely and proportionately, Baltimore's share of the total tobacco trade declined between 1784 and 1790 (see table 5-3). Mer-

[32]For Wallace, Davidson, and Johnson's shipments see table 2-5.

[33]For the efforts of Buchanan and Son see chapter 2. For a good indication of how the Scottish merchants used purchase to enter a market see the letter books of William Cuninghame & Co., Microfilm 52, Colonial Williamsburg Collection, Williamsburg, Va. For example, see the letter to Mr. Bennett Price of Fauquier, Virginia dated October 7, 1767. "By all manner of means endeavour to extend your sales before Marten Pickett opens store in the spring. . . . If a man be good it is not material although he cannot pay you any thing/next year by selling Goods to such men you no doubt encrease your debts but at the same time you will extend your influence and lay a sure foundation for a larger purchase hereafter and indeed there seems to be no doing any business of consequence without sinking a large sum." I am indebted to Gregory Stiverson of the research staff of Colonial Williamsburg for this reference.

[34]The manifests for Baltimore at the Hall of Records, Annapolis, Md., show that the three mentioned Baltimore firms were buying tobacco on the Patuxent and shipping it at their own risk to Amsterdam. For example, see the manifest for the *Christina*, July 1786, in which Robert Gilmor shipped 110 hogsheads of Patuxent and Elkridge tobacco to Amsterdam.

Table 5-5   Thomas Tillard's Tobacco Purchases, 1784–1785

(£ Currency)

Ship	Hhds (#)	Price Range (per cwt) (S/d)	Total Paid	Net Proceeds	Loss	Year
Nantes	4	15/– to 45/–	79.09.00	74.09.00	5.00.00	1784
Sally	26	20/– to 47/6	636.09.09	345.05.00	291.04.09	1784
Isabella	1	50/–	26.08.06	24.10.00	1.18.06	1784
Nantes	1	35/–	23.06.07	8.12.00	14.14.07	1785
Chance	1	40/8	19.00.00	13.12.00	5.08.00	1785
Sally	8	42/6 to 45/–	171.10.09	116.02.00	55.17.09	1785
Commerce	3	40/– to 45/–	64.15.04	43.16.00	20.19.04	1785
Antelope	9	35/– to 40/–	164.09.08	108.17.00	55.12.08	1785
Nantes	29	35/– to 42/6	395.11.10	270.04.00	125.07.10	1785
Total	73		1,584.05.11	1,005.10.00	578.15.11	

Source: Chancery Papers, Hall of Records, Annapolis, Md., 5231.

chants engaging in the purchase of quality tobacco for export directly to Holland were disillusioned when prices began to fall and they were forced to make public sale of their stock. By April 1786, Johnson was writing his partners that "Tobacco still remains dull & so it will continue I fear until after the Public Sales of the new American Merchants are over in Amsterdam . . . ."[35] During 1784 and 1785, anyone who purchased tobacco in Maryland at the prevailing country prices probably lost money.[36] Table 5-5 shows the tobacco Thomas Tillard at Pig Point purchased in those years and consigned to Wallace, Johnson and Muir, the prices he paid, and the net proceeds of the sale in London. On a total of seventy-three hogsheads, Tillard estimated he lost £578.15.11, an experience that was only confirmed by the plight of other adventurers such as Rutland.[37]

The Annapolis merchant, Thomas Rutland, used his extensive inherited estates as collateral for tobacco bought on credit and, in the process, lured two of Wallace, Johnson and Muir's most prominent customers, Charles Carroll and George Mason, into selling their crops in exchange for the promise of an exorbitant price. Rutland explained the nature of the debt in court when Carroll sought to gain possession of the land because Rutland had paid interest only once or twice, and never anything· on the principal. In 1783, unable to find cash to pay for goods he had imported but could not sell, Rutland found himself:

[35]WJM 5:67.

[36]*Ibid.*, p. 18, where Johnson notes that Baltimore merchants "will sink an imense deal of money" by their purchase. On this point see also Stuart Weems Bruchey, *Robert Oliver Merchant of Baltimore, 1783–1819* (Baltimore, 1956).

[37]Chan. Pap. 5231.

greatly distressed to procure a quantity of Tobacco to ship to the City of London and understanding that the complainant [Carroll] had some to dispose of, the defendant [Rutland] applied to him to purchase the same upon credit and after several meetings for that purpose the defendant purchased from the complainant . . . 100,000+ pounds of Tobacco at the rate or price of £2.5.0 current money per hundred weight and 4% for cask, which price this defendant was constrained from his necessities to give, although Tobacco of equal quality could have been then procured for ready money at the price of 40/-current money per hundred weight.[38]

In spite of Rutland's plea for equity from the Chancery Court to save him from the loss of land three times the value of the debt, Carroll got the property.[39] Other creditors were not as fortunate. In his quest for tobacco, Rutland was not reluctant to pledge the same piece of property twice as security for tobacco bought on time. Unknowingly, George Mason held a second mortgage on the same piece of property as Carroll for tobacco he had sold Rutland but, as Carroll had a prior claim, Mason did not recover more than a fraction of his money from Rutland's bankrupt estate.[40]

Against merchants like Rutland, some consignment merchants turned to purchasing in self-defense. John Muir was wary of buying, and in public noted that "it ought not to be pursued by them who push the consignment business," but, by the summer of 1785, he had changed his mind.[41] As competition for tobacco reached its seasonal peak, Wallace and Muir were pressed to load all their ships, but especially the *Mary* and the *Antelope*.[42] At that point, they welcomed investors who were willing to entrust funds for a purchase to their partners at Queen Anne, Tyler and Duckett, consoling themselves with the thought that at least the tobacco would be sent on consignment to Johnson, at the risk of the investors.[43]

But if the purchase of tobacco by others made it difficult for Wallace, Johnson and Muir to fill their ships at the peak of the season, by their own estimation their major competitors before 1786 were the consignment merchants themselves, some of whom made deep inroads into their market. Wallace, Johnson and Muir's major competitors in the consignment trade were American merchants, such as Uriah Forrest, Benjamin Stoddert, Benjamin Contee, and

[38]Chancery Records, Hall of Records, Annapolis, Md. (hereafter cited as Chan. Rec.), 16:314 ff.
[39]*Ibid.*
[40]Chan. Pap. 3464.
[41]WJM 4:273.
[42]WJM 5:21.
[43]WJM 4:314.

Thomas Contee. They came from planter backgrounds or had been minor merchants before 1776.[44] They made money during the Revolution which they sought to invest in the postwar tobacco trade. They organized themselves as Wallace, Johnson and Muir did, opening stores, employing riding captains, and establishing a partner in London. Uriah Forrest left for London in June 1783 with his first cargo. A sketch of his career and the purpose of his journey were indicated in a letter he carried with him.

The person to whose care this will be committed is Lieut. Col. Forest, a Native of St. Mary's or Cha[rles] Cty. When the War broke out he quitted the business of storekeeping and became an officer in the Maryland Troops. Having lost a leg in consequence of a wound he received at the Battle of German Town he was appointed to a lucrative office but quitting that soon afterwards became a trader and was pretty fortunate towards the end of the War. He has now loaded a ship with tobacco partly by purchase and partly with consignments and intends to proceed with it to London.[45]

The firm of Forrest and Stoddert made rapid progress in the consignment trade because of their ability to get their tobacco to a good market as fast as Wallace, Johnson and Muir could, and because of the closer attention they were able to pay to the needs of their consignment customers. Largely unhindered by the demands of cargo customers, they rapidly became Wallace, Johnson and Muir's major competitor.

London merchants also returned to the consignment trade. Christopher Court and Thomas Eden both tried to reestablish themselves, but with only moderate success. Apparently they made the most headway with planters, such as John Galloway, who had been their customers before the war, and who perhaps looked with some regret on the separation that had taken place between Britain and her former colonies.[46] A new London firm, Dedruzina and Company, did better than Eden or Court, but by September 1785, Johnson could write his partners that the major competitors were the Americans, Forrest and Stoddert and Contee and Company, with Dedruzina third.[47] In fact, Forrest and Stoddert did so well as to frighten John-

---

[44]For the Contee family, see Effie Gwynn Bowie, *Across the Years in Prince George's County* (Richmond, 1947).

[45]June 22, 1783, #114, Ridout Pap.

[46]Wallace, Johnson and Muir Letter Book, 1787–1788, Manuscript Division, New York Public Library, New York, N.Y. (hereafter cited as WJM 6), pp. 116, 119 where Joseph Galloway is suspected of spreading rumors about Wallace, Johnson and Muir's affairs. In 1771, John Galloway was supplied by the London merchant James Russell. See Samuel Galloway to James Russell, July 21, 1770, Galloway, Maxcy, Markoe Papers, Box 75c, Library of Congress, Washington, D.C.

[47]WJM 5:12.

son, who wrote in November 1785 that four of their ships had arrived and that "they will do great things & much more than I expected."[48]

Because a large percentage of the consignment trade was conducted on chartered ships, it is impossible to determine without the manifests whether or not any of Wallace, Johnson and Muir's competitors exported as much tobacco as they did.[49] From the Wallace, Johnson and Muir letter books the impression is that no one did, although Forrest and Stoddert came the closest. What is certain and is confirmed from extant manifests from Georgetown and Baltimore, is that Americans, among whom Wallace, Johnson and Muir were the most prominent, were able to maintain control over the bulk of the tobacco consignment business, at least until 1786, when the merchant community was confronted with a widespread economic crisis that affected not only the tobacco trade but the whole of American commerce as well. In June 1786, after Forrest had left London in a hurry without informing his creditors, Johnson summarized the situation of the remaining Americans engaged in the tobacco trade.

I find a smile on the countenance of many. They will naturally look on the step of Forrest an acquisition to their interest & represent it in the most heinous light. I hope that my countrymen may have too much good Sense to be duped by their report & continue to him & the House their favours & countenance, if they do not & that House & ours are overset, no other American will be able to make an Establishment in this Country.[50]

A GROWING CRISIS IN THE ECONOMY AND IN THE AFFAIRS OF WALLACE, JOHNSON AND MUIR, 1783–1786

As soon as it became clear that peace was at hand, Americans began to engage in a spending spree of magnificent proportions. In more sober times and upon reflection, it seemed as if people became obsessed with purchasing "carriages, furniture, silks, lace, jewelry, gegaws and frippery."[51] In the fall of 1783, as the Continental Congress was assembling in Annapolis for ratification of the peace

---

[48]WJM 5:27.

[49]Ownership as given on the Naval Office returns is not sufficient to gauge the success of consignment merchants. Much of their shipping was chartered and it may or may not have been entered with the Naval Office in their name. Consignment merchants also sent tobacco on the ships of others as partial cargoes and these too would be hidden from the Naval Office returns.

[50]WJM 5:91.

[51]*Maryland Journal* (Baltimore), article by "Mentor," August 3, 1786, cited by Louis Maganzin in "Economic Depression in Maryland and Virginia, 1783–1787" (Ph.D. dissertation, Georgetown University, 1967), p. 28.

treaty, the Maryland Senate admonished (with little effect) "improvident citizens who too frequently indulge in the pernicious practice of involving themselves in debt . . . to purchase luxuries . . . to the utter ruin of their families."[52]

Such extravagance was not a new phenomenon. After the French and Indian War, the colonists, especially those in the South, also had overindulged themselves in the importation of goods.[53] In 1768, Christopher Lowndes, a merchant of Bladensburg, could sense the guilt some of his customers felt and had advertised a full column of goods prefaced with the comment: "Ostentation (as yet) not being in universal Disesteem, the subscriber takes this method of acquainting those it may concern that he has on hand the following articles."[54] By 1769, when merchants found they still could not clear their inventories as fast as they would like, they had joined in a nonimportation agreement in the hopes of preventing any further influx.

We the Subscribers, his Majesty's loyal and dutiful Subjects, the Merchants, Traders, Freeholders, Mechanics, and other inhabitants of the Province of *Maryland*, seriously considering the present State and Condition of the Province, and being sensible, that there is a Necessity to agree upon such measures, as may tend to discourage and as much as may be, prevent the use of foreign Luxuries and Superfluities in the consumption of which, we have heretofore too much indulged ourselves, to the great Detriment of our private fortunes, and, in some Instances, to the Ruin of Families; and, to this end, to practice ourselves, and as much as possible, to promote countenance and encourage in others, a Habit of Temperance, Frugality, Economy and Industry; and considering also that measures of this Nature are more particularly necessary at this time as the Parliament of Great Britain by imposing taxes upon many articles imported . . . has left it less in our power, than in Time past, to purchase and pay for the manufactures of the Mother Country.[55]

Undoubtedly the same sentiments were felt by merchants beginning in 1783 and 1784, but a nonimportation agreement was not a viable option by that time. The import trade was no longer concentrated in the hands of a few merchants who were enabled by their control over exports to decide arbitrarily not to import goods. After

[52]*Ibid.*, citing Maryland, *Votes and Proceedings of the Senate*, November Session (Annapolis, 1783), p. 16.

[53]The Boston Nonimportation Agreement of August 1, 1768, *The Annual Register*, 1768, p. 235, makes it clear that in New England the problems of trade were not seen as stemming from overindulgence in luxury goods, a stark contrast from how Marylanders viewed things in 1769. See note 55 below.

[54]*Maryland Gazette*, March 17, 1768.

[55]*Maryland Gazette*, June 29, 1769.

1783, the "cloud of Murchants foreign and domestic," as one planter characterized them, descended upon the state armed with goods supplied by trusting London tradesmen.[56] Established merchants mistakenly thought that the first arrivals would be the last, and that importations would settle back to a manageable level but, as Wallace and Muir were to point out some years later, expectations were disappointed:

J[oshua] J[ohnson] removed to London in May 1783 and was so handsomely received by the Tradesmen, as to incline him to think the House had a fair opportunity to do a great deal of business. Mr. J[ohnson] and we took up the opinion that the first adventures to America would soon be sickened and abandon their schemes—and very unhappily we all calculated that the British Tradesmen had suffered so much by former dealings with America, that they would credit only solid men—this error in Judgment has brought infinite distress on us all; for credit was given to almost all who asked for it.[57]

Planters, and other Americans like Thomas Rutland, who had little in the way of capital, used their persuasiveness and, in Rutland's case, misrepresentation of his landed wealth, to convince tradesmen such as the wine merchants, Petty and Yates, to advance them goods on the promise of speedy remittances.[58] Some tradesmen even took on themselves the responsibility of sending out cargoes to people whom they thought could sell them. Morgan Gould, a London hatter, was convinced he could make money by sending a cargo of goods to Annapolis addressed to John Ridout's care. Ridout explained the circumstances and his difficulties in marketing the goods in a letter written in February 1785 to a friend of Gould's.

With the letter you were pleased to write to me the 10th inst. I received one by the last post from your friend Mr. Gould of much the same import with that he addresst to yourself and which really gives me very great uneasiness, though 'tis some satisfaction to me to know that with whatever ill consequences his shipping goods last year to this country may be attended I have nothing to blame myself with on that score as I never invited or advised him to become an adventurer, and have since his goods came to my hands endeavoured to dispose of them for his advantage to the best of my

[56]M. J. Stone to Walter Stone, May 3, 1783, Stone Papers, Library of Congress, Washington, D.C.

[57]Chan. Pap. 2893.

[58]For Rutland's dealing with Petty and Yates see Chan. Pap. 3943. In *Lowndes London Directory, for the Year 1786* . . . (London, 1786), p. 199, Yates & Petty are listed as Wine Merchants, 6 Crown Court, Old Broad Street.

judgment. If you have resided any time in North America you [know] that immense quantities of goods beyond the people's wants or at least beyond their ability to pay for have been imported since last winter; the first parcel that Mr. Gould to whom I am a stranger thought fit to consign to me though shipped some months before did not come to my hands till April last [1784], at which time a great number of vessels arrived together full freighted with British manufacturers. Those which I then received amounted to £854.18.9 including the package. I immediately offered them for sale and in the course of a few months sold a considerable part of them at a moderate advance to persons who I apprehended were likely to dispose of them by retail in a reasonable time and who would I believed pay for them as soon as it should be in their power or as soon as they could convert them into cash. They did accordingly from time to time make some payments though far short of what both they and I hoped they would have been able to make. . . .[59]

On the advice of Gould's friend, Ridout returned the goods he had not sold and spent the next eight years trying to collect from storekeepers who had great difficulty in paying for what they had agreed to buy. It is quite probable that other tradesmen felt as Gould did, and his letter to Ridout of September 15, 1792, undoubtedly speaks for many.

God only knows what I have experienced by this fatal adventure! . . . . Your readiness in adjusting my affairs . . . is a matter I hope will meet your wishes and may contribute to relieve me in part from the difficulties that have been too long the lot of your unfortunate humble Morgan Gould.[60]

The public was unable to pay for the influx of goods because of heavy taxes and the acute shortage of coin. The taxes were imposed to pay the costs of the war effort. They became a burden on the planters in 1782, with the implementation of effective enforcement of the tax laws by Daniel of St. Thomas Jenifer, who had been given extensive powers by the general assembly to improve the finances of the state.[61] Planters were hard pressed to pay the taxes and one, Samuel Chew, wrote a complaining letter to Jenifer from his plantation on Herring Bay in Anne Arundel County.

[59]John Ridout to William Blackburn, February 24, 1785, #214, Ridout Pap.

[60]Morgan Gould to John Ridout, September 15, 1792, #380, Ridout Pap.

[61]No one has written about the important role Daniel of St. Thomas Jenifer played in the finances of the state after his appointment as intendant in 1782. For the act appointing Jenifer see chapter 27, "An Act to Appoint an Intendant of the Revenue, and All Public Monies," *Laws of Maryland Made and Passed at a Session of Assembly, Begun and Held at the City of Annapolis, on Monday the fifth of November in the year of our Lord one thousand seven hundred and eighty-one* (Annapolis, 1782).

How Times are altered since we used to meet often at our City [Annapolis] but so it is. Things are turn'd upside down & when they will come Right again, God knows. If there be not some Alteration in affairs soon I do not know what will be ye Consequence. These heavy Taxes; we shall never be able to Comply with, unless ye Country Produce will fetch a better Price. Is it not something Extraordinary that our assembly should suffer ye Tax to be collected before we were able to get our grain out off ye straw. . . . I am heartly tier'd of ye Times & have paid enough for them, but I am afraid ye worst is not come Tho Bad enough at present for I am shure this Tax cant be Collected for never was money so scarce. . . . Every gentleman who has a large Country Estate of Lands & Negros must Sink for they will not pay ye assessment. I am shure it will not be long before I shall be obliged to sell mine. . . . As I am pushed so hard at this time by ye Sherriff I am at a loss to comply with his demand. . . . Therefore I taken ye liberty to beg it as a favour of ye to lend me as much as will answer ye Purpose which is about 120£ & an Order on ye Sherriff will answer. . . .[62]

With the large importation of goods that took place after 1783, the plight of planters and merchants worsened. In April 1784, John Ridout wrote to former Governor Sharpe in England:

You will easily conceive how much distress't the people are in general & how unable to pay the heavy taxes imposed on them in consequence of the late unhappy ruinous War. Money was never more scarce, much having been exported last year by the foreign adventurers who poured in Quantities of goods from Europe on the Cessation of Hostilities & got for them most of the specie that was then in Circulation.[63]

Adventurers were not the only ones taking specie out of Maryland. Until the summer of 1786, Wallace and Muir shipped as much as they could obtain. In December of 1784, for instance, they sent Johnson 12,588 Spanish dollars worth about £5,400 sterling.[64] They did it in an effort to pay off their London debts, which had grown to momentous proportions, largely on account of credit extended by the firm to cargo customers. The cargo customers were experiencing great difficulty in collecting their debts. Planters had little hesitation in taking goods on open account, and merchants were more than eager to give the credit in hopes of being able to collect the debt, if not immediately, at least after the standard grace period of one year allowed by law had elapsed. What the cargo customers found to their dismay, however, was that planters could not pay and, when refused

[62]Herring Bay, Sepr. ye 5th, 1782, Scharf Col.
[63]John Ridout to Horatio Sharpe, April 17, 1784, #119, Ridout Pap.
[64]WJM IV, pp. 60, 77, 87. One dollar was worth £.42976 sterling.

further credit, they simply changed stores, leaving the merchant to find ways to bring the debtor to account in courts reluctant to act.

By 1785, Wallace, Johnson and Muir's London debt totaled about £240,000 sterling, five times the total volume of business conducted by Wallace, Davidson, and Johnson in a similar three-year period before the war and equal to 77 percent of the total British-held debt in Maryland in 1776. Only £15,000 of the amount owed was on account of the Annapolis partnership; the remainder had been incurred for the cargo customers.[65] £225,000 was a sizable sum and probably made Wallace, Johnson and Muir the largest importer of wholesale goods operating in the Chesapeake. In 1773, when the three largest London tobacco firms were faced with a grave financial crisis, none was as deeply in debt. John Buchanan and Son owed £70,000, Christopher Court £52,000, and James Russell £50,000.[66] After the Revolution, William and Robert Molleson, Wallace, Davidson and Johnson's major remaining competitor in the consignment trade in 1774, claimed they were owed over £84,000 in prewar debts by people in Maryland and Virginia, but their bonded debt was only £35,490, and probably about one third of what they claimed can be discounted as the percentage of bad debts with which any merchant had to contend when a business was brought to an abrupt halt. Although what the Mollesons owed their London creditors is not known, it is safe to assume that it probably did not amount to more than two thirds of £84,000, or £56,000 at most.[67]

The amount owed Wallace, Johnson and Muir by cargo customers put a severe strain on the partnership, but even before the extent of the debt was known in Annapolis, tensions were mounting. Managing an extensive consignment business, while at the same time attempting to meet the needs of cargo customers, ended in neither planter nor merchant receiving the attention he desired. Tobacco was left behind, goods were not shipped or, when they were, did not please.[68] In March 1785, for instance, John Muir described the reaction to one cargo sent to Annapolis.

[65]WJM 5:6, gives the state of the debt in 1785. See table 2–5 for the volume of business, 1771–1774, which was £47,637.17.0 sterling. For the total British-held debt as of 1776 with interest to 1790, see Great Britain, Public Record Office 30/80/343. For this calculation, an annual interest on the debt of 6 percent was assumed, making the principal £310,590 sterling.

[66]James Anderson to James Hollyday, June 25, 1773, date of receipt, Corner Collection, Maryland Historical Society, Baltimore, Md., cited by Ronald Hoffman, "Economics, Politics and Revolution in Maryland" (Ph.D. dissertation, University of Wisconsin, 1969), chapter 5, note 59.

[67]PRO, AO 13/40.

[68]See especially WJM 4:312, concerning Johnson's neglect of business.

I have had such a salute from the Annapolis Gentlemen who had goods by the *Chance* that I heartily wish all their muggs and Piss Potts had been Six Months ago at the Bottom of the ocean should it ever happen again (but I hope such a Circumstance will not Occur) that you have such a parcel of truck in your warehouse nine months for heavens sake give them to the Devil rather than send them here. . . .[69]

Wallace and Muir admitted that theirs had become an "unwieldy business."[70] Johnson wrote to one of his former clerks that the demands of his work were so great that "it brings fast on me the old Man & I warn you as a real & Sincere Friend to avoid ever entering into such extensive matters."[71] Each side of the Atlantic blamed the other for the crisis, but in later years, when the quarrel was adjudicated by three disinterested arbitrators, the evidence convinced them to side with Wallace and Muir.[72] Johnson had allowed the business to get out of control. He had failed to hire enough clerks, to maintain his correspondence, and to keep his books up to date. In April 1785, Charles Carroll of Carrollton, Wallace, Johnson and Muir's wealthiest and most influential customer, called John Muir to his Annapolis townhouse, where Muir found the study "strewed" with Johnson's letters. Carroll quickly let it be known that he was not happy with Johnson's recent performance.

. . . he had pleasure in acknowledging that formerly he had found Mr. Johnson very exact and more than commonly punctual in his correspondence but that latterly he had too plainly perceived a very great falling off for which he could not account he proceeded to say that though he much wishes to have his own matters regulated & conducted in future with exactness and Attention, yet he should not have given me the trouble to have called on him if he had not found in the Course of his late Journeys, that complaints against our House were very common and general every where and that as he had a Value and regard for the members of our firm, he thought it an act of friendship to give me information thereof. . . . You well know Mr. C's close attachment to his own Interest, you know also his value, he must be attended to most pointedly and pleased. Our rivals are making every Exertion to draw him off, but a little pains will keep him.[73]

By the time Muir wrote about his encounter with Carroll, Wallace had already left for London to try and straighten out the firm's af-

[69]WJM 4:25.
[70]WJM 4:209.
[71]WJM 5:11.
[72]Chan. Pap. 2893.
[73]WJM 4:312.

fairs.[74] To the public, Wallace and Muir said Wallace's journey was intended to establish contacts directly with the manufacturing towns in order that better, less expensive goods could be obtained for their customers; but to their agents they told the truth. Johnson needed to be reprimanded in person. Letters had not worked and now the senior partner was going to London to set matters in the right "line."[75] In June 1785, when Wallace returned, looking "better and younger for his trip," the Annapolis partners thought things would improve, but they soon found they were mistaken.[76] Johnson had not told Wallace how deeply indebted the cargo customers were, probably because he was still in the process of shipping the spring goods when Wallace left and had not settled the books. The balance sheet was at last dispatched in August 1785 and, when it arrived, Wallace and Muir were horrified at the extent to which Johnson had allowed the debt of the cargo customers to mount. As they explained in 1798 when the partnership's affairs were being settled by arbitration:

It was the contract with every Cargo connection, that payment was to be made within Twelve months, and that a third Cargo would not be shipped unless the first was paid for, or at least greatly cut down—JJ perfectly understood this—his letters to Cargo friends expressed his determination not to ship a third Cargo to any one who had not remitted handsomely on account of the first—His letter of 1st December 1784 to W&M declares his resolution to ship to none in the spring 1785, but those who had remitted well—JJ will contend that W&M urged him to ship goods—true they did; but never did they press him to ship *largely* to any one who had got *very deep* and had been *very backward in making remittances*—when W&M saw the balance sheet of 31st May 1785, they trembled to find how deep many persons had got— that their debt very far exceeded what they had contracted for—W&M early saw and represented to JJ, the impolicy and danger of stoping abruptly with such persons; they stated to JJ that it was necessary for the advantage of the House, that he should continue to ship to such persons small quantities of goods, say, a half, a third or a fourth of what they might order, to keep the wheel agoing, that we might get clear of them without loss—JJ always contended that it was *impossible to curtail orders*—he shipped *largely* to many who in prudence ought to have had *very few*, and in many instances even more than they ordered—and in many cases stopped shipping at once—JJ's breaking abruptly with heavy debtors, put some of these debts to great hazard—and we were under the necessity, in several cases to purchase small quantities of goods for such persons, to enable them to go on with their

[74]*Ibid.*, p. 126.
[75]*Ibid.*
[76]Ridout Pap., #124.

operations, and to enable them to pay their debt to WJ&M. Our conduct in such cases, we will take the liberty to say, was judicious, for we thereby saved much money for WJ&M which otherwise would have been lost—Mr. Johnson means to contend that he saved the House of WJ&M, assuredly he was not labouring for that object, or for the advantage of the concern, when he filled the minds of his advisers, the principal creditors of the House, with suspicions that W&M were not acting right & not doing their duty—it appears to us, that JJ forgot, that suspicions once rooted, are not easily eradicated—it appeared to us, that he had forgot that it was his duty and his interest too, to support and defend the character of his partners—it seemed to us that JJ imagined he might make a bed of thorns for his partners, and yet repose himself on roses—[77]

The struggle to pay the London debt put Wallace and Muir to a severe test. The drainage of specie from the country, high taxes, and a market glutted with goods made debt collection arduous. By January 1786, John Ridout was writing that "Mr. Wallace seems to be very uneasy at the extreme difficulty of collecting debts here and at the impracticability of making adequate remittances to his partner in London."[78] Wallace told Ridout that they were sending all the specie they could and advised him how it was done in case he cared to ship any, but there simply was little to be had.[79] By the summer of 1786, the shortage of a medium of exchange was most acute and people still were not able to pay their taxes, as the collector of Baltimore County explained in a letter to Samuel Chase, a leader of a movement to force the state to issue paper money.

I have taken the liberty of laying before you the distress'd Situation of the Inhabitants of this County, hoping that your influence with his Excellency and the Honourable Council may operate so far, as to get an indulgence to the Collectors until sometime after Harvest, and thereby in a great measure alleviate the distresses of the people at large.

I have Acted as Collector of this County for six Successive years, and in that time have made as good Collections as perhaps any other in the State; to have my Bond put in suit at this Critical Juncture, when the most Strenuous exertions have been made by me to inforce the Collections, would answer no other purpose whatever, than to ruin those unfortunate people, who happen to be in arrears—Considerable Balances are due, which I find impossible to Collect from the people, I have seized their effects, and exposed them to public sale, but no person will purchase, or even bid except in Baltimore

[77]Chan. Pap. 2893.
[78]John Ridout to Horatio Sharpe, January 28, 1786, #128, Ridout Pap.
[79]*Ibid.*

Town, where the property sells at not more than one half its value—This misfortune arises from a Real (not an Imaginary) scarcity of Cash, which so generally and unhappily prevails throughout every part of the State.

I therefore most earnestly entreat you Sir, to State this matter and my perplexing Situation to his Excellency and the Honble. Council, confiding that their goodness, and humanity will prompt them to extend a further indulgence to the people, by which means a Number of worthy Citizens, with their families, will be preserved from inevitable ruin.

Be assured, Sir, that many of them at present, have not bread to eat, but what is purchased with difficulty, and on Credit; Added to this the gloomy prospect of loosing one third of their present Crops by the Worm, renders their Situation Truly deplorable. I am Confident no good man would wish to see his fellow Citizens devoted to ruin.[80]

The emission of paper money and laws for debtor relief seemed to be the only cures, although in the minds of creditors like Wallace and Muir, paper money raised the spectre of inflation which had been such a problem during the war.[81] Ridout ascribed the support the paper money measure had on the Western Shore to "powerful advocates . . . several of them leading men who have purchased of the state large quantities of confiscated property to be paid for in 1790 and want paper money to pay for it."[82] In addition to owning confiscated property, Samuel Chase was involved in a mercantile partnership during the war which, by 1786, was "indebted above £42,000 curt. Money," classing him among the debtors who would benefit most from a depreciated medium of exchange.[83] But whatever the motivations of the leaders of the paper money forces in Maryland, it seemed apparent that the general assembly would take positive action when it convened in the fall of 1786, as those delegates in favor on the Western Shore seemed likely to be joined by members from the Eastern Shore whose constituents were experiencing a general failure in the wheat crop.[84]

The fact that paper money was not issued in the fall of 1786 has always baffled historians of the period, but the reasons are quite simple.[85] In England the severe financial crisis (that Johnson, in No-

---

[80]William A. McLaughlin to Samuel Chase, July 8, 1786, Box 1, Pforzheimer Collection, Hall of Records, Annapolis, Md.

[81]WJM 5:78, 152.

[82]John Ridout to Horatio Sharpe, August 9, 1786, #132, Ridout Pap.

[83]Chan. Rec. 26:211-26. A fugitive item from this case that contains a breakdown of Chase's debts in the Perkins Library, Duke University, Durham, N.C. I am indebted to Professor Ronald Hoffman for loaning me a copy of the Duke University manuscript.

[84]Ridout Pap., #132.

[85]Philip A. Crowl, *Maryland during and after the Revolution: A Political and Economic Study* (Baltimore, 1943), chapter 4, pp. 83–110, describes the "Struggle for Paper Money and Debtor Relief," but lamely explains its resolution in terms of its being over-

vember 1785, argued was as bad as the time of the Fordyce Bank failure of 1773), which had been caused in part by the inability of American debtors to remit to their London creditors, was eased by the payment of three million pounds worth of dividends on government securities. The amount of money in circulation in Britain was greatly increased, and the hard-pressed London tradesmen were relieved. As Joshua Johnson explained in July 1786:

> The long succession of Easterly Winds has kept the shipping out from every quarter & of course the Tradesmen continue distressed, tho I do not find that there is a scarcity of Money, indeed the dividends paid in this month, has thrown three millions into Circulation which will prove a great easement & now if our shipping were to be coming in I should hope to see the distress removed in a very great measure. . . .[86]

With tradesmen more willing to extend credit and wait more patiently for debts overdue, American merchants were given more time to induce their own debtors to pay, relieving somewhat the necessity of pressing hard for cash payments for specie remittances to London. More important, however, was the increased circulation of a new medium of exchange in Maryland and to London, which emanated from Philadelphia.

Robert Morris's contract to supply the French tobacco monopoly provided him with a considerable credit balance in Europe and allowed his personal bills of exchange and notes to circulate freely in tobacco-growing areas. Morris notes and bills began to have an effect in Maryland in the summer of 1786, principally through efforts of merchants such as Wallace, Johnson and Muir, who borrowed Morris's bills on credit to send to London and who began to use their specie plus additional credit from Morris to purchase lower grades of tobacco on Morris's account. In August, Ridout noted Wallace, Johnson and Muir's change of plans, explaining why he was unable to ship specie to a creditor in England.

> . . . I intended to remit in specie by the first of Messrs. Wallace and Co.'s ships that might sail from Patuxent had not Mr. Wallace and his partner here when I lately [January] spoke to them on the subject told me that in conse-

---

shadowed by the question of the Constitution. Nowhere does he even mention Morris's notes and bills.

[86]WJM 5:97. See also WJM 4:157, where Johnson's description of the situation in London is retold by Wallace & Muir. "We shall say nothing in Addition only that credit in England is at least as much effected by the late failures as it was at the time of the famous Fordyce Stopped. . . ."

quence of letters from Mr. Johnson they had altogether dropped and abandoned the plan of remittance which they had mentioned to me last winter
and thought it more advisable to purchase at 77 1/2 percent advance some
bills from Mr. Morris of Philadelphia (one of the contractors for supplying the
farmers General of France with tobacco) tho payable at so long a sight as a
hundred days in order to make remittances to Mr. Johnson than to remit any
more specie and that they should not remit any this summer as what is now
remaining in circulation here consists mostly of half Joes and guineas shamefully clipt and cut. . . .[87]

The Morris purchase of the poorer grades of tobacco, while gradually bringing the price down (see table 5-6) because more and more
lower-grade tobacco was grown to meet the demand, released
money into the sector of the economy where it was needed most:
among the poorer planters, who were thus enabled to pay something on their accounts at the country store.[88] With money from their
least affluent customers, the country storekeepers were able to discharge in part their debt to such merchants as Wallace, Johnson and
Muir, from whom they bought goods wholesale. The Morris purchase
also meant that the poorer planters were less concerned about the
emission of paper money and debtor relief laws because they now
were able to begin meeting the demands of their creditors. By the
time the general assembly that had convened in April 1787 adjourned
in May, the demand for paper money and debtor relief had evapo-

[87]John Ridout to Horatio Sharpe, August 9, 1786, Ridout Pap., #132.

[88]Thomas Jefferson argued that the Morris monopoly with the French brought the
price of tobacco down, but for Johnson, the Morris monopoly kept the price of Maryland
tobacco up. WJM 5:228. William Graham Sumner, who was no friend to Morris's
paper money schemes, has a lengthy discussion of the French contract in which he
accepts Jefferson's argument that the price of Virginia tobacco was depressed by
Morris's contract but argues that Morris lost on the contract because of currency
manipulations that failed. William Graham Sumner, *The Financier and the Finances
of the American Revolution* (New York, 1970 [1891]), 2:169-74. Jefferson won the
right to have other American merchants import an additional 15,000 hhds into France
in 1786 and probably was instrumental in preventing a renewal of Morris's contract
in 1788. See WJM 5:87, and Jefferson's letter to the Governor of Maryland, Box 59,
Executive Papers, Hall of Records, Annapolis, Md. (hereafter cited as Exec. Pap.). The
evidence supports Johnson. Morris's contract kept the price of Virginia tobacco up at
a time when production was increasing rapidly. It is no wonder that the French
refused to renew when they could buy large quantities of Virginia tobacco in the
London market at a price considerably below that which they had to pay Morris and
those covered by the Jefferson agreement. By August 1787, the French refused to buy
any more under the terms of the Jefferson pact saying that the 15,000 quota had been
filled. WJM 5:198. In that same month there were several thousand hogsheads of
tobacco in the London market from Virginia and the ruling price was 3d sterling per
pound, 8/10 of a pence less than the French price to Morris. WJM 5:280.

Table 5-6 Tobacco Shipped by Tench Tilghman for Robert Morris, 1784–1786

Date	Hhds (#)	Ship	Cost of Cargo (in £ Currency)	Average Cost per Hhd (in £ Currency)
12/22/84	374	*Arthusa*	9,275.4.6	24.7994
6/18/85	150		2,871.4.5	19.1400
6/21/85	152	*Hannibal*	2,835.0.0	18.6500
9/15/85	552	*D'Artois*	10,566.15.0	19.1426
9/15/85	350	*George*	6,538.3.1	18.6800
10/18/85	280	*Patsy, Rutledge*	4,982.2.6	16.8216
10/31/85	157	*Unicorn*	2,641.5.4	16.8216
12/24/85	250	*Margaretta*	4,359.5.3	17.4360
1/21/86	540	*Hanover*	9,517.9.2	17.6240
4/18/86	20	*Philadelphia*	265.2.7	13.2500
4/20/86	200	*Bache & Lee*	2,647.7.0	13.2300
4/20/86	4	*Independence*	53.7.6	13.2500
Total	3,029			
Total for 1785	1,891			

Source: Chancery Papers, Hall of Records, Annapolis, Md., 1060.

rated, although the previous fall the legislature had made it easier to declare insolvency for those who were so far in debt that even the guarantee of a good market for their crop offered no hope of redemption. On May 28, 1787, Wallace and Muir wrote Johnson:

Our Assembly has just Risin. The paper money scheme was laid aside & we hope may not be ever taken up again. A very decided majority of the People were found against it. The proposed Installment law has been rejected and we have good hopes that future assemblys will endeavour to avoid interfering with private contracts and will be zealous to restore credit & confidence.[89]

A year later, Wallace and Muir could write that even the insolvency law "which has done so much mischief is repealed. This is an happy event and has saved us from much loss which would have happened under its continuance."[90] By then the Morris purchase was almost complete and his contract with the French at an end, but, for two years, it served a most useful purpose in Maryland's economy and, for one year, proved to be a critical factor in keeping Wallace, Johnson and Muir from bankruptcy.

[89] WJM 6:19.
[90] *Ibid.*, p. 389.

THE STRUGGLE TO PAY THE
LONDON DEBT, 1786-1789: AID FROM PHILADELPHIA

During the Revolution, Wallace and Muir had often been partners with Robert Morris in speculative trading ventures, and after the war, Wallace and Muir borrowed from Peter Whiteside's Philadelphia bank in which they held shares; but it was not until Wallace and Muir were confronted with an enormous debt in London that they began to rely heavily upon Philadelphia credit and advice.[91] When it became abundantly clear that they could not solve their financial crisis alone, Wallace and Muir turned to Morris and Whiteside for relief.

In January 1785, Le Normand, receiver general of finances for France, agreed with Robert Morris on behalf of the French tobacco monopoly to purchase 60,000 hogsheads of tobacco over three years: 1785, 1786, and 1787. One fourth of the quantity per year (5,000 hogsheads) was to come from Maryland and be "fit for smoking," but at the same price as the rest which would come from Virginia: 36 livres tournois per hundredweight (3.78d sterling per pound), with a deduction of 2 livres per hundredweight (.21d sterling per pound) to defray a million livre advance placed in the hands of the bankers Messrs. Couteaulx & Company for Morris's use in the purchase. The knowledge that Morris had a guaranteed market and a cash advance of £43,750 sterling in the hands of a French bank made people more than willing to accept his bills. The bills circulated freely as his agents began to purchase tobacco, a process that was not fully under way in Maryland until the summer of 1786.[92]

In the beginning, Morris's principal partner in Maryland was Tench Tilghman of Baltimore, who was joined later by James Carey. Tilghman shipped his initial cargo on Morris's account to France in December 1784, before the contract with the French had been signed, but he did not forward any more until the following June when, secure in the knowledge of the contract, he began shipping in earnest (see table 5-6).[93] In all, Tilghman shipped 1,891 hogsheads in 1785, far short of Morris's Maryland quota for that year. Some of the difference was made up by subcontracting to Thomas Howe Ridgate,

[91]WJM 4:300, 356, concerning the loan from Whiteside's bank.

[92]The Morris contract with a covering letter from Thomas Jefferson of May 31, 1786 and a copy of Jefferson's agreement with De Vergennes, is in Box 59, Exec. Pap. An exchange rate of 10-1/2d to the livre was used to convert the contract prices to sterling, WJM 3:459.

[93]Chan. Pap. 1060.

a merchant in Port Tobacco, Charles County. In November 1785, Wallace and Muir acted as intermediaries between Tilghman and Ridgate, who probably needed someone to vouch for his credit.[94] Ridgate had had a checkered career. He had been the infamous partner of John Barnes, who had left Barnes to suffer in a London jail during the depression of 1773, while he fled to safety in America.[95] Apparently Wallace and Johnson overlooked Ridgate's shortcomings. Before the Revolution one of Johnson's clerks, Christopher Richmond, had gone out to be Ridgate's storekeeper at Port Tobacco, and during the war Richmond had risen to the powerful and influential post of auditor general of the state.[96] Perhaps Richmond encouraged Wallace and Muir to recommend Ridgate to Tilghman but, whatever the circumstances, Tilghman sent Ridgate £1,500 in specie by Wallace and Muir's clerk, Francis Charlton, and over the next two years, Charlton was to be the courier for an additional £11,000 sterling in Morris's bills.[97]

Ridgate's efforts to supply Tilghman still did not meet Morris's Maryland quota.[98] At the prevailing price of £16.82 currency per hogshead (see table 5-6), at best another 892 hogsheads could be purchased with the £1,500, making the total secured for Morris in 1785 2,783 hogsheads. Although no correspondence between Morris and Wallace and Muir has survived for most of 1786 and five months of 1787, it is not unlikely that Morris was as eager to have Wallace and Muir's assistance in purchasing tobacco as they were to receive his bills.[99] Sometime after January 1786, a contract with Morris was signed allowing Wallace and Muir two and one half percent on all tobacco purchased and, in March, the first of Tilghman's drafts on

[94]*Ibid.*

[95]WDJ 1:131.

[96]Ridgate Letter Book, 1771–1772, Arents Collection, New York Public Library, New York, N.Y., letter of June 25, 1772, notes that Christopher Richmond is going out to take charge of Ridgate's store. Richmond was of great help to Johnson during his illness in the spring of 1772 and Johnson praised him highly when he left to go out to America for Barnes & Ridgate. WDJ 1:84, 126. For Richmond's public career see [List of Civil Officers] "84" 1777–1795, pp. 4, 203, Hall of Records, Annapolis, Md.

[97]Chan. Pap. 4207.

[98]WJM 5:24. Johnson notes that the French are in the market in a letter dated November 2, 1785, and that he hopes they will buy 4,000 to 5,000 hogsheads even though they are only paying 2-1/2d sterling per pound. A total of 2,985 hogsheads of tobacco were shipped directly to France from Baltimore in 1785, according to RG 36, NARS, and probably represent the extent of Maryland exports to the bulk tobacco market for that year.

[99]Johnson too was very keen on getting Morris's bills. In May 1786, he wrote: "I am very intimately acquainted with Mr. Morris's Partner here—he informs me that Mr. Morris can draw very largely, I wish that you could get five or six thousand pounds of his Bills it would be of a prodigious service to us." WJM 5:73.

Morris in their favor for £1,500 currency enabled Wallace and Muir to begin a new venture into the market for poorer grades of Maryland tobacco.[100]

How much tobacco Wallace and Muir purchased for Morris is difficult to determine without his or their books, but it probably amounted to approximately 4,106 hogsheads over the twenty-two month period from March 1786 to January 1788. Wallace and Muir borrowed £18,046 currency (£10,615 sterling) from Morris in bills on Philadelphia and bank notes which they used to purchase tobacco.[101] They also borrowed £21,000 sterling of Morris's bills of exchange drawn on Couteaulx and Morris's London partner, John Rucker, which they sent to Johnson to pay off the debt.[102] Although ultimately about £11,000 of the bills sent to London were protested, Morris paid interest on the amount not honored, acknowledging the fact that he indeed owed the sum to Wallace, Johnson and Muir, which in all probability was for tobacco they had shipped on his account.[103] Together, the total amount borrowed from Morris and employed in the purchase of poorer quality tobacco was about £32,000 sterling. At the prices Morris paid for tobacco in April 1786, the last date for which quotations are available (see table 5-6), Wallace and Muir would have been able to buy 4,106 hogsheads, or a yearly average of 2,240 hogsheads.

In terms of the amount of tobacco Wallace and Muir shipped on consignment from Maryland, the Morris purchase meant a yearly increase of 62.6 percent over what they normally might handle.[104] The shift to purchasing poorer quality tobacco, in addition to their consignment trade, meant reorganizing the business and expanding it to encompass the poorer tobacco lands on the Eastern and Western shores. Apparently Wallace and Muir exerted every effort to keep their purchases separate from their consignment trade. Rather than load Morris's ships at the same landings where they were filling their own vessels with quality consignment tobacco, they or their agents, such as Nicholas Kerr and Company on the Eastern Shore, shipped the purchased tobacco by flats and other bay craft to Tilghman and Carey at Baltimore or to their own dock in Annapolis.[105] At Anna-

[100]WJM 6:325, and Chan. Pap. 1060.
[101]WJM 6:144.
[102]WJM 5:175.
[103]Wallace, Johnson and Muir, *Journal, 1791–1795*, Gift Collection, D 796, Hall of Records, Annapolis, Md. (hereafter cited as Journal, 1791–1795). The entry for Phineas Bond on September 5, 1791, notes a credit for interest on Robert Morris's bills on Rucker amounting to £1,154.16.11. If this represents one year's interest at 6 percent, the principal would have been approximately £11,323 sterling at the going rate of exchange (170), or approximately the value of the protested bills.
[104]See table 5-2.
[105]WJM 6:11, 23, 38.

polis, Wallace and Muir probably were the principal backers of the reestablishment of the town as an inspection point, and they built a stone warehouse on the dock near the new inspection house to hold their tobacco in readiness for the arrival of Morris's ships.[106] In 1787, they even chartered one of their own newly acquired ships, the *Sally*, to Morris, which they loaded with approximately 500 hogsheads exclusively at Annapolis and dispatched to Bordeaux.[107] If only briefly, the port of Annapolis was again directly involved in an export trade and an international dimension was added to her growing regional market function.

Although Morris's bills helped relieve the monetary crisis in Maryland in the summer of 1786, the effects of Wallace and Muir's contract with Morris and the loan of Morris's French bills did not begin to affect the London debt significantly until January 1787, when Morris's bills on Couteaulx in Wallace, Johnson and Muir's favor began to arrive in quantity. In the meantime, the partners had reached an impasse in their personal relationship. In August 1785, Johnson sent the alarming news concerning the size of the London debt, which amounted to £240,000 sterling, and casually mentioned that Matthew Ridley was helping him with the London business.[108] The extent to which Johnson had allowed the cargo customers credit dismayed Wallace and Muir, but their patience was exhausted by the knowledge of Johnson's reliance on Ridley. Neither Wallace and Muir nor Johnson's brothers, Baker and Thomas, trusted Ridley, and when they heard that Ridley was now a partner in Johnson's half of Wallace, Johnson and Muir, all four wrote stinging letters of rebuke.[109] Why Ridley was so disliked is not clear but the advice was uniform: the connection must be dissolved. So stunned was Johnson by his brothers' reprimands that he refrained from answering their letters until the following Valentine's Day, when he could announce Ridley's imminent departure from London, but he replied to Wallace and Muir almost immediately.[110] In December 1785, he wrote acknowledging their letters of September 12 and October 7, in which they told him of their determination to withdraw from the partnership on June 1, 1786, and ordered him to sever all connections with Ridley.[111] Johnson expressed his dismay and pleaded with Wallace and

---

[106]Wallace and Muir loaded the *Kitty* at Annapolis with 420 hogsheads. WJM 6:11.

[107]*Ibid.*, p. 163.

[108]WJM 5:6.

[109]*Ibid.*, p. 32, "I have felt much pain at the manner of your mentioning Mr. Ridley as my Partner." Johnson claimed he had taken Ridley into his half "without prejudice to yours."

[110]*Ibid.*, p. 42.

[111]*Ibid.*, p. 32.

Muir to change their minds, urging them to find the funds to pay the debt and to engage some "rich country man" to take his place.[112]

Undoubtedly encouraged by the prospect of their contract with Morris, Wallace and Muir could not be swayed and were intent upon ending the partnership by June 1st, although they were not adverse to heeding part of Johnson's advice.[113] Sometime in the spring of 1786, they began negotiations with Peter Whiteside over the terms of a new partnership which would exclude Johnson altogether.[114] Whiteside, whose bank had failed, probably was not opposed to a change of scene, although he was slow in making up his mind.[115] An agreement had not been reached by April and Wallace and Muir were forced to ask Johnson to extend the old partnership for another six months. Their request did not arrive until after the June 1st deadline had passed, and Johnson was not in a humor to be told his partners had "plans" without any hint of the details.[116] Clerks were leaving in anticipation of the firm's dissolution. Promises were made of Morris bills but, as late as December 6, only £600 worth had arrived.[117] In November 1786, Johnson had £18,000 sterling to pay and only £3,000 on hand which he had received by pawning a cargo of tobacco.[118] He was almost dunned to death. "It is a Hell of a Life," he wrote, and if his partners did not do something to relieve him soon, he told Ridley, he might be driven to hang himself.[119] To Francis Charlton he wrote: "I begin to feel myself an old man, care, anxiety & Fatigue has filled my face with wrinkles & my head with white hairs."[120] From July to December 1786, Wallace and Muir persisted in not revealing what they were going to do after the first of January and the partnership was dissolved.[121] Johnson guessed that they intended to "connect with another House,"[122] and finally by the November packet, which arrived three weeks before the partnership of Wallace, Johnson and Muir was to end, Johnson at last was told of his intended replacement. The new firm was to be known as Wallace, Whiteside and Muir and would be capitalized at £10,000 sterling.[123]

[112]*Ibid.*
[113]*Ibid.*, p. 42.
[114]*Ibid.*, p. 93.
[115]WJM 4:300–301, 317, 356–57.
[116]WJM 5:93, 96.
[117]*Ibid.*, pp. 88, 122.
[118]*Ibid.*, p. 140.
[119]*Ibid.*, pp. 88, 89.
[120]*Ibid.*, p. 104.
[121]*Ibid.*, p. 132.
[122]*Ibid.*, p. 102.
[123]*Ibid.*, p. 132.

Johnson was incensed. Only a small token (£600) of the promised Morris bills had arrived.[124] The debt was as great as ever and there was little prospect of its being eradicated in the near future. Rather than meekly acquiesce, he decided to make it as difficult as possible for his partners' new scheme to succeed. He explained his intentions to Ridley in a letter written on December 6, 1786.

Wallace & Muir says that the Capital is £10,000—Ster & that they find it. The question asked by me, where does it come from, is it not WJ&M money? if so . . . it is not honest . . . the money ought to be distributed amongst the Creditors. This will be put to Mr. Whiteside on his arrival & if he has such a Sum it will be demanded. In short, both of us are placed in the most auquard situation. I have consulted some of my Creditors about giving up the affairs of the House to a Trust. They all say no I must not that the confidence that People has in me will carry us through if W & M does common Justice. However should I find their Mr. Whiteside on his arrival interfears as much with me as I have reason to expect I shall not hesitate calling the whole together & laying our Correspondence before them that they may Judge of my conduct & determine whether I deserve the treatment I have received from W & M. by raising up an unfavourable opinion of me in the Tradesmen by striking out my name & establishing another House under my nose.[125]

From December 1786 until May 1787, Johnson operated on the assumption that the new partnership of Wallace, Whiteside and Muir was to be launched upon Whiteside's arrival in London.[126] In February, Johnson's assets were down to £500 and he had £13,000 in bills to pay.[127] He borrowed all he could from his friends, but one persistent creditor threatened to arrest him. Johnson felt he had no recourse but to seek help informally from four of the firm's major creditors. As he explained to Francis Charlton on February 26:

I cald four of my Friends viz. Mr. Petrie of Cheap Side, Mr. Streatfield of Sothbury, Mr. Boak of Ledden Hall Street & Mr. Thorp of Oldgate, all whom you must remember, & asked them what I was to do, informing them at the same time that it was the opinion of many others that I had better ask time, after a careful investigation of our situation & taking into consideration the arrangement W & M has made with P[eter] W[hiteside]. They advised me to go on until he arrived & each lent me a Sum of money to enable me. They ground their advise on a supposition that W & M would never be so mad as to attempt the establishment of a new House without extracating the old

---

[124]*Ibid.*, p. 122.
[125]*Ibid.*, p. 133.
[126]*Ibid.*, p. 170.
[127]*Ibid.*, p. 159.

one & therefore they think Mr. P.W. will bring the necessary Funds or Credit with him, if he does not, by my struggling until then will prove to the World that I had not adopted any measure to defeat their views & that I may then give up with undoubted Credit to my self, this advice I shall follow, & as I have no Idea that neither Money or Credit will be forwarded by Mr. W. I shall prepare to lay our affairs under a Trust & make the best terms in my power.[128]

In the meantime, confronted with Johnson's hostile rejection of their plans, Wallace and Muir retreated. On May 2, 1787, Johnson learned that the agreement with Whiteside was dissolved.[129] His joy was brief. Three days later a new crisis in Wallace, Johnson and Muir's affairs occurred which forced Johnson into a formal capitulation to his creditors and ended the last vestige of independence from the London capital that Johnson had established sixteen years before. John Rucker, Morris's agent in London, fled the country on May 5 and Morris's bills began to be noted for nonacceptance.[130] The news reached Wallace and Muir in July, when they wrote Johnson that they had

just heard that in consequence of some quarrel or misunderstanding with the Farmers General, a large amount of Mr. Morris's bills will be returned. We have not learnt on what account this has happened but spring from what it may, if true it will prove a most embarrassing affair to you and us, it will derange our affairs exceedingly. . . .[131]

Approximately £21,000 sterling in Morris bills had been sent to Johnson, of which £10,000 had been accepted and applied to the debt.[132] When Johnson heard that £11,000 in all probability would be protested and no more bills forthcoming, he was forced to take drastic measures to meet his creditors' demands. On May 7th, he called together his thirteen major creditors and placed himself in their hands.[133] The creditors established themselves as trustees over Wallace, Johnson and Muir's London affairs and agreed to meet every week to review Johnson's correspondence and to decide what orders for goods he should be allowed to execute.[134] On May 31st, Johnson balanced the

[128]*Ibid.*, p. 160.
[129]*Ibid.*, p. 170.
[130]*Ibid.*, p. 173.
[131]WJM 6:51.
[132]WJM 5:293. In this letter Johnson says he still (11/88) has £10,240 sterling in Morris's bills on his hands.
[133]WJM 6:106-107. This letter to Stephen West written by Wallace & Muir on August 10, 1787, gives a good overall picture of the firm's indebtedness. There were 160 creditors altogether. All but 10 signed an agreement to leave the firm in peace for two years and not sue for their debt. WJM 5:253. Although the West letter mentions only 12 major creditors, Johnson refers to 13. *Ibid.*, p. 245.
[134]*Ibid.*, pp. 197ff.

accounts, revealing that the debt owed to his London creditors had been reduced to £170,000, of which £133,000 was owed London tradesmen and the remainder owed people who had lent Johnson money.[135] In two years, some progress had been made in overcoming the deficit, through consignments and the commission gained from the Morris purchase. In their letter informing Johnson that the agreement with Whiteside had been abandoned, Wallace and Muir asked for a continuation of Wallace, Johnson and Muir until January 1789 or July 1789, depending upon their ability to remove the debt.[136] On June 6, a month after he had precipitated creditor control of the firm's London business, Johnson agreed to the extension, informing his partners that the support of the major creditors placed Wallace, Johnson and Muir on a secure footing, as long as remittances were forthcoming.[137]

Wallace and Muir's reaction to Johnson's arrangements with the thirteen creditors who held over one half of the London debt was largely favorable, because it gave them time to pursue the cargo customers and to indulge themselves in a scheme to manipulate bills of exchange to their advantage.[138] On September 9, 1787, Wallace and Muir signed a secret partnership agreement with Peter Whiteside and Richard Caton, Charles Carroll's son-in-law. Caton was to be the acting partner in Maryland with a store in Baltimore. Whiteside was to go to London, this time to cooperate with Johnson instead of replacing him. It was to be a tripartite arrangement, each third to be capitalized at £2,000 sterling.[139] The main purpose of the partnership was a scheme for securing the debts owed Wallace, Johnson and Muir by their large debtors, most of whom were cargo customers. Caton would approach the debtor, offering to take his tobacco on consignment and provide goods. Caton would give the debtor bills of exchange for the tobacco drawn on Whiteside in London in favor of Wallace, Johnson and Muir. In this way, cargo customers, who were unable to get goods from Wallace, Johnson and Muir because of the London creditors' insistence that outstanding debts be paid first, were able to get goods from Whiteside; and, assuming Whiteside received tobacco or some form of remittance before the bills came due, Wallace, Johnson and Muir would be given good bills of exchange.[140] Realistically, Wallace and Muir expected many of the bills

---

[135]*Ibid.*, pp. 177, 188.
[136]*Ibid.*, p. 170.
[137]*Ibid.*, p. 182.
[138]The grace period was two years. *Ibid.*, p. 253.
[139]Chan. Pap. 1065.
[140]The bill of exchange scheme is discussed in WJM 5:266, 294, and WJM 6:166–67, 225, 244. Apparently Francis Charlton was a master at the game. See a curious letter

to be protested, but now that the courts were willing to support the collection of debts, "A protested bill in the eye of the Laws of Maryland and Virginia is more respectable than any other specialty."[141] In addition, the charges for the protest were 15 percent of the bill's value, three times the interest paid on Wallace, Johnson and Muir's London debt.[142] Johnson agreed to the drawing of bills on Whiteside, although he at first did not suspect that his partners had actually advanced capital and were partners in Caton and Whiteside.[143] As John Muir explained in a letter to Caton written on May 19, 1788:

What has hung most heavily on our minds, is the possibility of Mr. Johnson or some of our creditors coming at the knowledge of a Connection existing between P[eter] W[hiteside] and us—M. J[ohnson] and his advisors we find strongly suspect this to be the case and if they by any chance should obtain proofs it would certainly injure us much.[144]

In fact, Johnson initially welcomed Whiteside, once he felt his own position in the affairs of Wallace, Johnson and Muir was secure. He even went so far as to buy the ship *Potomac* jointly with Whiteside, and took great care to keep the fact from his creditor-trustees, although he kept Wallace and Muir fully informed of the venture.[145]

THE STRUGGLE TO PAY
THE LONDON DEBT, 1786-1789:
DISAPPOINTMENTS IN THE CONSIGNMENT TRADE

After May 7, 1787, with the firm's London affairs under the benevolent tutelage of their thirteen major creditors, who were bound by an agreement with Johnson not to bring suit on the debt for two years,

---

by Johnson in WJM 5:189-90, where he says Charlton had been involved in a bill of exchange swindle before he went to work for Johnson. A good example of how the scheme worked with one cargo customer is discussed in WJM 6:445-46, where Wallace and Muir note that they convinced Nichols, Kerr, & Chamberlain to draw £2,200 sterling on Peter Whiteside in expectation that when they came due remittances would be in Whiteside's hands to cover them. It was seen as a "mode of managing our tardy people," *ibid.*, pp. 475-76.

[141]WJM 5:166-67.

[142]Journal, 1791-1795, entry under August 27, 1792, where Nichols, Kerr, & Chamberlain are charged 15 percent interest on bills they drew on Whiteside which were protested.

[143]WJM 6:225.

[144]Chan. Pap. 1065.

[145]The one half share of the *Potomac* cost Wallace, Johnson and Muir £1,100 sterling. WJM 5:206.

Wallace, Johnson and Muir continued in the consignment trade. To their dismay, they found that there was too much competition, and that operating costs were mounting rapidly. Their agent in Calvert County, Joseph Wilkenson, demanded a higher salary, as did Francis Charlton. Both were valuable men and Wallace and Muir were forced to accede in order to keep them from taking better-paying posts with their competitors.[146] There was also the threat of losing valuable consignments from their cargo customers. As Wallace and Muir explained to Johnson, it was necessary to keep Thomas Tillard, the Pig Point merchant, friendly by shipping him a few goods because "Joseph Court is pressing there."[147] By the fall of 1787, Joseph Court and other British investors, such as the Lloyd banking family, Donald and Burton, Trecothick, Thwaites and Wheelwright, Dedruzina and Clerk, Oxley and Hancok, and Thomas Eden, had reentered the competition for quality tobacco with fresh capital and a desire to overset the Americans who had dominated the trade since the beginning of the Revolution.[148]

The return of British capital to the quality tobacco trade was induced by the failure of paper money schemes, the increasingly stringent attitude of Maryland's courts toward debtors, and finally the prospects of a strong national government that began to emerge in the fall of 1787. Ultimately those who purchased or advanced unwisely were defeated by declining prices in Europe, but while the influx of British capital lasted, American merchants such as Wallace, Johnson and Muir suffered severely. In December 1787 the American merchants, Forrest and Stoddert and Thomas Claggett, followed by their old British competitor, Thomas Eden, were still Wallace, Johnson and Muir's "Grand Opponents."[149] But a year later the situation had changed dramatically. Those who had sunk large sums of money into purchasing tobacco or paying exorbitant advances to planters had greatly curtailed Wallace, Johnson and Muir's shipments and had driven Forrest and Stoddert out of business.[150]

In order to load their ships, Wallace and Muir were forced to make large advances to the planters. They insisted that Johnson allow bills to be drawn on him to the planters at one half to two thirds of the value

[146]WJM 6:457, where Wallace and Muir comment that if they did not give Wilkenson a raise and he left their employ the bulk of the Calvert planters would follow him.

[147]*Ibid.*, p. 194.

[148]WJM 5:149, and the discussion of the Lloyds on pp. 84, 88, 89, 185.

[149]*Ibid.*, p. 233.

[150]WJM 6:510 where Wallace & Muir note the end of Forrest and Stoddert and express the hope they can take over their "shipping friends."

of the tobacco sent, arguing that otherwise they would have to abandon soliciting consignments altogether.[151] Reluctantly Johnson agreed, but even with the advances, Wallace and Muir were not able to do what they expected. Although they promised Johnson 3,000 hogsheads in 1788, they failed to meet their goal, sending a total of 2,750 instead, 23.4 percent less than what they had received on consignment in 1785.[152] Wallace and Muir were conscious of their failure as early as the fall of 1787, when in a letter to Johnson they tried to rationalize their performance in terms of what the other consignment houses were doing.

Though the quantity of Tob we have this year obtained on consignment is far short of what we had for years past, yet we think ourselves well justified in saying that it is equal to the amount obtained by all other houses together.[153]

Ironically, one of Wallace, Johnson and Muir's major competitors, whose advances to planters and purchases greatly hindered their consignment trade in 1787 and 1788, was an Annapolis firm, Cracroft and Hodgkin, who were agents of the British firm of Trecothick, Thwaites and Wheelwright.[154] Initially, Cracroft and Hodgkin had been cargo merchants, selling goods in Annapolis and at Upper Marlboro which they bought from the American merchant, Richard Contee, or from Trecothick, Thwaites and Wheelwright.[155] In November, 1786, Cracroft and Hodgkin decided that they could do well in the consignment trade with Trecothick, Thwaites and Wheelwright's backing. They voiced great optimism about their ability to find planters willing to ship; Francis Cracroft had only

one request to make which is that you would this year send us a ship into each of the Rivers we mention, those for Patuxent & Potomac to arrive by the 1st June & that for Patapsco by the 1st July as they are later bringing their Tobo. to that River than the other. I will forfeit my Existence if we do not load them in due Time & without embarrassing you & do but desire you to try it this year. In future I am confident we shall be able to load double the Num-

[151]*Ibid.*, p. 17.

[152]*Ibid.*, pp. 288, 486. The latter reference does not account for the *Betsey*, which may have taken as many as 500 hhds to London in 1788. *Ibid.*, p. 91.

[153]*Ibid.*, p. 180.

[154]William Cooke Papers, MS 195, Maryland Historical Society, Baltimore, Md. (hereafter cited as Cooke Pap.), Box 3. "The violent exertions of our neighbors Cracroft & Hodgkin & others have forced us to draw." WJM 6:128.

[155]Cooke Pap., Box 3.

ber of Vessells, but shall rest satisfied in doing a little for the present. Depend upon it you shall never be lead into any Visionary schemes by

yrs most sincerely
F. Cracroft.[156]

Perhaps the schemes were not visionary, but Cracroft and Hodgkin found themselves advancing closer and closer to the actual value of the tobacco shipped until sometime in the summer of 1788, when they actually were advancing more than the tobacco was worth on the London market! Other consignment merchants found themselves in the same predicament. Dedruzina and Clerk, a new British firm, failed. Forrest and Stoddert withdrew from trade just in time to save themselves. In fact, Cracroft and Hodgkin met their ultimate downfall in trying to take over Forrest and Stoddert's customers. As they tried to explain to Trecothick, Thwaites and Wheelwright in December, 1788:

> The sums advanced them [Forrest and Stoddert's customers] are much beyond the value of their present shipment, but we have taken their Bonds to make you ample consignments next year to cover the deficiency. . . . Indeed we shall not require much money in future, as we have laid the foundation for extensive consignments on moderate advances, which we are determined shall never exceed £3,000.[157]

Sanguine as their hopes may have been about the ensuing year, Cracroft and Hodgkin, like most others engaged in large advances, had overreached themselves. Trecothick, Thwaites and Wheelwright, after allowing two year's grace in which the debts incurred by the advances remained unpaid, turned the whole matter of debt collection over to William Cooke.[158] Hodgkin moved to Baltimore and managed to escape bankruptcy, but Cracroft declared himself an insolvent debtor in 1794 with £12,000 sterling still owed to the London firm.[159]

In addition to advances, British capital also was employed in the direct purchase of tobacco. Cracroft and Hodgkin bought tobacco outright as well as soliciting consignments.[160] The prewar consignment

[156]*Ibid.*
[157]*Ibid.*
[158]*Ibid.*
[159]For Cracroft see his petition as an insolvent debtor, January 18, 1794, in Chan. Pap. 1031 B. Hodgkin died in Baltimore, apparently free from the Cracroft & Hodgkin debt. *Maryland Gazette*, March 7, 1805.
[160]Cooke Pap., Box 3.

houses of Court, Eden, and Lloyd purchased tobacco, using it as a vehicle to reestablish themselves in the consignment trade.[161] Interest also revived in purchase for the direct trade to Amsterdam which, by the summer of 1788, was siphoning off at least 3,000 hogsheads of quality tobacco a year (probably 18 percent of the amount exported).[162] At Amsterdam the tobacco was sold at prices below the London market and consequently caused London prices to fall. When Watson and Company sold their tobacco at Amsterdam at one stiver per pound less than the going price, Johnson remarked, "I wish he [Watson] was over the Allegany Mountains & all such fellows."[163] All Wallace and Muir could do was to use advances judiciously and shrug their shoulders with the comment that "the purchasers, who seem mad fellows, have cut pretty deep into our expectations. . . ."[164]

THE END OF THE PARTNERSHIP, 1789

The failure of Morris's bills, mounting competition from other consignment merchants and from purchasers, and a growing desire to use any liquid assets of the firm to invest in speculative ventures at home combined to convince Wallace and Muir that they would do better to decline the tobacco business altogether. In November 1787, they wrote Johnson that:

our minds have been Continually employed with the plan of lessening the Amt of our Debt by securities here, and we in the most powerful terms intreat you to consider the matter with close attention, and to do everything possible to bring it about—there must be many of our creditors very rich, others in very easy Circumstances, all of them have reaped amazing Profits by their dealings with us, and we do conceive that they would in full and proper statement be well Contented to receive one half of their Debts, in perfectly solid Securities on which they would regularly receive their Interest Annually upon receiving the other half or thereabouts in money in the course of next year. . . . When the Gentlemen perceive the plan of Federal Government proposed and know that there is every probability that it will be adopted, we have a hope that Confidence in America will be in some degree

---

[161]WJM 5:84, 88, 89, 185, 191, 192. "In short, all the spirits of our opponents are up." *Ibid.*, p. 196.

[162]*Ibid.*, p. 279. The amount of quality tobacco exported from Maryland in 1788 probably did not exceed 17,000 hogsheads.

[163]*Ibid.*, p. 272.

[164]WJM 6:105.

Advertisements from the *Maryland Gazette,* 1767–1790.

strengthened (and if it is fully adopted) fully restored. On the whole therefore we trust you will not reject this matter as a Visionary Scheme.[165]

Wallace and Muir suggested that the creditors send a power of attorney to Mr. Carroll of Carrollton, Mr. D. Dulany, or "any other Gentlemen here high" in the creditors' confidence, with instructions to receive such securities as they deemed solid.[166]

The idea was not a new one. Johnson himself had suggested a similar plan in July 1786, when he advised Wallace and Muir to place £100,000 sterling collateral for the London creditors in the hands of George Washington and Charles Carroll, but Wallace and Muir chose a connection with Robert Morris instead as a more profitable solution to the debt question.[167] Nor was Johnson adverse to Wallace and Muir's using partnership funds to speculate in government securities which were certain to rise on the adoption of the Constitution. In April 1788, he wrote: "I notice what you say about American Securities. My Idea is that should the new Constitution be adopted . . ." securities "will rise, then fall," and he urged Wallace and Muir to "secure the rise."[168] Unfortunately, the London creditors were not yet convinced that American credit was as sound as Wallace, Johnson and Muir insisted, and they preferred that business proceed as usual, expecting that continued consignments of tobacco would bring new orders for goods as well as dependable remittances to pay the standing debt.[169]

Confronted by what was a hostile reception to their plan on the part of the London trustees, Wallace and Muir quickly retreated. In April 1788, they wrote a long letter of apology in which they stated their willingness to continue in trade and their "fair" prospects of remitting handsomely in the usual way.[170] By the fall of 1788, it was clear that they were mistaken. Consignments were off by almost a quarter from what they had predicted for the year and the London debt, instead of being reduced, was increased by about £10,000 sterling to approximately £143,000.[171]

The failure to reduce the London debt was not due solely to a decline in Wallace, Johnson and Muir's consignment business. Wallace and Muir diverted cash collected from debtors into domestic

---

[165]*Ibid.*, p. 198.
[166]*Ibid.*
[167]WJM 5:93.
[168]*Ibid.*, p. 264.
[169]*Ibid.*, p. 273.
[170]WJM 6:332–34.
[171]WJM 5:177, 276.

investments and limited sterling remittances to London to bills of exchange on Whiteside that both Johnson and his partners realized probably would be protested. In June 1789, when Johnson discovered that his partners were taking mortgages, bonds, and other forms of securities from people who had debts on the London books and transferring the debt to themselves without sending any money to London, he was much annoyed, and he brought the matter to the attention of the trustees. On June 30, the trustees wrote to Wallace and Muir: "Upon posting up the entries to November [1788], we observe the balance due from the Annapolis House is upwards of Eighty thousand pounds, we wish to know what this large balance consists of and what prevents you remitting it here."[172] Wallace and Muir contended that:

Some of the London debts so charged to the Annapolis House were secured by Mortgages &ca. Some were in train of being secured and others were in suit, he [Johnson] knew that this was the sole object of such transfers. He knew that none of them had been received by W&M, if any part of them had been paid, he had as full information of it, as W&M had, in their waste Books.[173]

They went on to complain that Johnson's action made their dealings with the London creditors all the more difficult, and made it impossible for them to draw on London for advances to the planters. As Wallace and Muir pointed out later, when reflecting upon this period of the partnership:

Suspicions were so strongly rooted, that W&M were in 1788 restricted from drawing on the London House on any emergency—this unexpected measure Crippled our Operations very much and we were obliged to fix credits at Philadelphia, Baltimore, Alexandria and Richmond, where on to draw occasionally. No sooner did JJ see our Waste Books, the entries relative to such drafts, than he took alarm—but instead of calling upon us for information, as he in prudence ought to have done, he selected these entries and laid them before his Advisers, as wild, dangerous and dishonorable measures pursued by his partners, was it at all to be wondered at, that creditors should view their [Wallace and Muir's] conduct with distrust?[174]

Although Wallace and Muir felt Johnson's actions were hostile, he probably had some justification for doing what he did. Wallace and Muir were well aware that, as a result of Johnson's agreement with

---

[172]Chan. Pap. 2893.
[173]*Ibid.*
[174]*Ibid.*

the trustees, there was little fear of prosecution over the London debt for two years between May 1787 and May 1789. Instead of remitting, they invested their collections in various ventures, including a flour mill they had purchased in 1785, a partnership with John F. Brice and Company of Richmond, Virginia for the purchase of tobacco, and above all, in the various securities of the states issued as a means of funding the war debt.[175] As E. James Ferguson has demonstrated, when the federal government assumed the debt of the states in 1790, Wallace and Muir had accumulated $56,578.00 worth of the debt in Maryland, second only to their old competitors, Forrest and Stoddert, who held $96,417.00.[176] It was an advantage which Johnson prevented Wallace and Muir from exploiting to the full. When transfer securities representing the amount of the state debts Wallace and Muir held began to rise in value, Johnson made it impossible to sell a significant number.

When we received United States certificates of stock, we had the comfort to find that we had by our judicious management, gained for WJ&M, Twenty five thousand pounds and upwards—and if M. J had had a proper confidence in us, we could have made with ease, a hundred thousand pounds.—On the score of the abovesaid stock, a very great loss arose (also, as we think, from M. J's want of confidence in us) in this way—so soon as we obtained the Stock, M. J urged that the certificates should be sent to London—we were very anxious to remit to London, but we trembled at the possible chance of a loss of the certificates, well knowing that a cent could not be Transfered, by any possible means until the original certificate was produced.—On this subject we consulted our good friend P[hineas] Bond Esquire [British consul in Philadelphia] and he agreed to receive a Transfer in his name, and to send to London triplicate certificates, that he had received such stock from W&M, and that it was held by him, subject to the control, disposal, direction and assignment of J. Johnson. Mr. Bond and ourselves, always thought, Mr. J might have made sale of (or have raised money on) the Stock on that footing—Mr. J. thought differently—The stock was not sold in London, nor authority given by JJ to sell in America, until September 1792, when we were glad to get 20/- p[er] pound for Six p[er] cent and in proportion for the other kinds—Mr. Bond could have had 27/- . . . on 5 months credit, in January 1792—Capt Campbell offered us, July 1791, 25/- p[er] pound, in Bills on London at par, stock to be held until the bills were paid—But Mr. Bond's hands and ours were tied up, we could not avail ourselves of these advantageous offers.[177]

[175]*Ibid.*
[176]E. James Ferguson, "Speculation in the Revolutionary Debt: The Ownership of Public Securities in Maryland," *Journal of Economic History* 14 (1954), 41.
[177]Chan. Pap. 2893.

The acrimonious debate between Annapolis and London over the management of partnership funds, which continued until Johnson died in 1802, began a new phase in 1789, when it became clear that Wallace and Muir were not able to collect debts and also conduct extensive new business. The final crisis in the partnership was precipitated in 1789 by the failure of Peter Whiteside and the collapse of Wallace and Muir's bill of exchange scheme. Whiteside's capital was largely in Morris's bills, which proved worthless when too many of the cargo customers to whom Caton and Whiteside extended credit failed to make remittances. Bankruptcy and jail were Whiteside's only alternatives.[178]

By 1790, it was obvious to the trustees that to insist upon the continuation of Wallace, Johnson and Muir was a mistake. At least one of the thirteen already had gone bankrupt, in part because of credit extended to the firm.[179] Allowing Wallace and Muir to concentrate on debt collection and leaving Johnson to try business on his own seemed the only solution. With what must have been a sign of relief on both sides of the Atlantic, the partnership of Wallace, Johnson and Muir came to an end on January 1, 1790.[180]

THE DEATH OF THE CONSIGNMENT TRADE

In January 1790, Johnson sent out a circular to all his friends and old customers in Maryland announcing that he was going to continue the consignment business on his own. He proposed to use the same agents and to follow the same pattern of shipping goods as before, although he carefully noted that it was "far from my intention to further myself with the shipment of cargoes. . . ."[181] Wallace and Muir even agreed to advance bills of exchange on London to anyone who was willing to consign. But changes were taking place in the attitudes of the planters that, by 1797, frustrated Johnson's plans and

---

[178]*Ibid.*; WJM 5:273, and WJM 6:301. Charles Carroll wrote Johnson on July 7, 1789, "I am sorry for poor Whiteside if this misfortune has not been occasioned by his own fault. Who conducted his business during his confinement? At whose suit is he confined? I am afraid Mr. Caton will be a Sufferer by him." Charles Carroll Letter Book, Arents Collection, New York Public Library, New York, N.Y. (hereafter cited as Carroll Letter Book).

[179]WJM 5:272. Jones and Boake failed in part because Johnson could not pay them. Later the trustees, or "inspectors" as Johnson sometimes called them, guaranteed the £1,600 sterling debt. *Ibid.*, p. 274.

[180]Chan. Pap. 2893.

[181]Charles Ridgely Papers, MS 692, Maryland Historical Society, Baltimore, Md.

ultimately caused the demise of the consignment tobacco trade altogether.

The major foreign competition for quality tobacco, which came from British merchants active in 1787 and 1788, and the major domestic competition, which came from Baltimore merchants engaged in purchasing for the Amsterdam market, were no longer a threat by 1790. The British and Baltimore merchants were undone by falling tobacco prices in Europe. Johnson's prediction that Trecothick, Thwaites and Wheelwright and the other adventurers would burn their fingers was proven correct.

By 1790, Baltimore merchants engaged in the tobacco trade already had turned their attention to the lower grades destined for the bulk market in France. Although the total amount of tobacco shipped from Baltimore steadily declined between 1780 and 1790, the number of hogsheads exported to France increased.[182] Initially, the major cause for the shift to poorer quality tobacco was the orders Robert Morris placed in the hands of his Baltimore agents, but other merchants took over the reexport trade when the Morris contract expired in 1787. Before long, practically all Eastern Shore tobacco (always considered inferior to that grown on the Western Shore) and some of the poorer grades from the Western Shore made their way first to Baltimore before being shipped abroad.[183] By 1788, if a tobacco ship arrived in London from Baltimore it was assumed to carry "ordinary" tobacco, and buyers would offer a farthing less per pound than for tobacco shipped directly from the Patuxent.[184] In the same year, at a time when Wallace and Muir were willing to settle their outstanding debts by taking quality tobacco at the going purchase price, they rejected one offer from a cargo customer in St. Mary's County on the grounds that the tobacco was not good enough. Instead, they encouraged the firm to sell at the price the firm claimed they could get in Baltimore and give the proceeds as payment for their debt: "We shall be equally as well pleased, as to have it here, for really with the money we can purchase superior tobacco for less price."[185] In 1790, the bulk of the tobacco shipped from Baltimore was composed of inferior grades from the Eastern and Western shores (see table 5-7). Of 8,184 hogsheads exported, 5,085 (62 percent) came from the Eastern Shore, while another 261 hogsheads (3 percent) were brought

---

[182]Naval Office returns for Baltimore in 1784 and 1785 show that exports to France increased from 2,345 hogsheads to 2,985, while total exports of tobacco declined from 15,958 hogsheads to 11,712 hogsheads. RG 36, NARS.

[183]WJM 6:96, 97.

[184]WJM 5:267.

[185]WJM 6:380.

Table 5-7 *Internal Migration of Maryland Tobacco Prior to Export, 1790*

(in hhds)

| County Where Grown | Naval District | | |
	Patuxent	Georgetown	Baltimore
Anne Arundel	1,492	7	1,851
Baltimore	66		539
Calvert	1,208	13	106
Charles	378	412	242
Frederick	9	260	
Montgomery	32	4,412	188
Prince Georges	2,207	1,721	154
St. Marys	72	255	19
Caroline			574
Dorchester	14	38	666
Kent			184
Queen Annes	50	2	848
Somerset	6	11	1,304
Talbot	171		1,069
Worcester		4	440
Total	5,705	7,135	8,184
Total Western Shore	5,464	7,080	3,099 (38%)
Total Eastern Shore	241	55	5,085 (62%)

Source: Archives of Maryland (Baltimore, 1883-), 72: 157-58, 160, 205.

from the inferior tobacco lands of Charles and St. Mary's counties on the Western Shore.

If British and Baltimore competitors were less of a threat to Johnson than they had been to Wallace, Johnson and Muir, the planters themselves offered a new, insurmountable problem. Those who would normally be expected to consign found they could get goods cheaper in the country. As Charles Carroll explained in a letter to Johnson written in 1789:

> You will observe that I have greatly curtailed my invoice this year. Most of the articles I can buy in the Country of a better quality and several of them much cheaper than what they cost me imported from London. . . .[186]

From that point on, Carroll bought much of his cloth and other goods from Baltimore merchants, or imported them from Connecticut.[187]

[186]November 11, 1789, Carroll Letter Book.
[187]Carroll to Josiah Burr, New Haven, Conn., November 11, 1791, *ibid.*

Planters did not want the consignment merchant's goods, and neither did cargo customers who were competing with stores established by Baltimore, Philadelphia, and New England houses that vended goods of foreign and domestic manufacture at prices below what similar goods cost to import from London. Samuel Davidson, who had left Annapolis to establish himself in business at Georgetown in 1783, first ordered goods from Wallace, Johnson and Muir. When, like a great number of their other cargo customers, he allowed his debt to mount and Johnson refused further shipment, Davidson switched to the new London firm of Donald and Burton, leaving the Wallace, Johnson and Muir debt to be settled in court.[188] By the fall of 1790, Donald and Burton were no longer able to supply goods at competitive prices, and Davidson decided it was time to retire from the drygoods business altogether. On November 28, he wrote Donald and Burton to inform them of his decision.

I have . . . finally declined further importation of Dry Goods, which are become a mere drugg in this country—you may depend on it, that a general cargo of Goods shipped at the usual prices in London, would not now command, even in the retail line in this town, an average of cost and charges yet, there are a number of *New Stores* daily fixing here from Baltimore, Philadelphia and New England. Our town [Georgetown] now absolutely stinks with Cod Fish . . . [i.e., the New Englanders].[189]

A familiar pattern was being repeated in the Chesapeake. American merchants in the retail trade were offering devastating competition to London tobacco merchants who were, in turn, forced to accommodate or withdraw. In contrast to the prewar situation, some of the London merchants were Americans, but the consequences were the same. As retail merchants backed by American capital took over the market for drygoods, they also began to move into the tobacco trade. Before the war, Annapolis had served as the source of sufficient capital to allow a challenge to the London middleman. After 1793, when fundamental changes in Maryland's economy took place, Baltimore became the center of a movement that led to the demise altogether of the London middleman in the Chesapeake retail import trade and culminated in a total reorganization of the tobacco export trade.

---

[188]General Court of the Western Shore Papers, October Term, 1787, Wallace, Johnson & Muir vs Samuel Davidson, Hall of Records, Annapolis, Md. Davidson owed £3,650.18.2 sterling. Samuel Davidson Letter Book, p. 12, Library of Congress, Washington, D.C., contains a letter to Donald & Burton concerning the state of the tobacco trade.
   [189]*Ibid.*, p. 51.

Fundamental changes in the organization of trade were paralleled by changes in agriculture in Tidewater Maryland that had their origins in the crop diversification encouraged by wartime demands for wheat to feed the army and the difficulties of shipping tobacco to its European market. After the Revolution, the demand for wheat declined because of the Algerian pirates and abundant harvests in Europe, and planters returned to the production of tobacco.[190] Tobacco exports gradually climbed until 1791, when they nearly reached prewar levels (see table 5-3). Most of the growth in tobacco exports came from the lower grades of tobacco raised on marginal lands and, in the short run, had little effect on the nature of opportunity confronting the consignment tobacco merchant. He competed for a limited quantity of quality tobacco and, when the French market for bulk tobacco revived, explored ways of handling the poorer grades of tobacco in place of the diminishing supply of wheat consignments. In the long run, however, the experience of wheat production on tobacco lands and the ease with which planters found they could diversify hastened a change in agriculture and the marketing of crops of enormous consequence to the planters and merchants.

During the Revolution, Maryland tobacco planters found they could become wheat farmers with little difficulty when tobacco prices were too low. After 1793, when the demand for poorer quality tobacco fell precipitously (see tables 5-8a and 5-8b) because of the European wars and the collapse of the French market, planters became farmers once more, with especially disastrous consequences for those with poorer lands and limited capital resources. While the lull in the market for lesser quality tobacco had lasted for a decade dur-

Table 5-8a   *Tobacco Exports from the United States, 1790-1823*

(in hhds)

1790	118,460	1800	78,680	1810	84,134	1820	83,940
1791	101,272	1801	103,758	1811	35,828	1821	66,858
1792	112,428	1802	77,721	1812	26,094	1822	83,169
1793	59,947	1803	86,291	1813	5,314	1823	99,009
1794	72,958	1804	83,343	1814	3,125		
1795	61,050	1805	71,252	1815	85,337		
1796	69.018	1806	83,186	1816	69,241		
1797	58,167	1807	62,232	1817	62,365		
1798	68,567	1808	9,576	1818	84,337		
1799	96,070	1809	53,921	1819	69,247		

Source: Lewis Cecil Gray, *History of Agriculture in the Southern United States to 1860* (Gloucester, Mass., 1958), p. 1035.

[190]WJM 5:5, 95.

Table 5-8b Destination of Tobacco Exports
of the United States for Selected Years, 1790-1798

(in hhds)

Country	1790	1793	1795	1798
Low Countries	23,448	7,290	11,015	10,832
Austrian Neth.		3,239		
Great Britain	73,708			
England		24,700	32,769	16,980
Scotland		2,394	3,982	2,194
Ireland		3,112	6,951	2,405
Germany	5,612	3,427	10,138	13,711
France	10,876	8,897	2,070	4,881
Spain	568	1,541	629	
Total all countries	118,460	59,341	72,958	58,167

Source: *American State Papers, Class IV, Commerce and Navigation* (Washington, D.C., 1831-1862), 1:32, 289, 310, 383.

ing the war, it continued for almost a generation beginning in 1793. Planters with marginal lands ceased production of tobacco. The effect was noticed immediately by merchants such as Robert Ferguson. Ferguson, backed by Glasgow capital, had opened a store after the Revolution at Port Tobacco in Charles County and was active in trading goods for inferior grades of tobacco, much like other Scottish merchants had done before the war. In August 1793, he observed that:

The shortness of last grown crop will be greater in this neighbourhood than was expected, not more than 200 hhds are yet inspected at this warehouse and from what I learn not much more to bring, however it will not exceed another hundred. Before the war the qty inspected here was 1000 hhds.[191]

Instead of tobacco, the planters overworked their marginal lands by planting grain. They ploughed deeper and more often, cultivating as much area as their labor supply would permit, which for grain crops meant at least five times the ground that they formerly were able to plant with tobacco.[192] The rains washed their soils away into the streams that once carried their tobacco to market. With the streams and rivers silted up there was no turning back again, even if the demand for marginal grades of tobacco increased once peace returned to Europe. The land was gone and the poorer planters had

[191]Port Tobacco Letter Book, 1792-1793, Glassford Papers, Volume 122, p. 161, Manuscript Division, Library of Congress, Washington, D.C.

[192]Gregory A. Stiverson, "Landless Husbandmen: Tenants on the Maryland Proprietary Manors in the Eighteenth Century: an Economic Study" (Ph.D. dissertation, Johns Hopkins University, 1973), p. 290.

Table 5-9 *Population of the Tobacco*
Counties of Maryland's Western Shore, 1790-1820

County	1790	1800	1810	1820
Anne Arundel	22,598	22,623	26,668	27,165
Calvert	8,652	8,297	8,005	8,073
Charles	20,613	19,172	20,245	16,500
Prince Georges	21,344	21,185	20,589	20,216
St. Marys	15,554	13,699	12,794	12,974

Source: Arthur Eli Karinen, "Numerical and Distributional Aspects of Maryland Population, 1631-1840" (Ph.D. dissertation, University of Maryland, 1958), p. 208.

no alternatives but to leave for wheat farms in western New York, for tobacco plantations in the West, or for jobs in Baltimore.[193] Between 1790 and 1820, large numbers of people left southern Maryland (see table 5-9), extinguishing any prospects of a growing market for mercantile goods and severely hampering any mercantile venture that depended upon the marginal planter for even a portion of its clientele.

The depression and out-migration of planters from the poorer tobacco lands in the 1790s did not affect the production of quality tobacco, as can be seen from the export figures for inspection houses located in the prime tobacco lands along the Patuxent (see table 5-10). Although silting up of the streams and rivers restricted the size

Table 5-10 *Prince George's County*
Patuxent River Warehouses: Tobacco Exports, 1791-1801

Year	Queen Anne	Upper Marlboro	Nottingham	Magruders
1791	n.a.	911	544	496
1792	n.a.	1,086	828	420
1793	862	473	315	279
1794	1,689	1,148	1,137	300
1795	1,052	842	671	n.a.
1796	1,061	954	886	541
1797	752	613	489	n.a
1798	1,505	1,057	898	553
1799	1,551	871	823	n.a.
1800	1,416	889	772	n.a.
1801	2,064	1,617	977	n.a.

n.a. = not available.

Source: Table compiled by B. H. Brune from Prince George's County, Maryland, County Court Tobacco Inspection Records, 1781-1802, Hall of Records, Annapolis, Md. I am indebted to Mr. Brune for this table.

[193]There has been no study of the migration patterns of Maryland planters after 1790, although undoubtedly much of the growth of Baltimore was due to a movement from farm to city between 1790 and 1810.

of ships that could navigate to many inspection landings, the consignment trade might have continued to flourish from points where the major rivers were still navigable, if it had not been for the competition from Baltimore merchants, who first supplied goods cheaper than could be imported directly from London and then, when profits from the reexport trade became plentiful after 1793, moved in to aggrandize the quality tobacco market.[194]

Statistically, the speed with which Baltimore took over the quality tobacco trade is difficult to measure because the data are fragmentary. By 1823, even though production of quality tobacco was almost as high as it had ever been in the state, most of it went first to Baltimore to be inspected before shipment abroad (see table 5–11).[195]

Table 5–11 *"Statement of the Tobacco Inspected at and delivered*
from the Several and Respective Inspection Warehouses . . . from the 6th
of October 1822 to October the 6th 1823 as per the reports made by the inspectors . . ."
(in hhds)

County or City	Names of the Warehouses	Domestic	Out of State	Reinspected	Total
Anne Arundel	Indian Landing	3			3
	Tracys Landing	309			309
	Pig Point	360			360
	Taylors Landing	72			72
Prince Georges	Piscattaway	989		2	991
	Queen Anne	572			572
	Upper Marlboro	710		6	716
	Nottingham	664			664
Calvert	Lower Marlborough	46			46
Baltimore City	Calhouns	6,087	121	768	6,976
	Smiths	3,830	42	86	2,777
	Dugans	1,048	138	118	1,737
	Sheppard	1,807	18	60	2,636
	Williams & O'Donnell	2,181	96	113	2,747
Total		18,678	415	1,153	20,246

Total inspected at Baltimore: 16,513 hogsheads
Percentage of tobacco inspected at Baltimore: 79.7 percent.

Source: Scharf Collection, Maryland Historical Society, Baltimore, Md.

[194]For the role of the reexport trade in the economic growth of the United States see: Douglass C. North, *The Economic Growth of the United States 1790 to 1860* (Englewood Cliffs, N.J., 1961), especially pp. 1–35. See also Curtis P. Nettels, *The Emergence of A National Economy 1775–1815* (New York, 1962), and David T. Gilchrist, ed., *The Growth of the Seaport Cities 1790–1825* (Charlottesville, Va., 1967).

[195]See notes 21 and 22 above. In 1772, the peak year of production for the colonial period, Maryland produced 33,495 hogsheads weighing on the average 1,000 pounds,

Literary evidence suggests that Baltimore's domination of the tobacco trade was well established by 1823. In 1807, Joseph Scott, a geographer, described Queen Anne, the town on the Patuxent where Wallace, Johnson and Muir once maintained a store.

The town has gone much to decay, as well as all the other towns on the Patuxent, since the surprising growth and consequence of Baltimore, which is swallowing up in its vortex the trade of all the towns in Maryland, and taking to itself all the mercantile importance of the state.[196]

The control of the quality tobacco trade by the Baltimore merchant community that became permanent after 1793 brought an end to the short, but illustrious, period when local merchants throughout the Chesapeake were given the opportunity to assert their independence from British capital. The brief two decades of freedom that had begun with Wallace, Davidson and Johnson's entry into the consignment trade in 1773 ended almost where it had begun, when capital for commerce again became concentrated in a large urban center, only now that center was Baltimore, and Tidewater merchants were loading small bay craft for the trip to the Patapsco instead of filling ocean-going vessels destined for the Thames.

---

or 33,495,000 pounds total. In 1792, Maryland produced 28,292 hogsheads weighing on the average 1,000 pounds, or 28,292,000 pounds total. In 1823, Maryland produced 19,831 hogsheads weighing on the average 1,500 pounds, or 29,746,500 pounds total.

[196]Joseph Scott, *A Geographical Description of the States of Maryland and Delaware* . . . (Philadelphia, 1807), p. 128.

CHAPTER 6

OPPORTUNITY in a QUIET MARKET TOWN: FROM PLANTER'S MERCHANT to FARMER'S BANKER, 1790–1805

A FTER 1793, Annapolis settled into the sleepy routine of a quiet market town. The city fathers devoted themselves to maintaining the public dock for the reception of farm produce and goods carried by the growing number of small bay craft that called at the town from Baltimore.[1] Scales were erected so that the city could regulate and tax the hay, fodder, and straw that was purchased by residents or was passing through.[2] Retail merchants, such as John Randall and Jonathan Pinkney, kept their stores on the dock con-

[1] The number of coasting vessels that entered and cleared from Annapolis increased after 1789, peaking in 1798 and 1807, as can be seen from the following table derived from "Abstract of Duties" bound with "Accounts Current, Annapolis 1745–1821," Record Group 36, National Archives, Washington, D.C.

	Vessels			Vessels	
Year	Coasting	Traders	Year	Coasting	Traders
1789	25	1	1803	58	
1790	27	3	1804	51	1
1791	18	5	1805	47	5
1792	18	1	1806	47	
1793	26		1807	66	4
1794	37		1808	52	
1795	45		1809	43	
1796	47		1810	44	9
1797	52	7	1811	50	
1798	65	5	1812	47	10
1799	61	5	1813	60	
1800	56	1	1814	36	
1801	57		1815	27	
1802	54		1816	59	

[2] Hay scales were first erected outside the town gate on West Street in 1784. They were later moved to the dock. See Annapolis Records, 9:21, 8:49, Hall of Records, Annapolis, Md. Large quantities of hay were moved through the town. See the accounts kept by the town weigher in Annapolis Treasurer's Papers, Hall of Records, Annapolis, Md. (hereafter cited as Treas. Pap.), Box 1.

venient to the new market house and stocked their shelves with goods supplied wholesale by Baltimore merchants.[3]

The efforts of the city to foster the marketing function of Annapolis were impeded by one member of the old merchant class, James Williams, who still claimed much of the land running on one side of Annapolis harbor adjacent to the public wharf, and whose entrepreneurial spirit had been crushed by the decline in mercantile opportunity. In 1803, John Muir reported on the work just completed on the public quay facing Williams's property.

> The City Commissioners beg leave to report that they have completed the wharf in a strong and handsome maner, and so as to prevent further injury to the Dock. . . . The Commissioners take leave to represent at the moment, the dock was secured on one side—the wharf of Mr. James Williams on the other, or Eastern side, was entirely destroyed and carried off—in consequence of which the Basin is exposed to certain destruction—for no doubt can be entertained that six months will wholly choak up the entrance to the Dock and thus render useless the efforts to preserve it. . . . The Commissioners . . . have stated to Mr. Williams the certain injuries which would result from his wharf not being immediately repaired, that Mr. Williams has decidedly declared his resolution not to repair his wharf. . . .[4]

Ultimately, the Williams property was taken over by the city and the basin was kept open for the sheltering of bay craft, but the once-proud spirit of the merchant community which initiated and promoted the development of the harbor area was gone. The city became the caretaker of the port and was left to fight a never-ending battle to maintain a status quo.

Not all of the old merchant class, however, were as sullen and resigned as Williams. Charles Wallace and John Muir found that the business of debt collection could be profitable, and their counting house on Green Street became the center of an informal, but exceedingly complex, financial institution. In 1791, a year after they formally ended their partnership with Joshua Johnson, Wallace and Muir's books showed assets of £228,145 currency, of which approxi-

---

[3]As early as 1789, John Randall bought goods from Oliver & Thompson, Baltimore. See his journal for December 1787 to April 1789, MS 1688, Maryland Historical Society, Baltimore, Md. Between November 1800 and March 1803, Jonathan Pinkney bought drygoods from Mr. Friese, a Baltimore merchant. See Friese Account Books, p. 189, MS 933, Maryland Historical Society, Baltimore, Md.

[4]Treas. Pap., Box 1.

mately £154,000, although transferred to Wallace and Muir for collection, still was owed, at 5 percent annual interest, to London creditors.[5]

Over the next six years, Wallace and Muir worked diligently to reduce the London debt and to reinvest their capital in profitable enterprises. Their first and foremost objective was to obtain as good security as possible from their debtors in order that they could sequester any real or personal property in the event that neither interest nor principal was paid. Wallace and Muir took notes, bonds, public securities, mortgages on property, and anything else they could squeeze out of their debtors as pledges against the payment of long overdue accounts. When debtors were reluctant to pay even the interest on debts, Wallace and Muir took them to court, where judgments on most securities were easily obtained. The frequency with which Wallace and Muir resorted to the courts can be seen from table 6-1, which is derived from the fees they paid for actions completed in the general court of the Western Shore.[6] Their most active year was 1791, when they successfully prosecuted claims worth £14,887 currency, £5,752 sterling, and 16,604 pounds of inspected tobacco.[7]

Table 6-1 Fees Paid by Wallace, Johnson and Muir
for Actions in the General Court of the Western Shore, 1786-1805

Year	Amount (pounds of tobacco)	Year	Amount (pounds of tobacco)
1786	706	1796	n.a.
1787	n.a.	1797	4,716
1788	870	1798	3,224
1789	5,992	1799	5,386
1790	11,498	1800	4,256
1791	16,604	1801	4,886
1792	7,578	1802	3,248
1793	7,313	1803	2,842
1794	5,000	1804	2,204
1795	6,614	1805	1,768

n.a. = not available.

Source: Fee Books, General Court of the Western Shore, Hall of Records, Annapolis, Md.

[5]Wallace, Johnson and Muir, Journal, 1791-1795, Gift Collection, D 796, Hall of Records, Annapolis, Md. (hereafter cited as Journal, 1791-1795).

[6]*Fee Books,* General Court of the Western Shore, Hall of Records, Annapolis, Md.

[7]Derived from the *Cost Books* of the General Court of the Western Shore, Hall of Records, Annapolis, Md.

Once the debts were secured by a court decision or by some form of legally recognized instrument, it became Wallace and Muir's chief chore to collect interest and ultimately the principal, while regularly remitting to London to pay their creditors. Payment of interest and principal came in many forms, ranging from cash to stock in the United States and, in two cases, land in Georgia totaling 75,500 acres.[8] Remittances were largely in bills of exchange on which Wallace and Muir gained as much as 5 percent when the exchange was below par.[9] By January 1798, the London debt was reduced to £69,216.2.4 sterling, with £29,679.16.6 sterling in United States stock and securities pledged to its redemption, leaving a net sum owed of £39.536 sterling (£64,843.1.9 currency at the going exchange rate of 164). In seven years, Wallace and Muir had sent their London crediors approximately £88,862 currency, or an annual average of £12,644.57 currency.[10]

The success Wallace and Muir had in collecting money to pay their London debt was in stark contrast to Johnson's declining fortunes in the consignment trade. By 1797, his affairs were in such disarray that he was eager to have the partnership settled and the profits divided.[11] Beginning in 1796, with capital (at 2.5 percent interest)

[8]Journal, 1791-1795, entries for March 24, 1792 and December 15, 1792 concern Georgia lands. On December 31, 1791, Robert Bowie gave Wallace & Muir stock in partial payment of his debt. For a good example of how one former cargo customer paid interest and principal on his debt see the account of Thomas Tillard given in Chancery Papers, Hall of Records, Annapolis, Md. (hereafter cited as Chan. Pap.), 5331.

[9]For the profits made from bills of exchange purchased when the rate of exchange was below par, see the evidence provided in Chan. Pap. 2893.

[10]Based on Ledger F, Wallace, Johnson and Muir Account Book, Private Account Records, Hall of Records, Annapolis, Md. (hereafter cited as WJM Ledger F). Except where otherwise cited, the calculations on the nature of Wallace, Johnson and Muir's debt and the speed with which they paid it off are based upon a careful reading of Ledger F supplemented with fragments of daybooks and journals and hints on Scottish bookkeeping practices supplied by John Mair's *Bookkeeping Methodiz'd*, Sixth Edition (Edinburgh, 1793). Although I think my calculations are close to what Wallace & Muir were able to do, I had much the same problem as the Auditor in Chancery who wrote in 1823 that "Instead of the books of [Wallace, Johnson and Muir] . . . the Auditor is furnished with a Single Ledger only, . . . unaccompanied by the Day Book and Journal on which it depends, or Even an Alphabet—It is true that the Separate accounts of Wallace, Johnson and Muir, in the Company's Ledger F exhibit balances against them respectively as in the Bill set forth—and it is also true . . . according to their several interests in the Concern as stated . . . but [the calculations] . . . [are] the result of an examination of their accounts only, and not of a general settlement of all their partnership transactions upon which alone the Court could safely act." Chan. Pap. 2468.

[11]How Johnson got into such straitened circumstances is not clear, although Dr. Rhoda Dorsey, who is familiar with Johnson through his correspondence as consul in London in the 1790s, feels it was probably owing to his obtuseness when it came to speculating in matters of trade. Johnson managed to marry off his daughter Louisa

supplied by his bankers, Fludyer, Maitland and Company, Johnson bought up the remaining small creditors, and in the fall of 1797, after securities had been pledged for the remaining debt not in his bankers' hands, Johnson returned home to claim his profits.[12]

Until his death in 1802, Johnson pursued Wallace and Muir through the courts in an effort to obtain more than the arbitrated settlement that had been made soon after his arrival in Maryland.[13] It was to no avail. Ultimately, the judgment of the arbitrators, Uriah Forrest, James Carey, and James Mason, prevailed, although Johnson's executors tried valiantly to revive his cause.[14] In February 1798, the three arbitrators, called for by the terms of the original partnership agreement signed in 1781, decided that the assets of the firm were sufficient to allow Johnson credit for £1,200 sterling per annum interest free during the years of the partnership as compensation for living expenses. Wallace and Muir for their half share were to receive an equal amount. The remaining assets were to be divided among the partners proportionate to their shares, deducting sufficient securities to cover the London debt and placing them in the hands of William Cooke and John Coles for collection.[15] The division netted Johnson £42,468 currency in specie and land, while Wallace and Muir were left to draw £37,330 currency, a discrepancy that was to result in a Chancery case that dragged on until 1823.[16]

Johnson's efforts to obtain even more money from Wallace and Muir had so exasperated them by 1801 that, a few months before Johnson died, they distributed a handbill in an effort to prove that they had not withheld what was rightfully his.[17] If anything, Wallace and Muir had been working overtime to eradicate the London debt. By the time the accounts of Wallace, Johnson and Muir were balanced in December 1801, an additional £32,769 currency had been sent to Fludyer, Maitland and Company, and only £27,502 currency in

---

Catherine to John Quincy Adams just before disaster struck, a fact that was to haunt Louisa Catherine the rest of her life and possibly was the cause of her periodic deep depression. Conversation with Lyman Butterfield, Massachusetts Historical Society, September 1972; and Andrew Oliver, *Portraits of John Quincy Adams and His Wife* (Cambridge, Mass., 1970), p. 27.

[12]Chan. Pap. 2893.

[13]*Ibid.*

[14]Johnson appealed the decision of the Chancellor to the Court of Appeals where the case was abated by Johnson's death. See Court of Appeals Dockets, June Term 1802, Docket #14, Hall of Records, Annapolis, Md. Johnson's administrator revived the case in Chancery in 1811 only to have it abated by Charles Wallace's death. No further action was then taken by Johnson's heirs. Chan. Pap. 606.

[15]Chan. Pap. 2893.

[16]Chan. Pap. 2468.

[17]Used as an exhibit in Chan. Pap. 2893. See p. 230.

To the PUBLIC.

IT is with reluctance that we presume to call the attention of the public to our private affairs. Our disagreeable disputes with Mr. Johnson being in a way to be settled by the proper tribunal, it may, perhaps, be deemed improper for either party to say any thing to the public with respect to the merits of the controversy. We have, for our part, hitherto cautiously avoided the subject, even in private conversations with any, except our nearest friends. But we find that a report is in circulation, equally contrary to truth, and injurious to that reputation which it has always been our endeavour to establish, and our pride to maintain. It is not our intention to trace the report to its origin; but we take the liberty of presenting to you a plain statement of facts, which, we presume, cannot be denied, and which, we trust, will appear to every impartial person of intelligence, who shall take the trouble of perusing it, wholly inconsistent with the report, " that Wallace and Muir hold every thing in their hands, " to the great injury of their late partner, Mr. Johnson, and his family."

1st. The house of Wallace, Johnson and Muir, existed nine years, during which time Johnson did not put to the amount of one shilling into the concern.

Currency.

2d. Mr. Johnson has drawn, in specie, from the profits of the concern, (interest not included,) . . . . £. 36,900 0 0

3d. There are funds in the hands of William Cooke, Esquire, belonging to the concern, and not under the control of Wallace and Muir, which, when disposed of, according to their destination, will probably yield to Mr. Johnson, ... 7,000 0 0

4th. There are lands in Virginia and Georgia belonging to the company, and not further under the control of Wallace and Muir than they are under the control of Johnson. Johnson's proportion of the net cost of which land is, ... 5,551 0 0

Johnson's proportion of a house and lot in Green-street, Annapolis, occupied as the company's counting-house, is, ... 254 0 0

Johnson's proportion of the company's interest in the Patowmack canal, is 830 0 0

Johnson's proportion of the company's interest in the Susquehanna canal, is 501 0 0

£. 51,036 0 0

Say fifty-one thousand and thirty-six pounds specie. As to the residue of the company's funds, they consist of bonds, notes and other obligations, and open accounts, and the net money arising from them, as soon as it is collected, is applied, as it ought to be, towards the discharge of the debts of the company; Wallace and Muir enjoy from this no advantage of which Mr. Johnson is deprived. The whole trouble of collection rests on Wallace and Muir, and they receive no compensation for it. It is true, that the expences of collection, as is certainly just, are defrayed from the funds.

We are perfectly sensible of the impropriety of attempting to prejudice the public mind with respect to the merits of a cause depending before a court of justice, and therefore have avoided any information respecting it. We have, indeed, been told, that such an attempt has been considered as punishable by the court. But when our credit and reputation, and of course our dearest interests, depend on the refutation of a report industriously circulated; when that report is of such a nature, that a simple denial would have little or no weight; when, perhaps, even a decision of the court in our favour may not be deemed a full refutation; when it is considered that some considerable time may elapse before that decision shall be given, and that we have confined ourselves to a few undeniable facts, and have left it entirely to our readers to form the proper conclusion from these facts, we flatter ourselves that no person of candour will think we have done more than in our situation could reasonably be expected.

WALLACE & MUIR.

Annapolis, 12th June, 1801.

Wallace and Muir Handbill, 1801. Maryland Hall of Records, Chancery Papers 2893. Photocopy by M. E. Warren, Annapolis.

debts being collected by Cooke and Coles remained due to the London creditors.[18]

With net capital assets of approximately £40,000 currency earning interest of approximately 6 percent a year, Wallace and Muir were provided with a comfortable income of, at minimum, £2,400 currency a year, or approximately £400 currency more than they were allowed to draw for living expenses during the life of the partnership.[19] In terms of a retirement income, £1,200 each was respectable. In 1787, a judge of the general court estimated that a person of his rank and status would spend £700 currency a year to support an Annapolis family "consisting of ten persons (half of whom are servants) keeping two horses and one milch cow."[20]

In 1801, at the age of seventy-four, Charles Wallace was content to rest easy and allow John Muir to bring to a close Wallace, Johnson and Muir's accounts, while he collected interest on his share and managed other investments such as the property along Fleet and Cornhill Streets, which annually returned a modest income in ground rents.[21] Part of the time Wallace spent at his plantation, and the rest in an elegant Annapolis townhouse he had purchased as the confiscated property of Ann Tasker's estate. The staymaker-turned-merchant, who sometime in 1773 had come with hat in hand to the same house to borrow enough to save Wallace, Davidson, and Johnson from bankruptcy, now tended the gardens as his own and presided at a table where once only the most privileged of Maryland society had dined.[22]

John Muir was fourteen years younger than Wallace and, in 1801, was not yet ready to retire.[23] To some extent his need to work was dictated by the continuing problems of collecting the remaining debts owed Wallace, Johnson and Muir. In a deposition taken in 1823, one resident recalled seeing him hard at work at the counting

[18]Balance Sheet, December 31, 1801, loose in WJM Ledger F.

[19]Chan. Pap. 2893.

[20]*Maryland Journal and Baltimore Advertiser*, April 6, 1787.

[21]The amount collected in ground rents was approximately $200 a year. See an exhibit in Chan. Pap. 3054A.

[22]Wallace was the third person to hold the Tasker lots since they were first offered for sale as the confiscated property of Daniel Dulany of Daniel in August 1781. Dulany was the executor of Ann Tasker's estate and the property was considered to be in his possession and thus subject to confiscation, as he was a loyalist. Wallace came into possession of the lots in 1793 and received title in 1799, after paying the original sale price of £1,280. Hemphill Notes, Gift Collection, D563, Box 13, Hall of Records, Annapolis, Md. The house and its "falling Garden" are noted by Wallace's nephew, Charles Wallace Hanson in his manuscript introduction to "Pamphlets by Alexander Contee Hanson, 1784–1788 and Manuscript Notes, ..." Maryland Historical Society, Baltimore, Md.

[23]Obituary, *Maryland Gazette*, September 5, 1810.

house in Green Street, grumbling to anyone who stopped in about Wallace's neglect of Wallace, Johnson and Muir's affairs.[24] But Muir also perceived that his and Wallace's assets, if combined with the capital of others, offered an opportunity to make an even greater fortune. As early as 1794, Charles Carroll of Carrollton was using Muir's services as a banker and "deposited" large sums of money with him for his management.[25] By 1804, Muir had decided that what he was doing privately could be rendered even more profitable if he could obtain a charter for a bank and sell shares.

There is no direct evidence to prove that the idea of a farmers' bank was first conceived by John Muir, but it is difficult to believe otherwise of the man who became its first president and chief cashier. Trained in the methods of Italian bookkeeping and familiar with the banking procedures of his native land, Muir easily could have suggested the two Scottish precedents that were incorporated into the charter and that made the bank at its founding unique in America: interest-bearing private accounts and the ability to make loans available to property holders on a demand basis through "cash accounts" (similar to the guaranteed checking accounts of today).[26] Muir also was in a good position to lobby for the charter as a member of the assembly from Annapolis; he probably even penned the major defense of the bank which was repeated several times in the *Maryland Gazette* in 1805 under the title "Observations [on the] Farmers Bank of Maryland."[27] The "Observations" were written to answer the opponents of the bank who claimed that: "Banks are calculated solely to aid commercial operations and that agricultural interest neither requires nor can support an institution of this nature."[28] Few people were as sensitive as John Muir was to the devastating impact of Baltimore capital on the tobacco trade, or could write as earnestly about the need to allow farmers as well as merchants time at interest to settle their debts.

The "Observations" begin with the erroneous plea that a bank could help revive Annapolis as a commercial center. After stressing the virtues of a harbor free from ice during the winter, the author wrote:

[24]Chan. Pap. 2468.

[25]Journal, 1791–1795, entries for May 8, 1794 and May 7, 1795 for sums "deposited by him Today" amounting to £807.19.5 currency.

[26]"Observations on the act, entitled, An Act to establish a bank, and incorporate a company, under the name of the Farmers Bank of Maryland, . . ." *Maryland Gazette*, April 18 and April 25, 1805. Cited by Mary Jane Dowd in "The Role of the State Government in the Economy of Maryland, 1777–1807" (Master's thesis, Johns Hopkins University, 1959), p. 165.

[27]*Ibid.* and obituary, *Maryland Gazette*, September 5, 1810.

[28]*Maryland Gazette*, April 18, 1805.

Annapolis too, is situated in the heart of the country producing the fine tobaccoes, which in a great degree, peculiar to her soil, must long continue the principal staple of Maryland; she [Annapolis] is more convenient to the extensive peninsula, which stretches to the eastward of the route from Baltimore to Washington, than either of those cities, and she is situated precisely at the point of communication established by nature between the two shores into which Maryland is divided. A market opened here, devoted immediately to the object of vending abroad and procuring returns for the tobaccoes of Maryland, although it would interfere with a branch of trade but little regarded in the commerce of Baltimore would yet prove of inestimable advantage to the state at large. This trade, once steadily persued, that fluctuation of price must necessarily cease, which is now frequently ruinous both to the cultivator and the merchant, as the supply would soon be proportioned to the demand. This fluctuation is perhaps solely owing to the neglect of this commodity in the Baltimore market, until its scarcity produces a price abroad that promises an higher gain to a few adventurers than their ordinary objects of speculation; then the sudden rise of price diverts a great proportion of the labour of the community to the article than foreign consumption requires, and no longer yielding a profit, it will hardly command any price at all, to the great injury of the disappointed cultivator, and sometimes to the ruin of the merchant.[29]

How the bank would bring about the necessary regulation of the tobacco trade is never made clear in the "Observations," and the author ignored the fact that Baltimore was becoming increasingly important as the major collection and distribution point for tobacco. But if the "Observations" were weakest in their conclusion about the future commercial impact of the farmers' bank on Annapolis, their strength was in the advocacy of the need for capital to foster agricultural improvement. Citing Sir James Steuart and Adam Smith, the author noted that, "to become a great state, to be highly commercial and opulent, it is necessary to commence by giving every facility, every encouragement to agriculture; commerce will follow of course."[30] Farmers should be able to earn money on their profits as merchants did. They also should be able to borrow to improve their stock and their land or to tide themselves over from one crop to the next. Realizing that the failure of the Ayre Bank, which touched off the great depression of 1773 and brought so many tobacco houses to ruin, was often cited as an argument against agricultural banks, the author points out that the Ayre Bank failed because not enough property backed the "chimerical schemes" of speculators. The Farmers Bank of Maryland would be different; loans in the form of

[29]*Ibid.*
[30]*Ibid.*

"cash accounts" would only be allowed to people of substance and property as determined by the representatives of the bank in the county where the borrower resided.[31]

The chartering of the Farmers Bank of Maryland in 1804 represented the logical extension of almost fifteen profitable years spent by John Muir and, to a lesser extent, Charles Wallace, in the settling of the affairs of the once great consignment tobacco house of Wallace, Johnson and Muir. Even the enormity of the London debt proved lucrative. While Wallace and Muir paid 2.5 and 5 percent interest to their London creditors, their debtors were forced to pay 6 percent, and many found that difficult. For example, one cargo customer, Thomas Tillard, owed £3,275.6.10 sterling ($14,557.07) in 1778 and had paid only $5,267.28 of the principal by 1797, although he had paid $7,809.79 in interest.[32] Whatever they had left after remitting regularly to London, Wallace and Muir reinvested in stocks, bonds, and land which returned at least 6 percent interest, if not more. For instance, they purchased United States securities, collected 6 percent interest for three or four years, and then apparently sold them at twice what they had cost.[33] It was only common sense to John Muir that establishing a bank to borrow money at 3 and 4 percent from investors to loan out at 6 percent would work in Annapolis.[34] He had already tested and proved the principle.

It was also fitting that John Muir should be the pioneer in a new venture designed to serve the needs of a town and countryside greatly altered from 1771, when Wallace, Davidson and Johnson first challenged the British middleman. In thirty-four years, tobacco planters had become diversified farmers, and Annapolis had changed from an emerging commercial center to a small market town. Rather than fight change, Wallace and Muir adjusted, taking advantage of the new opportunities for capital investment. Measured by the wealth they left behind, both men fared well. When Muir died in 1810 at the age of sixty, he left personal property worth $6,206.00 and such extensive land holdings in Georgia that the administrator of his estate, Dr. James Murray, emigrated to oversee their management.[35] Wallace died at the

---

[31]*Ibid.*, April 25, 1805.

[32]Chan. Pap. 5231.

[33]Chan. Pap. 2893.

[34]"Articles of Association of the Farmers Bank of Maryland," *Maryland Gazette*, August 2, 1804.

[35]Anne Arundel County Administration Docket, 1787-1820, p. 84, Hall of Records, Annapolis, Md.; Chan. Pap. 2468; and Muir's obituary in the *Maryland Gazette*, September 5, 1810, which reads: "Died in this city on the 30th ult., John Muir, President of the Farmer's Bank of Maryland, in the 60th year of his age. This worth gentleman was a native of Scotland, and came to this country at a very early period of his life, from which

age of eighty-three in 1812, leaving personal property appraised at $23,774.20 and extensive real estate in Anne Arundel County and Annapolis.[36] Other merchants, caught in the commercial decline of Annapolis, did not have the assets of Wallace, Johnson and Muir. Most had to be content with smaller profits and declining prospects of accumulating wealth, although perhaps none saw the change as graphically as James Williams, whose wharf, long neglected, finally washed away in 1803 during a storm.

Although the writer of the "Observations" on the Farmers Bank of Maryland thought that the presence of the bank in Annapolis would help make it a reexport center for the tobacco trade, he was mistaken. For another forty years, until the founding of the Naval Academy, Annapolis was to remain undisturbed by change. About 1820, one writer provided a characterization of the town and its people that probably contained considerable truth. The earth's axis, he wrote, must surely be Annapolis. "It should be called the pivot-city . . . for while all the world around it revolves it remains stationary." It was easy to find. "To get to Annapolis you have but to cultivate a colossal calmness and the force of gravity will draw you . . . there." The people are like exclamation points. They always have their hands in their pockets, eat nothing but sea food which expands their brains, and talk nothing but politics. "Annapolis keeps the Severn River in its place. This will be useful when the harbour of Baltimore dries up. Annapolitans are waiting for this. They are in no hurry. . . ."[37]

Too often the story of urban growth and economic development in the Chesapeake is told in terms of the rise of Baltimore; but for at least two decades, 1773–1793, outport towns, of which Annapolis was the first and perhaps the most important, played a major role in the export of tobacco, Maryland's most valuable crop. Their

---

time he attached himself warmly to the cause of American Independence, and took an active part in that struggle which terminated in the freedom of the country. His services as a member of the Legislature of Maryland, for six years, entitle his memory to the grateful respect of his fellow-citizens, and more particularly to those of Annapolis, whose best friend he has ever been."

[36]Wallace was born in Annapolis in April 1727, the son of John and Anne Wallace. St. Anne's Parish Register, 1: 79, Hall of Records, Annapolis, Md. His obituary appeared in the *Maryland Gazette* for February 20, 1812. For the value of his personal estate, see Anne Arundel County Administration Docket, 1787–1820, p. 90, Hall of Records, Annapolis, Md. The division of his real property among his heirs led to a number of Chancery cases. For example, see Chancery Record, 104:333ff., Hall of Records, Annapolis, Md.

[37]Elihu S. Riley, *The Ancient City* (Annapolis, 1887), p. 145.

merchants wrested control from London of the quality tobacco export trade. They successfully contained Baltimore capital until market conditions dictated by the European wars of the 1790s gave Baltimore merchants the competitive advantage.

During the 1770s, Annapolis merchants were the first Americans backed exclusively with native capital to make marked progress in the consignment tobacco trade. During the 1780s, Annapolis merchants effectively utilized capital gained from wartime profits to place themselves among the most important of the postwar exporters of quality tobacco. Finally, during the 1790s and the first half decade of the 1800s, at a time when all hope of success in the tobacco trade was lost, Annapolis merchants moved their resources from commerce to agriculture and helped establish one of the first successful agricultural banks in the nation. It was a pattern of shifting investment and individual adjustment to altering opportunities that perhaps was not unlike that elsewhere in Virginia and Maryland, but it is one that has been sadly neglected by those who have concentrated on aggregate growth or on isolated studies of individual firms. It is hoped that by looking closely at the Annapolis merchant community during a period of both rapid economic growth and equally rapid economic decline it has been possible to redress the balance and place mercantile activity in the Chesapeake between 1763 and 1805 into its proper perspective.

APPENDIXES

Appendix A: Geographical Distribution
of Joshua Johnson's Correspondents, 1781–1783

(x means correspondence in that year)

Country	State	City or County	Correspondent	1781	1782	1783
France		Abbeville	Comasell, T. & fils		x	
			Homasset & fils		x	x
		Amiens	Laurent, Augustin	x		
		Bergerac	Brian, née Lugeion		x	
		Bordeaux	Barton, Johnston & Co.			x
			Borde, Beaux & Co.	x		
			Conner, John		x	
			French, V.& P.			
			& Nephew		x	x
			Gernon, Christopher		x	
			Langlade, M.			x
			MacCarthy & Brothers		x	
			Le Baron de Paellnitz		x	
			Prenat, Lambert frères		x	
			Ridout, Thomas	x	x	x
		Brest	Pelegrin, M.			x
		Calais	Isaac, Laurent	x		
		Croisic	Brouard, M.		x	x
			La Marque d'aine	x		
		Dunkirk	Hunter, Archibald		x	x
		Havre de Grace	Lemozine, Andrew	x	x	x
		Lamballe	Lechevalur du faure			
			du Provillac		x	
		La Rochelle	Verdier fils & Greig		x	
		Laval	Bealuire, Mozin		x	
			Besnier de Chambray	x	x	x
			Perier de la Corbiniere			
			Co.	x		
			Perier du Bignon			x
			Gerardiere & Co.	x	x	x
			Guicherit, G. B.		x	
			Les Frères Guitet	x	x	x
			Pichot, M.	x		
			Seyeuir Frères &			
			Dolsegaray		x	

Note: All names reflect Johnson's spelling.

Appendix A (continued)

Country	State	City or County	Correspondent	1781	1782	1783
France (*cont.*)		Lille	Badas, M. Lacher		x	
		Lorient	Barclay & Moylan		x	
			Berard, J. J. & Co.		x	
			Cuming, James	x		
			Cuming & Macarty	x	x	
			Erwin, Joseph		x	
			Gibbs, J. W. William		x	
			Grubb, James	x	x	
			Helso, Nathan		x	
			Jennings, Dr. M.		x	
			Kelso, Nathaniel			x
			Moylan, James	x	x	
			Neilson, Robert		x	
			Nesbitt, Jonathan & Co.	x	x	x
			Norfleet, Elisha			x
			Patterson, Thomas	x	x	
			Reinolds, Jackson	x		
			Siemen, Paul		x	
			Willson, Samuel	x		
		Lyon	Carlton, Francis		x	
			Dozall, W. C. frères		x	
			Ferrason, Jonathan & fils		x	
			Latour, J. L.		x	
			Saye Pedant, J. B. & Co.			x
			Souvène & Co.	x		
		Marseille	Curson, Samuel			x
		Mayenne	Benoiste frères & Co.	x	x	x
		Metz	D'or Manger & Co.	x	x	x
		Nantes	Bailly, M.		x	
			Brisard du Marthre		x	
			Guesdon, M.		x	
			Pierce, John Harvey	x		
		Nîmes	Forele, M., l'aîné		x	
		Orleans	Howdoward, M.			x
			Huguier, H. Benoit		x	
			Loche, M.	x	x	
			Peteau, Guinebaud		x	
			Robillard & fils		x	

Appendix A (continued)

Country	State	City or County	Correspondent	1781	1782	1783
France (*cont.*)		Paimboeuf	O'Dea, James		x	x
		Paris	Allen, Jeremiah		x	
			Baller, Giradot & Co.			x
			Cliptues, Lewis		x	
			Le Couteulx & Co.		x	
			Darcel, Nicols		x	
			Dumas, M.		x	
			Grand, M.	x	x	x
			Gregson, John		x	x
			L'Hommaud, M.		x	
			Mauchonée, M.		x	
			Mayo, Joseph			x
			Pucet fils & Co.	x		
			Ridley, Mathew		x	
			Tardy, Lewis	x		
			Tourton & Bauer		x	
			Van Dobleine, G. C.	x		
		Pouliguen	Brouard, fils		x	x
		Rennes	Galbois père & fils		x	
			Villegaud in le Boucher	x		
		Rheims	L'Escossais, Dusautoy	x		
		Rouen	Brunel, M.		x	
			Garvey, Robert & Co.		x	x
			Gorlier le Roux & Co.			x
		St. Malo	LeClerc, Ives		x	x
		St. Quentin	Debrissac Paulet & Nording		x	
		Sedan	Labauche, Louis & fils		x	
		Tours	Bacots fils & Co.	x		
			Delavan Bouresault & fils		x	
			Pelge & Co.	x		
		Troyes	Camurat & fils		x	
		Vannes	Sères, M.			x
		Versailles	Bussman & Co.		x	
Germany		Gottinburgh	Dickson, David	x	x	x

Appendix A (continued)

Country	State	City or County	Correspondent	1781	1782	1783
Great Britain		Belfast	Brown, Samuel		x	
			Wilson, Nathaniel		x	
		Bristol	Mallet, Thomas	x		
		Cambridge	Harrison, Robert		x	
		Ireland	Cruikshank, Charles			x
		London	Bartlett, B.N.	x	x	
			Caxson, Edward			x
			Harrison, William			x
			Prescotts, Grotes, Culverden, Hollingsworth	x	x	x
			White, James		x	x
			Whiteside, William		x	x
			William, Theophilus			x
		Oxford	Crookshank, Charles & Co.			x
			Nichols, Henry		x	x
		Westmoreland	Harrison, Christopher		x	
Holland		Amsterdam	Bell, William	x	x	
			Clifford & Teyssets		x	
			Cromling, Daniel & Sons		x	
			Hazehurst, Isaac	x		
			Hockshon, John	x		
			Lappenburg, Reinhold & Schmuman	x	x	x
			Larwood, Vanhasselt & Dansuthlelen		x	x
			Meyers, Moses & Samuel		x	x
			John de Neufville & Son	x	x	x
			Schneck, Hermann	x	x	
			Van der Tunk		x	x
		Flessingue	Jan van der Woordt	x		
		Rotterdam	Barker, Nicholas	x	x	x
			Curson, Samuel		x	
		Utrecht	Peterson, Henry		x	

Appendix A (continued)

Country	State	City or County	Correspondent	1781	1782	1783
Madeira			Lamar, Hill, Bissett Co.			x
Netherlands (Austria)		Gand [Ghent]	Buyck, B.		x	
		Ostende	Atkinson, Jasper			x
			Bell, William		x	
			De Cuyper, P. S.	x		x
			De Vink & Co.			x
			Edwards, Eziekiel		x	
			Hayman, Thomas			x
			Riddle, John		x	x
			Roy Roche & Co.		x	
			Smith, George			x
			Wilson, Stephen		x	
		Ypres	Michell, J. B. & fils			x
Portugal		Lisbon	Buckeley, John & Co.	x		x
			Burns, M.			x
Spain		Barcelona	Arabet, Gautier, Manning		x	
		Cadiz	Gough, Edward	x	x	
			Harrison & Co.	x	x	x
			Healthcoat, John		x	
		Madrid	Gueneau, Augustin		x	x
St. Martin			Fairholme & Luther		x	
U.S.	Md.	Annapolis	Ashton, John			x
			Carroll, Charles	x	x	x
			Davidson, John	x	x	x
			Davidson, John & Samuel	x	x	x
			Dowson, Joseph	x	x	x
			Eastman & Neth	x	x	
			Faris, William		x	x
			Galloway, John			x
			Hanna, Rev. William	x	x	
			Harwood, Benjamin	x	x	
			Harwood, Thomas	x		
			Harwood, Thomas & Benjamin	x	x	
			Johnson, John		x	

Appendix A (continued)

Country	State	City or County	Correspondent	Year 1781	1782	1783
U.S. (*cont.*)	Md. (*cont.*)	Annapolis (*cont.*)	Lloyd, Col. Edward	x	x	
			Lloyd, Richard Bennett		x	
			MacNamara, Michael		x	
			Muir, John	x	x	x
			Murray, Dr. James		x	x
			Neth, Lewis		x	
			Sprigg, Richard		x	x
			Stevenson, William	x	x	
			Wilkens, William	x	x	
			Wilkens & Muir	x	x	
			Williams, James	x	x	
			Williams, Joseph	x	x	
			Williams & Boyle	x	x	
			Williams, Joseph & John Muir	x	x	x
		Anne Arundel	Chew, Samuel			x
			Cowman, John			x
			Hopkins, Johns	x		
			Hopkins, Joseph	x		
			Hopkins, Richard			x
			Mackall, Benjamin			x
			Sprigg, Elizabeth		x	x
			Steward, Stephen			x
			Thomas, John			x
			Weems, David		x	x
		Baltimore City	Alexander, Mark		x	
			Allison, Patrick	x	x	
			Bowly & Stewart		x	
			Bowly, Daniel & Co.		x	x
			Buchanan, Andrew		x	x
			Buchanan, Archibald	x	x	x
			Buchanan, Robert & Ephriam Blaine	x	x	
			Burling & Van Wyck	x	x	
			Calhoun, James		x	x
			Callerson, William & Bro.	x		
			Coulter, Dr. John		x	x
			Crocketts & Harris	x	x	
			Croxall, Charles			x
			Curson, Richard	x	x	x

Appendix A (continued)

Country	State	City or County	Correspondent	1781	1782	1783
U.S. *(cont.)*	Md. *(cont.)*	Baltimore City *(cont.)*	Davly, Alexander William	x	x	x
			Dorsey & Wheeler	x	x	
			Gartner, George	x	x	x
			Gilmore, Robert		x	
			Grant, Mr.			x
			Hammond, William	x	x	x
			Hammond & Hudson	x		
			Harris, David	x	x	
			Hollingsworth, Jesse	x	x	
			Hopkins, Daniel & Co.	x	x	
			Hudson, Jonathan	x	x	x
			Johnson, Dr. Edward			x
			Johnston, Christopher	x	x	
			Johnston, Robert	x	x	
			Lewis, John Weems		x	x
			McGriffin, Joseph	x	x	
			McKim, Robert & A.	x	x	
			McLure, John	x	x	x
			McLure and Thomas Russell		x	x
			McLure and Hugh Young		x	x
			Merryman, John		x	
			Moale, Eleanor	x	x	
			Moale, John	x	x	x
			Neill, William	x	x	x
			Patterson, William & Bros.	x	x	
			Purveyance, Samuel & Robert	x	x	x
			Ridgely, Charles	x	x	
			Ridgely, Richard		x	
			Ridley & Pringle	x	x	x
			Smith, John	x	x	
			Smith, Samuel	x	x	x
			Smith, William & Samuel	x	x	x
			Smith, Johnston & Co.	x	x	
			Sterrett, James	x	x	
			Sterrett, James Jr.	x	x	
			Sterrett, John & Co.	x	x	x

Appendix A (continued)

Country	State	City or County	Correspondent	Year		
				1781	1782	1783
U.S.	Md.	Baltimore	Sterrett, John &			
(*cont.*)	(*cont.*)	City	Jeremiah Yellott	x	x	x
		(*cont.*)	Steward, David	x	x	
			Steward, Stephen &			
			Son	x	x	x
			Steyer, George	x	x	x
			Swan, Col. John	x	x	
			Taylor, William	x	x	
			Vanbibber, Abraham	x	x	x
			Vanbibber, Isaac	x	x	
			Welsh &			
			Eichelberger		x	
			Young, Hugh	x	x	x
		Baltimore	Ridgely, Charles	x		
		County	Rumsey, Benjamin			
			Joppa	x	x	x
		Calvert County	Darnall, Henry			x
			Lyles, A. C. William	x		
			Weems, John		x	x
		Cambridge	Pattison, Archibald	x	x	
		Carrollsburgh	Fenwick, Ignatius		x	x
		Chaptico	Key, Philip		x	x
		Prince George's	Contee, Thomas			x
		County	Cooledge, Judson			x
			Crawford, David	x	x	
			Fitzhugh, Peregrene		x	
			Fitzhugh, William		x	x
			Holland, Thomas			x
			Leek, Frank M.	x	x	x
			Rozer, Henry		x	x
		St. Mary's	Barnes, Col. Richard	x	x	
		County	Plater, George			x
		Somerset	Gale, Levin	x	x	
		County				
		Talbot County	Bordley, John		x	
			Chamberlain, James			
			Lloyd		x	
			Chamberlain, Samuel	x	x	x
			Sharpe, Samuel		x	x

Appendix A (continued)

Country	State	City or County	Correspondent	1781	1782	1783
U.S. (cont.)	Md. (cont.)	Worcester County	Dennis, Robert	x	x	x
	Mass.	Boston	Austin, Benjamin		x	
			Austin, John Loring	x	x	
			Black, Andrew	x	x	x
			Eaton & Benson			x
			Johonnot, Francis		x	
			Lamb, James & Thomas		x	
			Loring, John & Austin, Benjamin			x
			Mitchell, Henry	x	x	
			Russell, Thomas		x	x
			Sears, David			x
			Williams, Jonathan	x	x	
	N.H.	Kettery	Buckminster, Rev. Mr.	x	x	
			Sparhawk, Elizabeth	x	x	
			Stevens, Rev. Benjamin	x	x	x
		Portsmouth	Brackett, Dr. Joshua	x	x	x
			Whipple, William		x	x
	N.C.	Edenton	Allen, Nathaniel	x	x	x
			Bateman, Nehemiah	x	x	
			Langley, Willis	x	x	
			Webb, Bryer & Co.		x	x
	Pa.	Philadelphia	Armston & King		x	
			Bridges, Robert		x	
			Connor, John		x	
			Craig, John	x	x	
			Dunlap, James		x	x
			Fillet, A. J.			x
			Footman & Carmick		x	x
			Forde, Standish	x	x	x
			Gardner, Dr. Joseph	x	x	
			Hazelhurst, Isaac		x	x
			Hazelhurst, Robert	x	x	
			Henderson, Hazel		x	
			Ingles, Samuel & Co.	x	x	
			Lewis, Mordeccai & Co.		x	
			Marshall, John		x	x
			McClenachan, Blair		x	x

Appendix A (continued)

Country	State	City or County	Correspondent	1781	1782	1783
U.S. (cont.)	Pa. (cont.)	Philadelphia (cont.)	Morris, Jacob & Woodward, John		x	x
			Morris, Robert	x	x	x
			Moses, Isaac & Co.			x
			Moulder & Stewart	x	x	
			Nesbitt, J. M. & Co.	x	x	x
			Ogden, Titus		x	
			Ord, John	x	x	
			Paisly, Robert		x	
			Penrose, Isaac		x	
			Penrose, Samuel	x	x	
			Pringle, John	x	x	x
			Purveyance, John	x	x	x
			Ramsay & Cox		x	x
			Reed & Forde	x	x	
			Robinson, James	x	x	x
			Ross, John	x	x	x
			Seagrove & Constable		x	
			Searle, James	x		
			Snowdon, Isaac			x
			Stevenson, Robert		x	x
			Stewart, Alexander & Totten, Robert	x	x	x
			Stewart, James & Alexander		x	x
			Swanwich, John [attorney to Robert Morris]		x	x
			Vermily, Elizabeth		x	x
			Wharton, Joseph	x	x	x
			Whiteside, Peter & Co.	x	x	x
			Whiteside & Wharton, T.		x	x
			Wickoff, Isaac		x	x
	Va.	Alexandria	Adam, Robert		x	
			Conway, Richard & Adam, Robert	x	x	
			Fitzgerrold, Col. John		x	
			Hooe & Harrison		x	
			Mason, George		x	

Appendix A (continued)

				Year		
Country	State	City or County	Correspondent	1781	1782	1783
U.S.	Va.	Alexandria	Steward, Dr. David		x	x
(*cont.*)	(*cont.*)	(*cont.*)	Watson & Tandy		x	x
		Fredericksburg	Brownlow, John	x	x	x
			Chew, Robert Beverly	x	x	x
		Petersburg	Ross, David & Co.		x	
		Richmond	Steward & Hopkins		x	x

Appendix B
Part 1: Occupational Index to the 1783 Tax List,
Annapolis Hundred, Derived from Individual Career Profiles

I. Professionals and government employees (19.44%)

    A.   Doctors
1. Murray, James
2. Scott, Upton
3. Steuart, James

    B.   Gentlemen-planters
1. Brice, James, Esq.
2. Bullen, John
3. Campbell, William (Capt.)
4. Carroll, Charles (Carrollton)
5. Jenifer, Daniel of St. Thomas
6. Lloyd, Edward
7. Lloyd, Richard B.
8. McCubbin, Nicholas, Jr.
9. Paca, Aquila
10. Quynn, Allen, Esq.
11. Ramsay, Nathaniel
12. Ridout, John
13. Stoddert, Benjamin

    C.   Lawyers
1. Brice, John
2. Chase, Jeremiah T.
3. Chase, Samuel
4. Duvall, Gabriel, Esq.
5. Hammond, Matthias
6. Hanson, Alexander C.
7. Jenings, Thomas
8. Paca, William (His Excellency)

    D.   Merchants–public servants
1. Couden, Robert
2. Davidson, John
3. Harwood, Benjamin
4. Harwood, Thomas
5. Hodgkin, Thomas B.

    E.   Minister
1. Gates, Rev'd Mr.

    F.   Scriveners and clerks
1. Callahan, John
2. Dorsey, Joshua
3. Fairbrother, Francis

Appendix B, Part 1 (continued)

4. Fowler, Jubb
5. Harrison, William
6. Harwood, Nicholas
7. Howard, Samuel H.
8. Johnson, Thomas
9. Knapp, John
10. McCubbin, Moses
11. Ranken, George
12. Shephard, Nathaniel

II.   Merchants and storekeepers (14.35%)

A.   Merchants
1. Brown, William (merchant)
2. Dowson, Joseph
3. Eastman, Joseph
4. Hyde, Thomas
5. McCubbin, Nicholas, Sr.
6. Mackubin, James of Richard
7. Muir, John
8. Neth, Lewis
9. Randall, John
10. Ridgely, Absalom
11. Ringgold, James
12. Rutland, Thomas
13. Tootell, James
14. Wallace, Charles
15. Wilkins, William
16. Williams, James
17. Williams, Joseph
18. Wilson, Thomas

B.   Storekeepers
1. Biggs, William
2. Brewer, John
3. Brewer, Nicholas
4. Clarke, Joseph
5. Gassaway, Thomas
6. Golder, Archibald
7. Graham, Thomas
8. Hurst, Jacob
9. Hyde, William
10. Johnson, John
11. McCubbin, Nicholas (cordwainer)
12. Pinkney, Jonathan
13. Wilmot, John

Appendix B, Part 1 (continued)

III.   Craftsmen (20.37%)

    A.   Blacksmiths
        1. Harris, Isaac
        2. Retallick, Simon

    B.   Blockmaker
        1. Green, John

    C.   Bricklayer
        1. Nixon, Robert

    D.   Cabinetmakers
        1. Chisholm, Archibald
        2. Shaw, John

    E.   Carpenters
        1. Dalzal, Thomas
        2. Frazier, Joshua
        3. Minskey, Nicholas
        4. Thompson, Alexander
        5. Weedon, Oliver

    F.   Coachmakers
        1. Hutton, Samuel & Henry
        2. Parker, Jonathan
        3. Price, Thomas (Pryse)

    G.   Painter-glazer
        1. Tuck, William

    H.   Pumpmaker
        1. Lilley, William

    I.   Printers
        1. Green, Frederick
        2. Green, Samuel

    J.   Shipcarpenter
        1. Owens, Edward

    K.   Shoemakers
        1. Flemming, Richard
        2. Fowler, Daniel
        3. Henry, William and Thomas
        4. Howard, John
        5. Marshall, John
        6. Maw. William
        7. Williams, Joseph
        8. Williams, William
        9. Willshire, Jonathan

Appendix B, Part 1 (continued)

L. Silversmiths–engravers
   1. Chalmers, John
   2. Hogg, Charles
   3. Sparrow, Thomas

M. Staymaker
   1. Yeates, Vachel

N. Surveyor
   1. Brown, William

O. Tailors
   1. Callahan, Thomas
   2. Campbell, Frances
   3. Coe, William
   4. Slaughter, Thomas
   5. Thompson, Richard

P. Tanner
   1. Goldsmith, William

Q. Watchmakers
   1. Claude, Abraham
   2. Faris, William
   3. French, James
   4. Whetcroft, William

R. Wheelwright
   1. Fowler, John

IV. Service occupations (22.69%)

A. Bakers
   1. Grammar, Frederick
   2. Sibell, Henry

B. Barbers
   1. Jones, Richard
   2. Logan, William
   3. Reed, James
   4. Seibert, Justus

C. Butchers
   1. Bash, Adam
   2. Wells, Daniel

D. Ferrykeeper
   1. Thompson, Edward

Appendix B, Part 1 (continued)

E. Ship captains and mariners*
   1. Allen, John (m)
   2. Berry, Robert (c)
   3. Brown, Hugh (c)
   4. Bryan, Daniel (c)
   5. Dashiell, Capt. (c)
   6. Garston, George (?)
   7. Gordon, John (c)
   8. Gordon, William (c)
   9. Hanson, John (c)
   10. Levashier, John (c)
   11. Middleton, Joseph (c)
   12. Middleton, William (c)
   13. Pitt, John (c)
   14. Steuart, John (c)
   15. Stichbury, Philip (c)
   16. Valliant, Nicholas (c)
   17. Yieldhall, William (c)

F. Tavern, inn, and boardinghouse keepers
   1. Ashmead, Joseph
   2. Brewer, Joseph
   3. Brewer, Thomas
   4. Bryce, Frances
   5. Clarke, Robert
   6. Davis, George
   7. Fairbairn, Benjamin
   8. Fowler, William
   9. Gaither, Ann
   10. Ghiselin, Mary
   11. Hewett, Jane
   12. Howard, Mary
   13. McHard, Isaac
   14. Mann, George
   15. Maybury, Beriah
   16. Middleton, Gilbert
   17. Mills, Cornelius
   18. Rebb, Adam
   19. Reynolds, Robert
   20. Ridgely, Charles
   21. Sands, John
   22. West, James
   23. Wilkins, Deborah

*m=mariners; c=ship captains

Appendix B, Part 1 (continued)

V.   Laborers and unknowns (14.81%)

    A.   Laborers
        1.   Martin, John
        2.   Meeke, Vestal
        3.   Richardson, Adam
        4.   Sands, William
        5.   Townsend, Thomas

    B.   Unknowns
        1.   Adams, Miss
        2.   Adams, George
        3.   Barber, Charles
        4.   Barnhold, Henry
        5.   Beard, Richard
        6.   Callahan, James
        7.   Callahan, John
        8.   Christian, John
        9.   Cotter, Daniel
      10.   Dowds, Charles
      11.   Henley, Zachariah
      12.   Leeke, Richard
      13.   Lang, Robert
      14.   Massey, Henry
      15.   Mills, John
      16.   Munroe, Daniel
      17.   Owens, Richard
      18.   Pinkney, Anthony
      19.   Piper, Thomas
      20.   Purdy, John
      21.   Ross, Nathaniel
      22.   Sears, Tissue
      23.   Smith, Richard
      24.   Stevens, Joseph
      25.   Tyers, Richard
      26.   Valliant, Elcock
      27.   Wells, John

VI.   Widows and spinsters (8.33%)
        1.   Adams, Elizabeth
        2.   Annis, Mary
        3.   Brewer, Rachel
        4.   Callahan, Sarah
        5.   Caton, Ann
        6.   Dulany, Mary
        7.   Fulk, Margaret

Appendix B, Part 1 (continued)

8. McCubbin, Elizabeth (Mackubin)
9. Pressley, Mary
10. Reynolds, Mary
11. Robins, Ann
12. Ross, Widow
13. Selby, Ann
14. Smith, Mary
15. Steuart, Mary
16. Unsworth, Mrs.
17. Vineyard, Widow
18. Wilmot, Dinah

Appendix B
Part 2: Alphabetical Index to the 1783 Tax List, Annapolis Hundred

Name	Lots	Acres	Land Value (£)	Slaves	Total Value of Property (£)	Households* WM	WF	AM
Adams, George	0	0	0	0	24.00.0	2	2	1
Allen, John	0	0	0	3	44.00.0	3	2	1
Annis, Mary	0	0	0	0	0	0	3	0
Ashmead, Joseph	0	0	0	3	249.03.4	5	4	1
Ashmead, Joseph (for Robert Johnson's estate)	2	1.25	483.0.0	0	483.00.0	0	0	0
Ball, John (estate)	1	.50	70.0.0	0	70.00.0	0	0	0
Barber, Charles	0	0	0	0	19.00.0	3	3	1
Barnhold, Henry	0	0	0	0	0.15.0	1	1	1
Bash, Adam	0	0	0	0	50.00.0	2	2	1
Beard, Richard	0	0	0	1	40.00.0	1	1	1
Berry, Robert	0	0	0	8	275.01.8	3	2	1
Biggs, William	0	0	0	1	147.00.0	1	0	1
Bordley, Elizabeth	5	5	617.0.0	6	792.00.0	0	0	0
Brewer, John	1	.50	516.0.0	5	764.06.8	2	4	1
Brewer, Joseph	0	0	0	7	276.00.0	4	4	1
Brewer, Nicholas	1	.25	228.0.0	2	335.01.8	1	0	1
Brewer, Rachel	0	0	0	1	47.00.0	1	3	0
Brewer, Thomas & Welch	1	.25	208.0.0	0	258.00.0	3	2	3
Brice, Francis	1	.50	115.0.0	0	120.00.0	1	2	0
Brice, James, Esq.	2	2	833.0.0	7	1,228.13.4	1	2	1
Brice, John	2	2	833.0.0	2	1,078.08.4	3	2	1
Brown, Capt. Hugh	0	0	0	4	180.00.0	1	1	1
Brown, William (merchant)	0	0	0	1	133.13.4	1	2	1
Brown, William, Sr.	0	0	0	2	310.00.0	5	2	1
Bryan, Daniel	0	0	0	0	40.00.0	2	1	1
Bullen, John	2	2	250.0.0	3	670.16.8	1	0	1
Callahan, James	0	0	0	0	0.15.0	0	0	0
Callahan, John	0	0	0	2	192.10.0	2	1	1
Callahan, Sarah	0	0	0	6	173.10.0	0	2	3
Callahan, Thomas	1	.50	363.0.0	0	363.00.0	1	0	1
Calvert, Benedict	15	12	180.0.0	0	180.00.0	0	0	0
Campbell, Frances	1	1	208.0.0	1	266.00.0	0	2	0
Campbell, William (Capt.)	0	0	0	2	178.03.4	1	3	1
Carroll, Charles (Barrister)	6	6	1,329.0.0	7	1,527.16.8	0	0	0
Carroll, Charles (Carrollton)	28	25	1,554.0.0	19	3,259.00.0	4	3	2
Caton, Ann	0	0	0	0	0	0	2	2
Chalmers, John	2	1.25	413.0.0	2	538.08.4	3	5	1
Chase, Jeremiah T., Esq.	1	1	66.0.0	8	491.00.0	1	4	1
Chase, Samuel (Glebe land)	4	3.75	120.0.0	5	1,089.13.4	3	6	1
Chew, Bennet	1	1	530.0.0	0	530.00.0	0	0	0
Chisholm, Archibald	1	.75	333.0.0	2	508.16.8	1	3	1

*WM=number of white male inhabitants of every age.
 WF =number of white female inhabitants of every age.
 AM =number of white male inhabitants from 16 to 50 years of age.

Appendix B, Part 2 (continued)

Name	Lots	Acres	Land Value (£)	Slaves	Total Value of Property (£)	WM	WF	AM
Chisholm, Archibald (for Mary Reynolds' Glebe land)	0	0	0	0	750.00.0	2	0	0
Christian, John	0	0	0	0	50.00.0	1	0	0
Clarke, Joseph (merchant)	0	0	0	2	530.00.0	4	1	1
Clarke, Robert (Glebe land)	0	0	0	2	296.05.0	2	1	1
Claude, Abraham	2	1.50	375.0.0	1	482.00.0	3	1	1
Coe, William, & Co.	1	.75	208.0.0	0	242.00.0	5	3	4
Cotter, Daniel	0	0	0	0	51.00.0	3	2	1
Couden, Robert	1	.50	485.0.0	10	1,139.11.8	2	3	2
Dalzal, Thomas	0	0	0	0	26.00.0	1	1	0
Dashiell, Capt.	0	0	0	0	0	2	2	1
Davidson, John	1	1	40.0.0	10	1,015.13.4	3	5	1
Davidson, John (for Joshua Johnson)	1	.25	376.0.0	0	376.00.0	0	0	0
Davidson, Samuel	0	0	0	0	80.00.0	0	0	0
Davis, George	0	0	0	1	113.00.0	3	0	1
Dick, James (estate)	1	.50	250.0.0	0	250.00.0	0	0	0
Dorsey, Joshua	0	0	0	0	0.15.0	1	0	1
Dorsey, Thomas	1	1	333.0.0	0	333.00.0	0	0	0
Dowds, Charles	0	0	0	0	50.00.0	2	1	1
Dowson, Joseph	1	.50	250.0.0	2	454.03.4	2	3	1
Dulany, Daniel, Sr.	10	9	820.0.0	0	820.00.0	0	0	0
Dulany, Mary	3	3	590.0.0	10	931.00.0	0	2	0
Duvall, Gabriel, Esq.	0	0	0	0	90.00.0	1	0	1
Eastman, Joseph	0	0	0	2	143.00.0	1	0	1
Fairbairn, Benjamin	1	n.g.	416.0.0	0	516.16.8	1	2	1
Fairbrother, Francis	1	.75	208.0.0	6	433.01.8	1	1	1
Faris, William (Glebe land)	0	0	0	3	275.16.8	5	4	3
Flemming, Richard	0	0	0	1	95.00.0	2	3	1
Fowler, Daniel	0	0	0	0	20.00.0	2	2	1
Fowler, John	0	0	0	0	0	1	1	1
Fowler, Jubb	0	0	0	5	110.00.0	4	4	1
Fowler, William	0	0	0	0	20.00.0	2	1	1
Frazier, Joshua	2	1.50	1,516.0.0	7	2,049.05.0	2	3	1
French, James	0	0	0	0	0.15.0	1	0	1
Fulk, Margaret	1	.50	125.0.0	0	132.00.0	0	3	0
Gaither, Ann	1	1	500.0.0	1	521.16.8	0	1	0
Galloway, Samuel	3	3.50	140.0.0	0	140.00.0	0	0	0
Garston, George (Glebe land)	1	.50	166.0.0	1	470.06.8	1	2	1
Gassaway, Thomas	1	.50	281.0.0	5	611.01.8	1	4	1
Gates, Rev'd Mr.	0	0	0	0	20.00.0	1	0	1
Ghiselin, Mary	1	.75	40.0.0	4	227.10.0	1	3	0
Golder, Archibald	1	1	416.0.0	0	416.00.0	1	1	1
Goldsmith, William	0	0	0	1	132.16.8	7	5	3
Gordon, Capt. John	0	0	0	5	131.00.0	1	1	1
Gordon, William	0	0	0	0	55.16.8	2	1	1
Graham, Thomas	2	.50	268.0.0	1	452.05.0	3	1	1
Grammar, Frederick	1	.50	166.0.0	0	320.05.0	4	3	1
Green, Frederick	4	4	510.0.0	9	922.16.8	3	7	2
Green, John	1	.25	209.0.0	0	238.00.0	3	3	1

Appendix B, Part 2 (continued)

Name	Lots	Acres	Land Value (£)	Slaves	Total Value of Property (£)	WM	WF	AM
Green, Samuel	0	0	0	0	0.15.0	0	0	0
Hall, John, Esq.	2	2	250.0.0	3	360.00.0	0	0	0
Hammond, John	1	1	50.0.0	0	50.00.0	0	0	0
Hammond, Matthias	4	4	410.0.0	0	410.00.0	1	0	1
Hammond, Nathan	2	2	166.0.0	0	166.00.0	0	0	0
Hammond, Philip	1	.75	208.0.0	0	208.00.0	0	0	0
Hanson, Alexander C.	0	0	0	2	246.13.4	1	3	1
Hanson, Capt. John	0	0	0	1	66.05.0	1	3	1
Harris, Isaac	1	1	316.0.0	4	584.13.4	1	2	1
Harrison, William	0	0	0	0	26.00.0	1	2	1
Harwood, Benjamin	0	0	0	0	51.00.0	1	0	1
Harwood, Nicholas	0	0	0	3	193.16.8	2	3	1
Harwood, Thomas	1	.25	557.0.0	4	947.13.4	5	4	1
Henley, Zachariah	0	0	0	0	0.15.0	1	1	1
Henry, William & Thomas	0	0	0	0	1.10.0	2	0	2
Hewett, Jane	1	.25	216.0.0	0	224.00.0	1	2	0
Hodgkin, Thomas B.	0	0	0	2	172.10.0	2	4	1
Hogg, Charles	0	0	0	1	51.00.0	3	1	1
Howard, John	2	1	220.0.0	4	302.00.0	1	2	1
Howard, Mary	0	0	0	7	366.13.4	0	1	1
Howard, Samuel H	1	1	140.0.0	2	305.00.0	2	2	1
Hurst, Jacob	1	.75	250.0.0	0	340.00.0	2	2	1
Hutton, Samuel & Henry	1	.50	99.0.0	0	149.00.0	4	1	2
Hyde, Thomas	3	1.75	1,470.0.0	4	1,726.00.0	2	1	1
Hyde, William	0	0	0	0	51.00.0	1	0	1
Jenifer, Daniel of St. Thomas	3	3	590.0.0	0	590.00.0	1	0	1
Jenings, Thomas	3	3	830.0.0	9	1,358.13.4	3	3	1
Johnson, John	1	.50	20.0.0	1	153.00.0	1	3	1
Johnson, Jonathan; Wright, S.	0	0	0	0	0	3	3	1
Johnson, Joshua; see Davidson, John								
Johnson, Robert; see Ashmead, Joseph								
Johnson, Thomas	0	0	0	0	255.18.4	2	5	1
Jones, Richard	0	0	0	0	50.00.0	3	1	1
Kingsbury, James (estate)	1	.75	30.0.0	0	30.00.0	0	0	0
Knapp, John	0	0	0	0	0.15.0	1	0	1
Lamb, Joshua (estate)	1	.50	183.0.0	0	183.00.0	0	1	0
Lang, Robert	0	0	0	0	21.00.0	1	2	1
Lee, Philip (estate)	1	1	340.0.0	0	340.0.0	0	0	0
Lee, Richard	1	1	340.0.0	0	340.0.0	0	0	0
Leeke, Richard	0	0	0	0	40.0.0	2	2	2
Levashier, John	0	0	0	1	75.00.0	0	1	0
Lilley, William	1	.50	45.0.0	0	66.00.0	1	1	1
Lloyd, Edward	2	2	833.0.0	2	1,003.00.0	1	2	1
Lloyd, Richard B.	0	0	0	9	622.06.8	4	3	1
Logan, William	0	0	0	0	130.06.8	1	1	1
McCubbin, Elizabeth (Mackubin)	1	1	440.0.0	4	601.00.0	1	4	0
McCubbin, Moses	0	0	0	0	83.00.0	3	2	1

Appendix B, Part 2 (continued)

Name	Lots	Acres	Land Value (£)	Slaves	Total Value of Property (£)	WM	WF	AM
McCubbin, Nicholas (Jr.)	0	0	0	2	180.00.0	1	0	1
McCubbin, Nicholas (Sr.)	4	4	1,761.0.0	11	2,475.13.4	4	1	1
McCubbin, Nicholas (Cordwainer)	1	1	80.0.0	2	237.00.0	3	1	1
McHard, Isaac	0	0	0	4	222.15.0	2	7	1
Mackubin, James of Richard	1	.25	150.0.0	4	605.00.0	1	1	1
Mann, George	2	2	120.0.0	4	465.00.0	2	2	2
Marshall, John	0	0	0	0	20.00.0	1	2	1
Martin, John	0	0	0	0	30.00.0	1	2	1
Massey, Henry	0	0	0	0	31.00.0	1	3	1
Maw, William	0	0	0	0	268.01.8	1	0	1
Maybury, Beriah	1	.50	620.0.0	3	876.11.8	1	2	1
Meeke, Vestal	0	0	0	0	88.00.0	2	2	1
Middleton, Gilbert	2	1.75	586.0.0	9	1,035.18.4	2	3	1
Middleton, Joseph	1	.75	210.0.0	4	570.05.0	4	3	1
Middleton, William	0	0	0	7	260.00.0	1	2	1
Mills, Cornelius	1	.50	416.0.0	0	511.00.0	2	2	1
Mills, John	0	0	0	0	50.00.0	1	1	0
Minskey, Nicholas	0	0	0	0	0	1	5	0
Muir, John	0	0	0	0	90.00.0	1	0	1
Munroe, Daniel	0	0	0	0	24.00.0	2	2	1
Munroe, William (estate)	1	.25	183.00.0	0	183.00.0	0	0	0
Murray, Dr. James	0	0	0	11	585.10.0	2	4	1
Neth, Lewis	0	0	0	0	0.15.0	0	0	0
Nixon, Robert	0	0	0	0	0	1	1	2
Ogle, Benjamin, Esq.	2	2	630.0.0	0	670.00.0	0	0	0
Owens, Edward	0	0	0	2	110.00.0	2	2	1
Owens, Richard	0	0	0	0	60.00.0	2	2	1
Paca, Aquila	0	0	0	5	243.00.0	2	2	1
Paca, William (His Excellency)	1	.75	83.0.0	11	863.06.8	1	1	1
Parker, Jonathan	0	0	0	0	18.00.0	2	1	2
Pinkney, Jonathan	0	0	0	5	268.15.0	3	2	1
Pinkney, William	0	0	0	0	21.00.0	1	0	1
Piper, Thomas	0	0	0	1	93.00.0	3	3	1
Pitt, Capt. John (Glebe land)	0	0	0	2	492.05.0	4	3	1
Pressley, Mary	0	0	0	0	0	1	3	0
Price, Thomas (Pryse)	1	.50	103.0.0	1	178.00.0	3	4	1
Purdy, John	0	0	0	0	0.15.0	1	0	0
Quynn, Allen, Esq.	1	1	360.0.0	5	635.10.0	3	4	1
Ramsey, Nathaniel	2.5	2.50	450.0.0	10	974.00.0	2	3	1
Randall, John	0	0	0	0	285.00.0	1	1	1
Ranken, George	0	0	0	0	34.06.8	1	2	1
Rebb, Adam	0	0	0	0	53.00.0	3	2	1
Reed, James	1	.25	223.0.0	0	286.00.0	3	2	2
Reeth, Robert (estate)	1	.50	103.0.0	0	113.16.8	0	2	2
Retallick, Simon	0	0	0	0	51.00.0	6	2	2
Reynolds, Robert	3	2.75	540.0.0	0	567.16.8	2	3	1
Richardson, Adam	0	0	0	0	40.00.0	1	3	1

Appendix B, Part 2 (continued)

Name	Lots	Acres	Land Value (£)	Slaves	Total Value of Property (£)	WM	WF	AM
Ridgely, Absalom	1	1	209.0.0	2	430.16.8	3	2	1
Ridgely, Charles	0	0	0	4	137.00.0	2	3	1
Ridout, John	2	2	900.0.0	1	1,125.08.4	0	0	0
Ringgold, James	0	0	0	8	1,250.03.4	3	3	1
Robins, Ann	0	0	0	0	20.00.0	1	2	0
Roper and Welch	0	0	0	0	51.00.0	0	0	0
Ross, Widow	0	0	0	0	0	0	3	0
Ross, Nathaniel	0	0	0	0	0.15.0	1	0	0
Rutland, Thomas	2	1.50	833.0.0	0	833.00.0	0	0	0
Sands, John	1	.75	210.0.0	3	414.05.0	3	3	2
Sands, William	0	0	0	0	33.00.0	1	2	1
Scott, Upton	2	2	558.0.0	0	558.00.0	0	0	0
Sears, Tissue	0	0	0	0	40.00.0	3	1	0
Seibert, Justus	1	.25	249.0.0	0	269.00.0	3	1	1
Selby, Ann	1	1	190.0.0	1	210.00.0	0	2	0
Shaw, John	1	.50	116.0.0	2	264.05.0	6	2	1
Shephard, Nathaniel	0	0	0	0	21.00.0	3	2	1
Sibell, Henry	1	.25	353.0.0	2	474.00.0	4	2	2
Slaughter, Thomas	0	0	0	1	51.00.0	2	2	1
Smith, Mary	0	0	0	0	0	2	1	0
Smith, Richard	0	0	0	2	98.00.0	1	1	1
Sparrow, Thomas	0	0	0	0	20.00.0	1	2	1
Sprigg, Richard	2	1.50	220.0.0	0	220.00.0	0	0	0
Steuart, Charles	2	1.50	1,000.0.0	0	1,000.00.0	0	0	0
Steuart, James	0	0	0	4	136.00.0	3	0	1
Steuart, John	0	0	0	1	104.13.4	1	1	1
Steuart, Mary	0	0	0	0	0	2	1	0
Stevens, Joseph	0	0	0	0	200.00.0	1	0	1
Stevens, Vachel	2	2	240.0.0	0	240.00.0	0	0	0
Stichbury, Philip	0	0	0	0	41.00.0	1	1	1
Stoddart, Benjamin, Esq.	0	0	0	5	305.00.0	3	1	1
Thompson, Alexander	0	0	0	0	0.15.0	1	0	1
Thompson, Edward	0	0	0	0	34.00.0	2	3	1
Thompson, Richard	1	1	90.0.0	0	97.16.8	3	2	1
Tootell, James	1	.50	566.0.0	4	969.06.8	3	4	1
Tootell, Richard (estate)	3	3	374.0.0	4	553.03.4	0	2	0
Townsend, Thomas	0	0	0	0	0	2	2	1
Tuck, William	0	0	0	1	86.13.4	3	3	1
Tyers, Richard	0	0	0	0	20.00.0	2	1	1
Unsworth, Mrs.	0	0	0	0	0	2	3	0
Vallette, Eli	1	.50	208.0.0	0	208.00.0	0	0	0
Valliant, Elcock	0	0	0	0	0.15.0	1	0	1
Valliant, Nicholas	1	.50	208.0.0	0	290.00.0	3	1	1
Vineyard, Widow	0	0	0	0	51.00.0	1	3	0
Wallace, Charles	2	1	208.0.0	5	537.06.8	1	2	1
Wallace & Davidson	1	.50	557.0.0	0	557.00.0	0	0	0
Weedon, Oliver	0	0	0	0	110.00.0	1	1	1
Welch & Roper; see Roper & Welch								
Wells, Daniel	0	0	0	2	386.05.0	3	6	1
Wells, John	1	1	208.0.0	0	267.05.0	1	2	1

Appendix B, Part 2 (continued)

Name	Lots	Acres	Land Value (£)	Slaves	Total Value of Property (£)	WM	WF	AM
West, James	0	0	0	1	159.05.0	3	1	1
Whetcroft, William	2	1.50	750.0.0	4	979.00.0	3	15	3
Wilkins, Deborah	1	.75	60.0.0	2	111.00.0	0	1	0
Wilkins, William	0	0	0	4	264.10.0	3	3	1
Williams, James	4	2	823.0.0	8	1,340.03.4	1	4	1
Williams, James (for Miss Adams)	1	.50	80.0.0	0	80.00.0	0	0	0
Williams, Joseph (merchant)	1	.50	557.0.0	1	876.03.4	1	0	1
Williams, Joseph	0	0	0	1	270.00.0	2	2	1
Williams, William	0	0	0	0	32.00.0	1	2	1
Willshine, Jonathan	0	0	0	0	50.00.0	2	2	1
Wilmot, Dinah	0	0	0	1	31.00.0	0	2	0
Wilmot, John	1	.25	140.0.0	1	238.13.4	3	3	1
Wilson, Thomas	1	1	250.0.0	4	420.11.8	1	1	1
Worthington, Nicholas	1	.75	200.0.0	2	285.00.0	0	0	0
Wright, S.; see Johnson, John								
Yeates, Vachel	0	0	0	0	53.00.0	1	2	1
Yieldhall, William	1	.50	145.0.0	1	313.16.8	1	3	1

Appendix B
Part 3: The Distribution of Total
Assessed Wealth in Annapolis from the 1783 Tax List

Carroll, Charles (Carrollton)	£ 3,259.00.0
McCubbin, Nicholas, Sr.	2,475.13.4
Frazier, Joshua	2,049.05.0
Hyde, Thomas	1,726.00.0
Carroll, Charles (Barrister)	1,527.16.8
Jenings, Thomas	1,358.13.4
Williams, James	1,340.03.4
Ringgold, James	1,250.03.4
Brice, James, Esq.	1,228.13.4
Couden, Robert	1,139.11.8
Ridout, John	1,125.08.4
Chase, Samuel (Glebe land)	1,089.13.4
Brice, John	1,078.08.4
Middleton, Gilbert	1,035.18.4
Davidson, John	1,015.13.4
Lloyd, Edward	1,003.00.0
Steuart, Charles	1,000.00.0
Whetcroft, William	979.00.0
Ramsey, Nathaniel	974.00.0
Tootell, James	969.06.8
Harwood, Thomas	947.13.4
Dulany, Mary	931.00.0
Green, Frederick	922.16.8
Maybury, Beriah	876.11.8
Williams, Joseph	876.03.4
Paca, William (His Excellency)	863.06.8
Rutland, Thomas	833.00.0
Dulany, Daniel, Sr.	820.00.0
Bordley, Elizabeth	792.00.0
Brewer, John	764.06.8
Chisholm, Archibald (for Mary Reynolds' Glebe land)	750.00.0
Bullen, John	670.16.8
Ogle, Benjamin, Esq.	670.00.0
Quynn, Allen, Esq.	635.10.0
Lloyd, Richard B.	622.06.8
Gassaway, Thomas	611.01.8
Mackubin, James of Richard	605.00.0
McCubbin, Elizabeth (Mackubin)	601.00.0
Jenifer, Daniel of St. Thomas	590.00.0
Murray, Dr. James	585.10.0
Harris, Isaac	584.13.4
Middleton, Joseph	570.05.0
Reynolds, Robert	567.16.8

Appendix B, Part 3 (continued)

Scott, Upton	558.00.0
Wallace & Davidson	557.00.0
Tootell, Richard (estate)	553.03.4
Chalmers, John	538.08.4
Wallace, Charles	537.06.8
Chew, Bennet	530.00.0
Clarke, Joseph (merchant)	530.00.0
Gaither, Ann	521.16.8
Fairbairn, Benjamin	516.16.8
Mills, Cornelius	511.00.0
Chisholm, Archibald	508.16.8
Pitt, Capt. John (Glebe land)	492.05.0
Chase, Jeremiah T., Esq.	491.00.0
Ashmead, Joseph (for Robert Johnson's estate)	483.00.0
Claude, Abraham	482.00.0
Sibell, Henry	474.00.0
Garston, George (Glebe land)	470.06.8
Mann, George	465.00.0
Dowson, Joseph	454.03.4
Graham, Thomas	452.05.0
Fairbrother, Francis	433.01.8
Ridgely, Absalom	430.16.8
Wilson, Thomas	420.11.8
Golder, Archibald	416.00.0
Sands, John	414.05.0
Hammond, Matthias	410.00.0
Wells, Daniel	386.05.0
Davidson, John (for Joshua Johnson)	376.00.0
Howard, Mary	366.13.4
Callahan, Thomas	363.00.0
Hall, John, Esq.	360.00.0
Lee, Richard	340.00.0
Lee, Philip (estate)	340.00.0
Hurst, Jacob	340.00.0
Brewer, Nicholas	335.01.8
Dorsey, Thomas	333.00.0
Grammar, Frederick	320.05.0
Yieldhall, William	313.16.8
Brown, William, Sr.	310.00.0
Stoddart, Benjamin, Esq.	305.00.0
Howard, Samuel H.	305.00.0
Howard, John	302.00.0
Clarke, Robert (Glebe land)	296.05.0
Valliant, Nicholas	290.00.0

Appendix B, Part 3 (continued)

Reed, James	286.00.0
Randall, John	285.00.0
Worthington, Nicholas	285.00.0
Brewer, Joseph	276.00.0
Faris, William (Glebe land)	275.16.8
Berry, Robert	275.01.8
Williams, Joseph	270.00.0
Seibert, Justus	269.00.0
Pinkney, Jonathan	268.15.0
Maw, William	268.01.8
Wells, John	267.05.0
Campbell, Frances	266.00.0
Wilkins, William	264.10.0
Shaw, John	264.05.0
Middleton, William	260.00.0
Brewer, Thomas & Welch	258.00.0
Johnson, Thomas	255.18.4
Dick, James (estate)	250.00.0
Ashmead, Joseph	249.03.4
Hanson, Alexander C.	246.13.4
Paca, Aquila	243.00.0
Coe, William & Co.	242.00.0
Stevens, Vachel	240.00.0
Wilmot, John	238.13.4
Green, John	238.00.0
McCubbin, Nicholas (cordwainer)	237.00.0
Ghiselin, Mary	227.10.0
Hewett, Jane	224.00.0
McHard, Isaac	222.15.0
Sprigg, Richard	220.00.0
Selby, Ann	210.00.0
Hammond, Philip	208.00.0
Vallette, Eli	208.00.0
Stevens, Joseph	200.00.0
Harwood, Nicholas	193.16.8
Callahan, John	192.10.0
Lamb, Joshua (estate)	183.00.0
Munroe, William (estate)	183.00.0
McCubbin, Nicholas, Jr.	180.00.0
Brown, Capt. Hugh	180.00.0
Calvert, Benedict	180.00.0
Campbell, William (Capt.)	178.03.4
Price, Thomas (Pryse)	178.00.0
Callahan, Sarah	173.10.0

Appendix B, Part 3 (continued)

Hodgkin, Thomas B.	172.10.0
Hammond, Nathan	166.00.0
West, James	159.05.0
Johnson, John	153.00.0
Hutton, Samuel & Henry	149.00.0
Biggs, William	147.00.0
Eastman, Joseph	143.00.0
Galloway, Samuel	140.00.0
Ridgely, Charles	137.00.0
Steuart, James	136.00.0
Brown, William (merchant)	133.13.4
Goldsmith, William	132.16.8
Fulk, Margaret	132.00.0
Gordon, Capt. John	131.00.0
Logan, William	130.06.8
Brice, Francis	120.00.0
Reeth, Robert (estate)	113.16.8
Davis, George	113.00.0
Wilkins, Deborah	111.00.0
Fowler, Jubb	110.00.0
Owens, Edward	110.00.0
Weedon, Oliver	110.00.0
Steuart, John	104.13.4
Smith, Richard	98.00.0
Thompson, Richard	97.16.8
Flemming, Richard	95.00.0
Piper, Thomas	93.00.0
Duvall, Gabriel, Esq.	90.00.0
Muir, John	90.00.0
Meeke, Vestal	88.00.0
Tuck, William	86.13.4
McCubbin, Moses	83.00.0
Davidson, Samuel	80.00.0
Williams, James (for Miss Adams)	80.00.0
Levashier, John	75.00.0
Ball, John (estate)	70.00.0
Hanson, Capt. John	66.05.0
Lilley, William	66.00.0
Owens, Richard	60.00.0
Gordon, William	55.16.8
Yeates, Vachel	53.00.0
Rebb, Adam	53.00.0
Vineyard, Widow	51.00.0
Slaughter, Thomas	51.00.0

Appendix B, Part 3 (continued)

Roper and Welch	51.00.0
Retallick, Simon	51.00.0
Hyde, William	51.00.0
Hogg, Charles	51.00.0
Harwood, Benjamin	51.00.0
Cotter, Daniel	51.00.0
Willshine, Jonathan	50.00.0
Mills, John	50.00.0
Jones, Richard	50.00.0
Hammond, John	50.00.0
Dowds, Charles	50.00.0
Christian, John	50.00.0
Bash, Adam	50.00.0
Brewer, Rachel	47.00.0
Allen, John	44.00.0
Stichbury, Philip	41.00.0
Beard, Richard	40.00.0
Bryan, Daniel	40.00.0
Leeke, Richard	40.00.0
Richardson, Adam	40.00.0
Sears, Tissue	40.00.0
Ranken, George	34.06.8
Thompson, Edward	34.00.0
Sands, William	33.00.0
Williams, William	32.00.0
Wilmot, Dinah	31.00.0
Massey, Henry	31.00.0
Kingsbury, James (estate)	30.00.0
Martin, John	30.00.0
Harrison, William	26.00.0
Dalzal, Thomas	26.00.0
Adams, George	24.00.0
Munroe, Daniel	24.00.0
Shephard, Nathaniel	21.00.0
Pinkney, William	21.00.0
Lang, Robert	21.00.0
Robins, Ann	20.00.0
Marshall, John	20.00.0
Fowler, Daniel	20.00.0
Sparrow, Thomas	20.00.0
Fowler, William	20.00.0
Gates, Rev'd Mr.	20.00.0
Tyers, Richard	20.00.0
Barber, Charles	19.00.0

Appendix B, Part 3 (continued)

Parker, Jonathan	18.00.0
Henry, William & Thomas	1.10.0
Dorsey, Joshua	0.15.0
French, James	0.15.0
Green, Samuel	0.15.0
Henley, Zachariah	0.15.0
Callahan, James	0.15.0
Barnhold, Henry	0.15.0
Neth, Lewis	0.15.0
Knapp, John	0.15.0
Purdy, John	0.15.0
Ross, Nathaniel	0.15.0
Thompson, Alexander	0.15.0
Valliant, Elcock	0.15.0
Unsworth, Mrs.	0
Townsend, Thomas	0
Steuart, Mary	0
Smith, Mary	0
Ross, Widow	0
Pressley, Mary	0
Nixon, Robert	0
Minskey, Nicholas	0
Johnson, Jonathan	0
Wright, S.	0
Fowler, John	0
Dashiell, Capt.	0
Caton, Ann	0
Annis, Mary	0

BIBLIOGRAPHY

1. ARCHIVES AND MANUSCRIPTS

ONLY those records cited in the text are listed, although at each repository a great number of other collections were consulted in the search for data. The arrangement is geographical, with collections in alphabetical order under each repository. Many of the sources consulted in reconstructing the careers of townspeople have not been included. Practically every record group at the Hall of Records and most collections at the Maryland Historical Society were used in some way and the bibliography would become unnecessarily cumbersome if it tried to cite everything examined. For a discussion and outline of the major sources used in career analysis see my discussion of methodology and sources in Part III C of "Final Report National Endowment for the Humanities Grant #H69-0-178" on deposit at the Hall of Records, Annapolis, Md. A useful guide to Maryland records is Eleanor Phillips Passano, *An Index of the Source Records of Maryland: Genealogical, Biographical, Historical* (Baltimore, 1940). Although much out of date and in great need of revision, the *Catalogue of Archival Material* (Annapolis, 1942), provides a helpful guide to the materials in the Hall of Records. It does not contain a description of probate and chancery records, however, which at the time it was published were in the land office.

As yet no one has done an adequate guide to the chancery records which were used extensively in this study. There are approximately 13,000 case files and about 200 bound volumes of recorded cases, not to mention the rerecordings among the case papers of the Court of Appeals. More than any other single source, chancery and equity materials make it possible to probe in detail all aspects and levels of economic life in Maryland. They contain bankruptcy cases, petitions for insolvency, disputes over partnerships, controversies over estate management, and data relating to a whole range of other economic and social questions.

Prerogative and land office records other than chancery are described in *Land Office and Prerogative Court Records of Colonial Maryland* (Baltimore, 1968), by Elisabeth Hartsook and Gust Skordas.

Many, but not all, of the indexes available to researchers at the Hall of Records are listed in "Bulletin No. 18 INDEX HOLDINGS," available free on request. Invaluable guides in the form of unpublished shelf lists are also available at the Hall of Records.

Most of the collections of the Maryland Historical Society are superbly described and indexed in Avril J. M. Pedley's *The Manuscript Collections of the Maryland Historical Society* (Baltimore, 1968), with subsequent accessions listed in the *National Union Catalogue of Manuscripts.* An exception to the rule is the Scharf Collection, which contains an enormous body of inadequately inventoried materials relating to the daily operations of the Maryland government during the eighteenth and early nineteenth centuries. Most of the Scharf Collection complements the Executive Papers at the Hall of Records, and one cannot be used profitably without the other.

A. Hall of Records, Annapolis, Md.

    Accounts
    Adjutant General's Papers
    Annapolis Plats
    Annapolis Records
    Annapolis Treasurer's Papers
    Anne Arundel County Administration Dockets
    Anne Arundel County Deeds
    Anne Arundel County Judgments
    Anne Arundel County Miscellaneous Court Papers
    Anne Arundel County Testamentary Papers
    Army Accounts
    Auditor General's Journal B
    Black Books
    "James Brice's Accounts as Treasurer of the Corporation of
       Annapolis"
    Chancery Papers [loose]
    Chancery Records [bound]
    Court of Appeals Dockets
    Executive Papers
    General Court of the Western Shore Cost Books
    General Court of the Western Shore Fee Books
    General Court of the Western Shore Papers
    Gift Collection
       James Brice Account Book G530
       Hemphill Notes D563
       Ridout Papers D371

Shipping Invoices of Lancelot Jacques D387
Wallace, Johnson and Muir, Journal 1791–1795 D796
Wilmot and West Account Book D553
Intendant's Papers
Inventories
Naval Office Returns [uncatalogued]
Parish Register, All Hallows Parish, Anne Arundel County
Parish Register, St. Anne's Parish, Anne Arundel County
Pforzheimer Collection
Port of Entry Records, Annapolis [Microfilm 1002]
Prince George's County Inspection Records
Prince George's County Inventories
Prince George's County Judgments
Private Account Books
    Wallace, Davidson, and Johnson;
    Wallace, Johnson, and Muir
Register of Civil Officers, 1777–1794
Revolutionary Papers [technically a part of the Executive Papers
    but boxed separately]
Testamentary Papers
Wills

B. Maryland Historical Society, Baltimore, Md.

Carroll Maccubbin Papers MS 219
Coffing Account Book MS 249
William Cooke Papers MS 195
Corner Collection MS 1242
Davidson Papers MS 281
Friese Account Books MS 933
Hammond Account Book MS 429
Charles Wallace Hanson manuscript introduction to the
    Collected Works of Alexander Contee Hanson, Rare Book
    Collection
Hyde Papers MS 1324
Issue Books of the Annapolis Commissary MS 1146
Naval Office Returns MS 1668
Journal of John Randall MS 1688
Charles Ridgely Papers MS 692
Scharf Collection MS 1999
Vertical File [miscellaneous material]
Wallace, Johnson and Muir Letter Book, 1784–1785 MS 1180
Thomas Williamson Account Book MS 913

C. New York Public Library, New York, N.Y.

Charles Carroll Letter Book, Arents Collection
Papers Relating to Maryland, Chalmers Collection,
    Manuscript Division
Ridgate Letter Book, 1771–1772, Arents Collection
Wallace, Johnson and Muir Letter Book, 1781–1783,
    Manuscript Division
Wallace, Johnson and Muir Letter Book, 1787–1788,
    Manuscript Division

D. Library of Congress, Washington, D.C.

Samuel Davidson Letter Book
Gabriel Duvall Papers
Galloway, Maxcy, Markoe Papers
Glassford Papers
Letter Book of Alexander Hamilton, 1773–1776
Saltworks Ledger, Force Collection
Stone Papers
Joshua Johnson's Letter Book, 1785–1788, Force Collection

E. National Archives, Washington, D.C.

"Abstract of Duties," bound with "Accounts Current, Annapolis,
    1745–1821," Record Group 36
"Accounts Current, Annapolis . . . ," Record Group 36
"Annapolis Registers, 1774–1798," Record Group 41
Carmichael Papers, Record Group 233
Census Schedules of Annapolis, Maryland for 1800, 1810, 1820,
    1830
Letters to Naval Officers, Record Group 56 [Microfilm #178]
Naval Office Returns for Baltimore, Record Group 36
"Report of the Commissioners of the Public Debt, June 27,
    1793," Record Group 53

F. Great Britain, Public Record Office

Audit Office Papers
High Court of Admiralty Papers
Treasury Papers

G. Other Repositories

Duke University Library, Durham, N.C.
    "Samuel Chase's Debts," Fugitive item from Chancery
        Record 26:211–26, Hall of Records, Annapolis, Md.

James Dick and Stewart Company Letter Book, 1773–1781
Massachusetts Historical Society, Boston, Mass.
Matthew Ridley Papers
Colonial Williamsburg, Williamsburg, Va.
William Cuninghame & Co. Letter Book [Microfilm 52]

2. NEWSPAPERS AND OTHER PUBLISHED RECORD MATERIAL

Acomb, Evelyn M., ed., *The Revolutionary Journal of Baron Ludwig Von Closen, 1780–1783.* Chapel Hill, 1958.
American State Papers, Class IV, Commerce and Navigation. Washington, D.C., 1831–1862.
The Annual Register. London, 1768.
Archives of Maryland. Baltimore, 1883——.
Balch, Thomas, ed., *Papers Relating Chiefly to the Maryland Line During the Revolution.* Philadelphia, 1857.
Baltimore Maryland Gazette.
Burnaby, Rev. Andrew. *Travels Through the Middle Settlements in North America in the Years 1759–60.* London, 1775.
The Gentleman's Magazine. London, 1764.
Griffith Map of Maryland, 1794.
[Hanson, Alexander Contee]. *Considerations on the Proposed Removal of the Seat of Government, Addressed to the Citizens of Maryland, By ARISTIDES.* Annapolis, 1786.
Kilty, William, ed., *The Laws of Maryland.* 2 vols. Annapolis, 1799.
Laws of Maryland Made and Passed at a Session of Assembly, Begun and Held at the City of Annapolis, on Monday the fifth of November in the Year of our Lord one thousand seven hundred and eighty-one. Annapolis, 1782.
Lowndes London Directory, for the Year 1786. . . . London, 1786.
Maryland Gazette. [Annapolis].
The Maryland Gazette: or The Baltimore Advertiser.
Maryland Journal and Baltimore Advertiser.
Maryland. *Votes and Proceedings of the Senate, November Session.* Annapolis, 1783.
Mifflin, Benjamin. "A Journal of Benjamin Mifflin on a Tour from Philadelphia to Delaware and Maryland, July 26–August 14, 1762." Edited by Victor H. Palsits. *Bulletin of the New York Public Library* 39 (June, 1935), 431–34.
[Oldmixon, John]. *The British Empire in America Containing the History of the Discovery, Settlement, Progress and State of the British Colonies on the Continent and Islands of America.* 2 vols. New York, 1969 [1741].

The Papers of Alexander Hamilton. New York, 1961 ——.

Rochefoucault-Liancourt, Duc de la. *Travels Through the United States of North America in the Years 1795, 1796, 1797*. London, 1800.

Scott, Joseph. *A Geographical Description of the States of Maryland and Delaware*. . . . Philadelphia, 1807.

INDEX

DATE DUE